Nationalism in a Transnational Age

Nationalism in a Transnational Age

—

Irrational Fears and the Strategic Abuse of Nationalist Pride

Edited by
Frank Jacob and Carsten Schapkow

ISBN 978-3-11-126776-0
e-ISBN (PDF) 978-3-11-072929-0
e-ISBN (EPUB) 978-3-11-072935-1
DOI https://doi.org/10.1515/9783110729290

This work is licensed under the Creative Commons Attribution-NonCommercial-NoDerivatives 4.0 International License. For details go to http://creativecommons.org/licenses/by-nc-nd/4.0/.

Library of Congress Control Number: 2021948490

Bibliographic information published by the Deutsche Nationalbibliothek
The Deutsche Nationalbibliothek lists this publication in the Deutsche Nationalbibliografie; detailed bibliographic data are available on the Internet at http://dnb.dnb.de.

© 2023 Frank Jacob and Carsten Schapkow, published by Walter de Gruyter GmbH, Berlin/Boston
This volume is text- and page-identical with the hardback published in 2021.
The book is published with open access at www.degruyter.com.

Cover Credits:
RapidEye/iStock/Getty Images Plus
nopparit/iStock/Getty Images Plus (Hintergrund)
Typesetting: Integra Software Services Pvt. Ltd.
Printing and binding: CPI books GmbH, Leck

www.degruyter.com

Contents

Frank Jacob and Carsten Schapkow
1   Nationalism in a Transnational Age: An Introduction —— 1

Section I: Old Wine in New Bottles: About the Continuities of Nationalism and Empire in the 21st Century

Frank Jacob
2   Turkish Nationalism: From Gallipoli to Contemporary
    Neo-Ottomanism —— 15

Sven Brajer and Johannes Schütz
3   Old Concepts in Changing Societies? Continuities and
    Transformation of Nationalism in East Germany, 1871–2019 —— 41

Alicja Curanović
4   The Phantomic Nature of Missionary Nationalism in a Former Empire:
    The Case of Russia —— 69

James Okolie-Osemene
5   New Transnational Pan-Africanism and Its Nationalist
    Limitations —— 91

Section II: The Fight For and the Creation of Identity: A Cultural Struggle Against the "Other"

Inessa Kouteinikova
6   Russia's Central Asia: Photographic Symbology of Nationhood —— 119

Irakli Chkhaidze
7   Georgia's Two Others: Nationalism and the Identity Struggle
    of a Post-Soviet Nation State —— 139

Muhammad A. Z. Mughal
8   New Media and the Narratives of National Identity and Nationalism:
    A Pakistani Case Study —— 157

Section III: **Globalized Nationalisms and their National Frontiers**

Tetiana Perga
9 Eco-Nationalism in the Soviet Union in the Late 1980s and Early 1990s: The Ukrainian Case —— 177

Anna Zadora
10 Teaching History in Belarus: Between Globalization and Authoritarian Confinement, Between Europe and Russia —— 195

List of Contributors —— 223

Index —— 227

Frank Jacob and Carsten Schapkow
1 Nationalism in a Transnational Age: An Introduction

We might believe we live in a postmodern and postnational world. And we might want to believe that a transnational age will secure peace, but the truth is, as political scientist and Princeton University professor Jan-Werner Müller emphasized in 2019, that "[t]here appears to be one indisputable global trend today: the rise of nationalism."[1] It is also true that regardless of the wish to establish a postnationalist, transnationalist political order that would represent a more global reply to the political issues of the 21st century,[2] we, as Andreas Wimmer, another political scientist, worded it, "[w]ith a few exceptions . . . are all nationalists today."[3] The latter, at the same time, emphasizes that "[n]ationalism provided the answer to the classic boundary question of democracy: Who are the people in whose name the government should rule?"[4] It is in particular the power question, or the related fear of people to lose power and status in their existent national order, that makes them fear the impact of changes, as they are representative of the globalization of the economy or increasing migration.[5] While, for philosopher Kwame Anthony Appiah, "[t]he modern nation-state has always been a community too large for everyone to meet face-to-face; it has always been held together not by literal companionship but by imaginative identification,"[6] today, the ingroup-identity resembling the nation is getting related to the fear of the out-group(s) instead of embracing migration as a chance to extend the spiritual principle of the nation to include other, different, and maybe foreign values.[7]

---

1 Jan-Werner Müller, "False Flags: The Myth of the Nationalist Resurgence," *Foreign Affairs* 98, no. 2 (2019): 35.
2 Frank Jacob, *#FUCK2020: Impulse zu den Krisen und Herausforderungen des 21. Jahrhunderts* (Marburg: Büchner, 2021).
3 Andreas Wimmer, "Why Nationalism Works: And Why It Isn't Going Away," *Foreign Affairs* 98, no. 2 (2019): 28.
4 Ibid., 30.
5 Jürgen Osterhammel, "Nationalism and Globalization," in *The Oxford Handbook of the History of Nationalism*, ed. John Breuilly, 2nd ed. (Oxford: Oxford University Press, 2016), 694–709.
6 Kwame Anthony Appiah, "The Importance of Elsewhere: In Defense of Cosmopolitanism," *Foreign Affairs* 98, no. 2 (2019): 26.
7 Michael Thumann, *Der neue Nationalismus: Die Wiederkehr einer totgeglaubten Ideologie* (Berlin: Die Andere Bibliothek, 2020).

∂ Open Access. © 2021 Frank Jacob and Carsten Schapkow, published by De Gruyter. [CC BY-NC-ND] This work is licensed under the Creative Commons Attribution-NonCommercial-NoDerivatives 4.0 International License.
https://doi.org/10.1515/9783110729290-001

When French historian and orientalist Ernest Renan (1823–1892) defined the nation in 1882, he focused on shared pasts and a consensus for the future that would determine its existence in the first place:

> A nation is a soul, a spiritual principle. Two things, which in truth are but one, constitute this soul or spiritual principle. One lies in the past, one in the present. One is the possession in common of a rich legacy of memories; the other is present-day consent, the desire to live together, the will to perpetuate the value of the heritage that one has received in an undivided form. Man, Gentlemen, does not improvise. The nation, like the individual, is the culmination of a long past of endeavours, sacrifice, and devotion. Of all cults, that of the ancestors is the most legitimate, for the ancestors have made us what we are. A heroic past, great men, glory (by which I understand genuine glory), this is the social capital upon which one bases a national idea. To have common glories in the past and to have a common will in the present; to have performed great deeds together, to wish to perform still more – these are the essential conditions for being a people. One loves in proportion to the sacrifices to which one has consented, and in proportion to the ills that one has suffered. One loves the house that one has built and that one has handed down. The Spartan song – "We are what you were; we will be what you are" – is, in its simplicity, the abridged hymn of every *patrie*.[8]

What in today's globalized age, as in moments of national formations of the past, e.g. upheavals against foreign rule, nevertheless still plays an important role in forging the bonds between people is the *Other* the nation is supposed to be abstracted from. Literary scholar and semiotician Yuri Lotman emphasized this opposition between the *I* and a culturally different *Other* in his work *Universe of the Mind: A Semiotic Theory of Culture* (1990) as well, when he states with regard to literary texts that "The laws of construction of the artistic text are very largely the laws of the construction of culture as a whole. Hence culture itself can be treated both as the sum of the messages circulated by various addressers (for each of them the addressee is 'another', 's/he'), and as one message transmitted by the collective 'I' of humanity to itself. From this point of view human culture is a vast example of autocommunication."[9] With regard to the creation and communication of the nation, one can also emphasize this self – or autocommunication within the group that shares a nation that is communicated in abstraction to a specific *Other*.

This *Other* could have been the colonial power that a nationalist movement was directed toward, it could have been the enemy of a war against which the

---

8 Ernest Renan, "A Lecture Delivered at the Sorbonne, 11 March 1882: 'Qu'est-ce qu'une nation'," in *Oeuvres Completes*, vol. 1 (Paris: Calmann-Lévy, 1947), 887–907.
9 Yuri Lotman, *Universe of the Mind: A Semiotic Theory of Culture*, transl. by Ann Shukman (Bloomington: Indiana University Press, 1990), 33. Also see Juri Lotman, *Culture and Explosion*, transl. by Wilma Clark (Berlin: De Gruyter, 2009), 136.

national spirit was assembled, but the nation was usually established in countering a different, foreign, and opposite identity. The fact that we are currently facing a tremendous increase in nationalist tensions around the world is therefore without any doubt related to the large numbers of international migrants – 260 million were counted by the UN in 2017[10] – who are often considered a threat to the national integrity of a nation state, although the latter is in no real danger. As much as the nation itself is imagined,[11] so is the menace it is facing from international migration.[12]

The nation, which needs to be abstracted from the idea of homeland that can be the base of an almost romantic idealization, i.e. patriotism,[13] must be considered as an idea with an implied political meaning and can be changed and redefined by every generation that needs to decide the extent to which the national values of the past are supposed to be the national values of the future. A nation is consequently nothing that is written in stone, although often related to semiotic images and codes,[14] but something that is in steady transformation. This also means that every generation has to redefine the canon of moral, ethical, cultural, and political standards that have to be applied when forging the new idea of a nation. The United States can serve as an example for this transformation here. While the US nation in 1776 was a white, Christian, male, and unfree one, the one at the end of the 20th century was supposed to be a multicultural, multireligious, human, and free one, although this idea was challenged by the Trump era of recent years that left a fractured and divided US nation.[15] National divisions within an existent nation state are nothing new if one takes a look into US history in particular, as the Civil War was one between two different national concepts as well. National segregation is a problem nation states could face in the

---

10 Appiah, "The Importance of Elsewhere," 26.
11 Benedict Anderson, *Imagined Communities: Reflections on the Origin and Spread of Nationalism* (London: Verso, 1983).
12 Frank Jacob and Adam Luedtke, "Introduction: Migration and the Nation State," in *Migration and the Crisis of the Modern Nation State?*, ed. Frank Jacob and Adam Luedtke (Wilmington, DE: Vernon Press, 2018), v–xiv.
13 For a theoretical reflection on these differences see, among others, Ivano Cavallini, ed. *Nation and/or Homeland: Identity in 19th-Century Music and Literature Between Central and Mediterranean Europe* (Milano/Udine: Mimesis, 2014).
14 See, among others, Umberto Eco, *Inventing the Enemy* (Boston: Mariner Books, 2013); Francesco Mangiapane and Tiziana Migliore, eds. *Images of Europe: The Union between Federation and Separation* (Cham: Springer 2021).
15 Frank Jacob, "Joe Bidens Krux: Die USA und die gespaltene Nation," November 25, 2020, https://jacobschreibtgeschichteonline.net/2020/11/25/joe-bidens-krux-die-usa-und-die-gespaltene-nation/.

21st century as well, e.g. with regard to the division of Sudan or to the nationalist independence movements in Catalonia in Spain or Scotland in the UK. It is especially in times of crisis that nationalist emotions gain ground, and the current COVID-19 pandemic seems to have triggered responses that were based on such nationalist feelings.[16]

Nationalism may have intensified, but the pandemic is different from one form of nationalism that determined the nation state-building experience of the "long" 19th century.[17] In general, it seems appropriate to divide between two different types of nationalism. The first one is a pre-nation state nationalism, a movement to establish a state based on a specific nation that is shared by those who drive the state-building process forward. The second type would then be a post-nation state nationalism, an overexpression of nationalist ambition that could either be directed against an internal minority living in the borders of the nation state or against an external competitor who, due to the necessary accumulation of capital and the securing of resources, becomes an enemy of the nation.[18] The rivalry of the superpowers in the era of the Cold War overshadowed or even catalyzed these nationalist rivalries into the struggle between two larger political systems. When the conflict was eventually over in the late 1980s and early 1990s, people were willing to believe that this would also mean the end of nationalism or, as American historian Jill Lepore worded it:

> The nation-state was in decline, said the wise men of the time. The world had grown global. Why bother to study the nation? Nationalism, an infant in the nineteenth century, had become, in the first half of the twentieth, a monster. But in the second half, it was nearly dead – a stumbling, ghastly wraith, at least outside postcolonial states. And historians seemed to believe that if they stopped studying it, it would die sooner: starved, neglected, and abandoned.[19]

Francis Fukuyama's most important achievement was probably nothing other than explaining to American readers the philosophical ideas of Immanuel Kant (1724–1804) and Georg Wilhelm Friedrich Hegel (1770–1831) about eternal peace as a

---

16 Stephan Lesenich, "Corona-Nationalismus: Auch die Solidarität bleibt daheim," in *Die Welt nach Corona: Von den Risiken des Kapitalismus, den Nebenwirkungen des Ausnahmezustands und der kommenden Gesellschaft*, ed. Dieter F. Bertz (Berlin: Bertz + Fischer, 2021), 143–148.
17 Franz J. Bauer, *Das "lange" 19. Jahrhundert (1789–1917): Profil einer Epoche*, 4th rev. ed. (Stuttgart: Reclam, 2017).
18 Rosa Luxemburg, *Die Akkumulation des Kapitals: Ein Beitrag zur ökonomischen Erklärung des Imperialismus* (Berlin: Paul Singer, 1913), https://www.marxists.org/deutsch/archiv/luxemburg/1913/akkkap/index.htm.
19 Jill Lepore, "A New Americanism: Why a Nation Needs a National Story," *Foreign Affairs* 98, no. 2 (2019): 10.

consequence of liberal ideas and the end of history, respectively,[20] and putting them in a modern-day context. Yet while Fukushima was "hardly alone in pronouncing nationalism all but dead,"[21] he was probably the most influential.[22]

Many other academics expected that humanity would reach a political order beyond the nation state, such as Jürgen Habermas, who anticipated a "post-national constellation,"[23] or others who regarded the nation to be an outdated concept.[24] At the same time, the thesis that nationalism has returned since the beginning of the 21st century is somehow misleading, as it had never really disappeared, although the political climate at the end of the 20th century seemed to promise a transnational future instead.[25] However, nationalism is strong again and might even intensify as a consequence of the present pandemic. Regardless of its rather bad connotation among intellectuals,[26] the end of the Soviet Union marked the starting point for a new rise of nationalist forces, and "the world has become a world of nation-states governed according to nationalist principles."[27] Wimmer warned readers in 2019 that "[i]n both the developed and the developing world, nationalism is here to stay,"[28] and as far as we can presently grasp the impact of the global pandemic, it seems safe to say that he will be right with regard to this evaluation.

The nationalism that has evolved in the last two decades is a new form that not only questions globalization as such but also the wish to live in a more transnational world.[29] Regardless of the dangers, and as US biologist Robert

---

20 Immanuel Kant, *Zum ewigen Frieden: Ein philosophischer Entwurf*, ed. Rudolf Malter (Stuttgart: Reclam, 2008 [1795]); Georg W. F. Hegel, *Philosophy of History* (New York: Dover, 1956). See also Howard Williams, "The End of History in Hegel and Marx," *The European Legacy* 2, no. 3 (1997): 557–566.
21 Lepore, "A New Americanism," 10.
22 Francis Fukuyama, *The End of History and the Last Man* (New York: Free Press, 1992).
23 Jürgen Habermas, *Die postnationale Konstellation: Politische Essays* (Berlin: Suhrkamp, 1998).
24 Ulrike Guérot, "Wir brauchen die Nation nicht mehr," *Der Standard*, May 2, 2017, https://www.derstandard.at/story/2000056814520/politologin-guerot-wir-brauchen-die-nation-nicht-mehr, cited in Sina Arnold, Sebastian Bischoff and Jana König, "Postnationale Potenziale: Praktiken jenseits der Nation," *Aus Politik und Zeitgeschichte* 68, no. 48 (2018): 2. A survey of the discussion is provided by Arnold et al. as well.
25 Christian Geulen, "Zur 'Wiederkehr' des Nationalismus," *Aus Politik und Zeitgeschichte* 68, no. 48 (2018): 4.
26 Wimmer, "Why Nationalism Works," 27.
27 Ibid., 28.
28 Ibid., 34.
29 Colin Crouch, "Der Nationalismus globalisiert sich," *ZEIT Online*, February 11, 2017, http://www.zeit.de/wirtschaft/2017-02/globalisierung-widerstand-rechte-nationalismus-donald-trump-marine-le-pen-is/komplettansicht.

Sapolsky correctly remarked, "[t]oday, this toxic brand of nationalism is making a comeback across the globe, spurred on by political leaders eager to exploit it for electoral advantage."[30] The rise of nationalism, however, not only happened in accordance with a crisis of our global age, but also because it was used in a variation, namely "nationalist populism."[31] Political leaders of right-wing movements and state leaders like Donald Trump, Vladimir Putin, and Recep Tayyip Erdoğan used people's concerns and anxieties in their countries to pave their own way to power, applying the "political business model is permanent culture war"[32] to represent a "very loud minority"[33] that fears to lose its own social standing within society and considers it threatened by transnational forces or an increase of progressive liberalism, democratic socialism, or other "menaces" like global migration. Through their political strategies, the new nationalists threaten the future of transnational visions like the European Union, which is still suffering from its primary forms of affiliation, i.e. the nation state.[34]

It was skepticism over Europe that made British Prime Minister Theresa May explain in October 2016 that "if you believe you are a citizen of the world, you are a citizen of nowhere."[35] And her successor Boris Johnson noticeably continued to intensify the nationalist emotions toward the final Brexit, leaving Britain alone in a time of crisis and facing new pro-European separatist nationalism within. While true Europeans in the sense of the word tried to defend a union based on values and a federation the different nations would find a new identity in, the nationalist ambitions in the respective nation states prevented a re-formulation of the single nations according to such a plan.[36]

Anti-European skepticism was also stimulated by the so-called "refugee crisis," which gave populist right-wing movements fodder for their anti-liberal cannons and a narrative to channel the fear and anxiety of people who felt a loss of status to be imminent and thereby to gain considerable support in many countries.[37] New

---

30 Robert Sapolsky, "This Is Your Brain on Nationalism," *Foreign Affairs* 98, no. 2 (2019): 47.
31 Müller, "False Flags," 35.
32 Ibid., 36.
33 Ibid., 38.
34 Geulen, "Zur 'Wiederkehr'," 8.
35 Appiah, "The Importance of Elsewhere," 20.
36 Bruno Latour, *Down to Earth: Politics in the New Climatic Regime* (Cambridge: Polity Press, 2018), 99–107.
37 Crouch, "Der Nationalismus globalisiert sich." See also Martin Sabrow, "Höcke und wir," *Zeitgeschichte-online*, January 25, 2017, http://www.zeitgeschichte-online.de/kommentar/hoecke-und-wir.

"politicians"[38] like Trump, Viktor Orbán, and others would use these fears, the rejection of a progressive democracy and its representatives also in the media, i.e. the "establishment," the rejection of an economic globalization that caused job losses for national economies, and the rejection of immigration in order to change the cultural demographics of a country.[39] The new political leaders that represent neo-nationalism, no matter if we call it Trumpism,[40] Orbánism,[41] or neo-Ottomanism,[42] in some way also represent a form of Orwellian "brute authoritarianism" steadily contesting facts and representing alternative narratives to history and contemporary issues alike.[43] Older national narratives not only in these authoritarian regimes but also in totalitarian ones, i.e. China and Russia, are replaced with new ones that put their focus on blood, faith – in the political or religious sense –, and heritage instead of moral values and solidary ethics.[44] The language they use for their claims is very different from what people expected from politicians in the past, but this is also what makes the populist nationalists so appealing for a loud group of supporters: "These men all constantly joke about private parts, fucking and shitting, often partnered with boasts about excessive screwing, eating and drinking. Their bawdy lingo tells us more about their political strategy and strengths than any manifesto: populism and penis jokes go hand in hand."[45]

---

38 Trump in particular argued that he was not a politician but a successful businessman, and always claimed he would "drain the swamp" of the political capital. Adam Soboczynski, "Donald Trump: 'Wir werden unsere Nation mit amerikanischen Händen wieder aufbauen'," *Die Zeit* 5 (2017), January 26, 2017, http://www.zeit.de/2017/05/donald-trump-politische-kommuni kation-rhetorik-sprache/komplettansicht.
39 Such views were often backed by populist authors. As an example, among others, see Ann Coulter, *Adios, America: The Left's Plan to Turn Our Country into a Third World Hellhole* (Washington, DC: Regnery Publishing, 2016). On the impact of such books in the American context, see Nicole Hemmer, *Messengers of the Right: Conservative Media and the Transformation of American Politics* (Philadelphia: University of Pennsylvania Press, 2016).
40 Regula Stämpfli, *Trumpism: Ein Phänomen verändert die Welt* (Basel: Münsterverlag, 2018).
41 Krisztina Koenen, "Orbánismus in Ungarn Ursprünge und Elemente der 'Illiberalen Demokratie'," *Osteuropa* 65, no. 11–12 (2015): 33–44.
42 Alexander Murinson, *Turkish Foreign Policy in the 21st Century: Neo-Ottomanism and the Strategic Depth Doctrine* (London: I. B. Tauris, 2020); M. Hakan Yavuz, *Nostalgia for the Empire: The Politics of Neo-Ottomanism* (Oxford: Oxford University Press, 2020).
43 Adam Gopnik, "Orwell's '1984' and Trump's America," *The New Yorker*, January 27, 2017, https://www.newyorker.com/news/daily-comment/orwells-1984–and-trumps-america.
44 Soboczynski, "Donald Trump." See also Adam Gopnik, "Trump's Radical Anti-Americanism," *The New Yorker*, February 13–20, 2017, https://www.newyorker.com/magazine/2017/02/13/trumps-radical-anti-americanism.
45 Peter Pomerantsev, "The False Lords of Misrule," *Granta* 137, January 20, 2017, https://granta.com/false-lords-misrule/.

To think that nationalism is a historical phenomenon we will not have to bother about in a few years or decades is wishful thinking. To quote Lepore once more:

> The endurance of nationalism proves that there's never any shortage of blackguards willing to prop up people's sense of themselves and their destiny with a tissue of myths and prophecies, prejudices and hatreds, or to empty out old rubbish bags full of festering resentments and calls to violence. . . . A nation founded on revolution and universal rights will forever struggle against chaos and the forces of particularism. A nation born in contradiction will forever fight over the meaning of its history.[46]

The present book, which assembles the extended papers that were presented at an international workshop at Nord Universitet, Norway – co-organized with the Center for the Study of Nationalism in the College of International Studies at the University of Oklahoma, USA – in November 2019, intends to address the problems nationalism causes in an age that was considered to be transnational already. It will analyze different national contexts and narratives to show which role nationalism still plays and which negative impacts the abuse of it by the populist nationalists of our time could create.

The first section aims to provide a closer look at the continuities of older nationalist narratives and their reframing in a more global 21st century. Frank Jacob opens the section with a discussion of the continuities and discontinuities of Turkish nationalism since the end of the First World War. He evaluates the role of Kemal Atatürk in the formation of the Turkish nation after the War of Independence (1918–1922) and how this national narrative is contested nowadays by neo-Ottomanism. Jacob's chapter highlights in what ways nationalisms can change and which events or factors determine these changes over a longer time period. The following chapter by Sven Brajer and Johannes Schütz follows a similar approach and offers a longue durée survey of East German nationalism, highlighting the continuities and transformations from the Imperial period until today and argues that the end of the Soviet Union forced not only formerly peripheral regions to redefine their idea of the nation[47] but also Russia to reinvent its nation and thereby to apply a reinterpretation of the past. Alicja Curanović's chapter focuses on the "phantomic nature of missionary nationalism" and its consequences for Russian politics and shows the extent to which the history of the pre-revolutionary Russian Empire is revived as a national narrative to

---

46 Lepore, "A New Americanism," 11, 19.
47 Ivan Krastev, *After Europe* (Philadelphia: University of Pennsylvania Press, 2017). See also Irene Götz, Klaus Roth and Marketa Spiritova, eds., *Neuer Nationalismus im östlichen Europa: Kulturwissenschaftliche Perspektiven* (Bielefeld: Transcript, 2017).

sanction Putin's expansionist policy. The last chapter in this section by James Okolie-Osemene switches to another geographical context and shows how far nationalism is limiting a "new transnational Pan-Africanism," highlighting one of the problems the African continent is facing as well and thereby stressing that the fight between nationalist and transnationalist ideas is truly a global conflict and not a purely Western and post-industrial one.

The second section takes the question of identity and the role of the Other in its creation into closer consideration. Inessa Kouteinikova shows how photographs were used to create a "symbology of nationhood" in the Russian context, especially with regard to the depiction and perception of Central Asia. That there can exist, as mentioned before, different national identities in one nation state that might come into conflict with each other is then presented via a case study about Georgia by Irakli Chkhaidze. National identities are, however, not only contested in the 21st century but also communicated, especially by using social media. This aspect is discussed in the third chapter in this section, a Pakistani case study by Muhammad A. Z. Mughal, who analyzes the role of new media for the national narratives shared by a new generation of women and men in Pakistan.

The final section of the book examines nationalisms in a global context, meaning that nationalisms can be embedded into larger global narratives or movements but are then torn between this globalizing process and the national frontiers within it. First, Tetiana Perga provides a study about eco-nationalism in Ukraine in the late 1980s and early 1990s that shows how nationalist ideas were a side-product of a transnational protest movement of the time. Anna Zadora's case study of Belarus also points out the nationalist limitations of globalization, as she discusses the conflict "between globalization and authoritarian confinement, between Europe and Russia," a conflict that has even been more intensified by the revolutionary process in Belarus, where the future of the nation state has still not yet been decided. People will continue to struggle there, as well in other national contexts, to find out if they are open enough to reach a transnational order of living or if they are too fearful to leave the comforting environment of their own nation.

Works Cited

Anderson, Benedict. *Imagined Communities: Reflections on the Origin and Spread of Nationalism*. London: Verso, 1983.

Appiah, Kwame Anthony. "The Importance of Elsewhere: In Defense of Cosmopolitanism." *Foreign Affairs* 98, no. 2 (2019): 20–26.

Arnold, Sina, Sebastian Bischoff and Jana König. "Postnationale Potenziale: Praktiken jenseits der Nation." *Aus Politik und Zeitgeschichte* 68, no. 48 (2018): 27–33.

Bauer, Franz J. *Das "lange" 19. Jahrhundert (1789–1917): Profil einer Epoche*. 4th rev. ed. Stuttgart: Reclam, 2017.

Cavallini, Ivano, ed. *Nation and/or Homeland: Identity in 19th-Century Music and Literature Between Central and Mediterranean Europe*. Milano/Udine: Mimesis, 2014.

Coulter, Ann. *Adios, America: The Left's Plan to Turn Our Country into a Third World Hellhole*. Washington, DC: Regnery Publishing, 2016.

Crouch, Colin. "Der Nationalismus globalisiert sich." *ZEIT Online*, February 11, 2017. http://www.zeit.de/wirtschaft/2017-02/globalisierung-widerstand-rechte-nationalismus-donald-trump-marine-le-pen-is/komplettansicht.

Eco, Umberto. *Inventing the Enemy*. Boston: Mariner Books, 2013.

Fukuyama, Francis. *The End of History and the Last Man*. New York: Free Press, 1992.

Geulen, Christian. "Zur 'Wiederkehr' des Nationalismus." *Aus Politik und Zeitgeschichte* 68, no. 48 (2018): 4–8.

Gopnik, Adam. "Orwell's '1984' and Trump's America." *The New Yorker*, January 27, 2017. https://www.newyorker.com/news/daily-comment/orwells-1984-and-trumps-america.

Gopnik, Adam. "Trump's Radical Anti-Americanism." *The New Yorker*, February 13–20, 2017. https://www.newyorker.com/magazine/2017/02/13/trumps-radical-anti-americanism.

Götz, Irene, Klaus Roth and Marketa Spiritova, eds. *Neuer Nationalismus im östlichen Europa: Kulturwissenschaftliche Perspektiven*. Bielefeld: Transcript, 2017.

Guérot, Ulrike. "Wir brauchen die Nation nicht mehr." *Der Standard*, May 2, 2017. https://www.derstandard.at/story/2000056814520/politologin-guerot-wir-brauchen-die-nation-nicht-mehr.

Habermas, Jürgen. *Die postnationale Konstellation: Politische Essays*. Berlin: Suhrkamp, 1998.

Hegel, Georg W. F. *Philosophy of History*. New York: Dover, 1956.

Hemmer, Nicole. *Messengers of the Right: Conservative Media and the Transformation of American Politics*. Philadelphia: University of Pennsylvania Press, 2016.

Jacob, Frank and Adam Luedtke. "Introduction: Migration and the Nation State." In *Migration and the Crisis of the Modern Nation State?*, edited by Frank Jacob and Adam Luedtke, v–xiv. Wilmington, DE: Vernon Press, 2018.

Jacob, Frank. "Joe Bidens Krux: Die USA und die gespaltene Nation." November 25, 2020. https://jacobschreibtgeschichteonline.net/2020/11/25/joe-bidens-krux-die-usa-und-die-gespaltene-nation/.

Jacob, Frank. *Impulse zu den Krisen und Herausforderungen des 21. Jahrhunderts*. Marburg: Büchner, 2021.

Kant, Immanuel. *Zum ewigen Frieden: Ein philosophischer Entwurf*, edited by Rudolf Malter. Stuttgart: Reclam, 2008 [1795].

Koenen, Krisztina. "Orbánismus in Ungarn Ursprünge und Elemente der 'Illiberalen Demokratie'." *Osteuropa* 65, no. 11–12 (2015): 33–44.

Krastev, Ivan. *After Europe*. Philadelphia: University of Pennsylvania Press, 2017.

Latour, Bruno. *Down to Earth: Politics in the New Climatic Regime*. Cambridge: Polity Press, 2018.

Lepore, Jill. "A New Americanism: Why a Nation Needs a National Story." *Foreign Affairs* 98, no. 2 (2019): 10–19.

Lesenich, Stephan. "Corona-Nationalismus: Auch die Solidarität bleibt daheim." In *Die Welt nach Corona: Von den Risiken des Kapitalismus, den Nebenwirkungen des*

Ausnahmezustands und der kommenden Gesellschaft, edited by Dieter F. Bertz, 143–148. Berlin: Bertz + Fischer, 2021.

Lotman, Juri. *Culture and Explosion*, transl. by Wilma Clark. Berlin: De Gruyter, 2009.

Lotman, Yuri. *Universe of the Mind: A Semiotic Theory of Culture*, transl. by Ann Shukman. Bloomington: Indiana University Press, 1990.

Luxemburg, Rosa. *Die Akkumulation des Kapitals: Ein Beitrag zur ökonomischen Erklärung des Imperialismus*. Berlin: Paul Singer, 1913. https://www.marxists.org/deutsch/archiv/luxemburg/1913/akkkap/index.htm.

Mangiapane, Francesco and Tiziana Migliore, eds. *Images of Europe: The Union between Federation and Separation*. Cham: Springer 2021.

Müller, Jan-Werner. "False Flags: The Myth of the Nationalist Resurgence." *Foreign Affairs* 98, no. 2 (2019): 35–41.

Murinson, Alexander. *Turkish Foreign Policy in the 21st Century: Neo-Ottomanism and the Strategic Depth Doctrine*. London: I. B. Tauris, 2020.

Osterhammel, Jürgen. "Nationalism and Globalization." In *The Oxford Handbook of the History of Nationalism*, 2nd ed., edited by John Breuilly, 694–709. Oxford: Oxford University Press, 2016.

Pomerantsev, Peter. "The False Lords of Misrule." *Granta* 137, January 20, 2017. https://granta.com/false-lords-misrule/.

Renan, Ernest. "A Lecture Delivered at the Sorbonne, 11 March 1882: 'Qu'est-ce qu'une nation'." In *Oeuvres Completes*, vol. 1, 887–907. Paris: Calmann-Lévy, 1947.

Sabrow, Martin. "Höcke und wir." *Zeitgeschichte-online*, January 25, 2017. http://www.zeitgeschichte-online.de/kommentar/hoecke-und-wir.

Sapolsky, Robert. "This Is Your Brain on Nationalism." *Foreign Affairs* 98, no. 2 (2019): 42–47.

Soboczynski, Adam. "Donald Trump: 'Wir werden unsere Nation mit amerikanischen Händen wieder aufbauen'," *Die Zeit* 5, January 26, 2017. http://www.zeit.de/2017/05/donald-trump-politische-kommunikation-rhetorik-sprache/komplettansicht.

Stämpfli, Regula. *Trumpism: Ein Phänomen verändert die Welt*. Basel: Münsterverlag, 2018.

Thumann, Michael. *Der neue Nationalismus: Die Wiederkehr einer totgeglaubten Ideologie*. Berlin: Die Andere Bibliothek, 2020.

Williams, Howard. "The End of History in Hegel and Marx." *The European Legacy* 2, no. 3 (1997): 557–566.

Wimmer, Andreas. "Why Nationalism Works: And Why It Isn't Going Away." *Foreign Affairs* 98, no. 2 (2019): 27–34.

Yavuz, M. Hakan. *Nostalgia for the Empire: The Politics of Neo-Ottomanism*. Oxford: Oxford University Press, 2020.

Section I: **Old Wine in New Bottles: About the Continuities of Nationalism and Empire in the 21st Century**

Frank Jacob
2 Turkish Nationalism: From Gallipoli to Contemporary Neo-Ottomanism

Turkish nationalism has gone through tremendous changes in the last century. While it was first expressed in the Young Turk revolution of 1908 and was important during the last years of the Ottoman Empire, it reached its first height during and after the Turkish War of Independence, when Mustafa Kemal, later known as Atatürk, became the incarnation of the Turkish nation. His rise to become the nation's strong man actually began with one decisive battle during the First World War, namely the battle for the Gallipoli Peninsula and the Dardanelles. Although the main focus of research related to the centennial of the First World War is still directed on the campaigns in Europe, in particular the Western Front, "the Gallipoli operations are the most famous and well-remembered today."[1] The memory of the events related to the Gallipoli campaign[2] has played an important role in Britain, as well as in Australia, where discussions about the reasons for its failure and the ANZAC (Australian and New Zealand Army Corps) myth, respectively, were at the center of commemorative events.[3] However, the victory at Gallipoli was as important for the Turkish memory as the defeat and shared suffering were for the Australian identity.[4] Ulrichsen emphasizes the role Gallipoli-related memories have played for the Australian and Turkish nations since the end

---

[1] Kristian C. Ulrichsen, *The First World War in the Middle East* (London: Oxford University Press, 2014), 75. For extensive discussions of the campaign, see Les A. Carlyon, *Gallipoli* (London: Bantam, 2003); Edward J. Erickson, *Gallipoli: Command under Fire* (London: Bloomsbury, 2015); Edward J. Erickson, *Gallipoli: The Ottoman Campaign* (Barnsley: Pen & Sword, 2015); Peter Hart, *Gallipoli* (Oxford: Oxford University Press, 2014); Philip J. Haythornthwaite, *Gallipoli 1915: Frontal Assault on Turkey* (London: Osprey, 1991); Peter Liddle, *The Gallipoli Experience Reconsidered* (Barnsley: Pen & Sword, 2015); Alan Moorehead, *Gallipoli* (London: Hamish Hamilton, 1956); Frank Jacob, *Gallipoli 1915/16: Britanniens bitterste Niederlage* (Berlin: De Gruyter Oldenbourg, 2020).
[2] Jenny Macleod, *Gallipoli* (Oxford: Oxford University Press, 2015).
[3] Jeff Hopkins-Weise, *Blood Brothers: The ANZAC Genesis* (Auckland: Penguin, 2007); Robin Prior, *Gallipoli: The End of a Myth* (New Haven, CT: Yale University Press, 2015).
[4] Frank Jacob, "The Construction of a Memorial Space: The Gallipoli Campaign and Spatial Remembrance," in *War and Memorials,* ed. Frank Jacob and Kenneth Pearl (Paderborn: Schöning, 2019), 189–207.

Note: Parts of this chapter have been used for a recent article published in Global Humanities 8 (2021): Identity and Nationhood.

of the First World War, as this military campaign "has come to symbolise the rise of a national consciousness in both countries, and the memory and bravery of those who took part continue to reverberate a century on."[5]

With their decision to join the war on the German side in 1914, the Ottoman leadership had originally intended to save the empire from partition and colonial rule, but the war would trigger its further decline and fall.[6] The Young Turks and their attempts to reform the empire had already stimulated a Turkish nationalism before the First World War,[7] but the Balkan Wars had weakened the empire, and their defeat in 1918 initially limited the chances for the Turkish national struggle, although the nation would be forged in wars continuing until 1922.[8] The rise of the Turkish nation from the ashes, to use a metaphorical expression, was related to another rise, namely that of Mustafa Kemal, a military officer who would begin to determine and decide the future of an independent Turkey in the aftermath of the First World War. His success was based on the victory at Gallipoli as well, because Kemal, who would become known as Atatürk, "Father of the Turks," was not only remembered as the defender of the Turkish nation in the post-war period, but also as someone who in 1915 had already defeated the imperialist attempt of the Entente to conquer the soil that would later belong to the Turkish nation. Kemal's rise to power was consequently related to his military successes that laid the foundation for his political reshaping of Turkey from 1922. Although his rule was autocratic, the nationalism Kemal represented and that continued to shape Turkey in his name during the 20th century was a secular and modernity-oriented one that longed for international ties to secure Turkey's standing within the international community, although it suppressed minorities like the Kurdish at the same time. This course, however, was eventually abandoned, and a new "strong man" in Turkey attempted to revert this course of nationalism, leading it back to one based on religious values and a strong Turkish stand in the region. The case of Turkish nationalism from the First World War to the early 21st century therefore shows how national ideas and the nationalisms that are supposed to express the post-nation state power and course of politics can be changed according to the agenda of ruling elites. The present contribution therefore intends to outline the building of the Turkish nation state, the role

---

5 Ulrichsen, *First World War in the Middle East*, 75.
6 Mustafa Aksakal, *The Ottoman Road to War in 1914: The Ottoman Empire and the First World War* (New York: Cambridge University Press, 2008), 2.
7 Feroz Ahmad, *The Young Turks: The Committee of Union and Progress in Turkish Politics 1908–1914* (New York: Oxford University Press, 1969); Carter V. Findley, *Turkey, Islam, Nationalism, and Modernity: A History, 1789–2007* (New Haven, CT: Yale University Press, 2010), 201–205.
8 Findley, *Turkey, Islam, Nationalism, and Modernity*, 219–226.

of Atatürk, and especially the commemoration of his military victories at Gallipoli and between 1918 and 1922, when he defended the new nation against foreign invaders and thereby stimulated an anti-imperialist nationalism, which was quite common in colonial and semi-colonial regions of the world in the interwar period.[9] The second part will show how Kemalist nationalism was eventually exchanged for a more aggressive and reactionary nationalism under the rule of Recep Tayyip Erdoğan. The chapter will consequently show that nationalisms are able to change and that attempts to overcome national categories by transnational ones can be reverted through crises and political changes that allow populist elements to reframe the nation and the aims of nationalism.

Kemal's Rise after Gallipoli

It was the victory at Gallipoli that proved that the Ottoman Army was not inferior, as many war planners in London had anticipated. In addition, the Ottoman military victory laid the ground for Kemal's reputation as a successful defender of national interests.[10] When the "British withdrew their entire expeditionary force in January 1916, Gallipoli had become synonymous with Allied humiliation and Turkish triumph,"[11] and Kemal's rise to power began, although the German commander of the defending troops, Otto Liman von Sanders, would later complain that the Turkish officer's role during the Gallipoli campaign had been overemphasized.[12] Regardless of such a critical view by a former German commanding officer after the First World War, the Turkish nation-building process centered around "two key victories: Gallipoli and the Turkish War of Independence of 1919–22, which culminated in the republic's recognition in the 1923 Treaty of Lausanne."[13] The defeat in the Balkan Wars had already made the

---

9 For example, for a discussion of Chinese nationalism in relation to the First World War and Japanese imperialism, see Frank Jacob, "China's Eruption after the First World War: Japanese Imperialism, Western Jingoism, and the Awakening of Chinese Nationalism," in *Zeiten des Aufruhrs (1916–1921): Globale Proteste, Streiks und Revolutionen gegen den Ersten Weltkrieg und seine Auswirkungen*, ed. Marcel Bois and Frank Jacob (Berlin: Metropol, 2020), 171–213.
10 Sean McMeekin, "World War I and the Establishment of the Republic," in *The Routledge Handbook of Modern Turkey*, ed. Metin Heper and Sabri Sayari (London: Routledge, 2012), 38.
11 Ibid.
12 Liman von Sanders to Carl Mühlmann, Munich, January 30, 1927, German Federal Archives, Military Archives (BArch MArch), RH61/1088.
13 Macleod, *Gallipoli*, 155.

Young Turks demand "a new spirit and enthusiasm"[14] for the army, and men like Kemal had tried to strengthen their political influence as well. However, the Ottoman Army was suffering from several problems, including insufficient logistics and diseases.[15] All in all, the Ottoman Army was nevertheless able to mobilize around 3,000,000 men during the First World War,[16] and the experience of the war was shared by many men who would later support Kemal's claim for independent power under his leadership.

Regardless of their large number, Beşikçi described several problems the Ottoman Army was weakened by:

> First of all, there was the problem of lack of standardization among regions regarding recruitment. [. . .] Secondly, although at the beginning a short war was generally expected, the Ottoman state began to have difficulty in sustaining a large-scale and permanent mobilization as the war continued. And, thirdly, resistance to conscription in the forms of draft-evasion and desertion became a major problem especially in the second half of the war.[17]

The victory at Gallipoli was consequently an outstanding experience, as it showed that the Ottoman Army was capable of winning battles if led by commanders like Kemal, who consequently became a kind of figurehead of Turkish nationalism during the First World War, since other military leaders, like Ismail Enver Pasha, had failed to secure victories, e.g. in the Caucasus region. For the "foundation myth [of the Turkish nation], the War of Independence is by far the more important, but the memory of Gallipoli is nonetheless interesting and the link between the two is Mustafa Kemal."[18] Kemal was therefore the central figure, and after playing a role in the pivotal moments of Gallipoli and the War of Independence "he then went on to lead the Turkish national movement which fought to overthrow the stipulations of the Treaty of Sèvres, end the Ottoman sultanate, and establish sovereign, secular, and democratic government in Turkey."[19] Although "nationalist historiography inaugurated by the republican regime in the 1930s" tended to

---

14 Mehmet Beşikçi, "Mobilizing Military Labor in the Age of Total War: Ottoman Conscription before and during the Great War," in *Fighting for a Living: A Comparative Study of Military Labour 1500–2000*, ed. Erik-Jan Zürcher (Amsterdam: Amsterdam University Press, 2014), 555.
15 Hikmet Ozdemir, *The Ottoman Army 1914–1918: Disease and Death on the Battlefield* (Salt Lake City, UT: University of Utah Press, 2008), 28–31, 48.
16 Turkish Military Archives, Ankara, BDH, Folder 62/File 309A/Index 005, cited in Beşikçi, "Mobilizing Military Labor in the Age of Total War," 558.
17 Beşikçi, "Mobilizing Military Labor in the Age of Total War," 558.
18 Macleod, *Gallipoli*, 155.
19 Ibid.

2 Turkish Nationalism: From Gallipoli to Contemporary Neo-Ottomanism — 19

not overemphasize the impact of Gallipoli as an important moment that triggered Turkish nationalism but rather "to present the emergence of Turkish nationalism as a process of 'awakening,' belated yet inevitable,"[20] it was also inevitable that Kemal's role as the central figure remained an important aspect of Turkish nationalism in the decades to come. When it emerged from the War of Independence in 1922, as Ugur Ümit Üngör correctly highlighted, "[m]entally, the young nation state was still blank and needed a memory. The continuous process of defining and fine-tuning a national identity entailed a parallel process for a national memory."[21] It was Kemal who provided an integrative nationalist figure, the "Father of the Turks," whose transition into Atatürk reached back to the last rearing up of the Ottoman Empire when fighting the Allied invasion forces at the Dardanelles and on the Gallipoli Peninsula.

During these battles, Kemal "galvanized the simple Turkish soldier with a new courage. They were ready to follow him to hell."[22] This would be part of the foundational myth of modern Turkey, as without Gallipoli there would have been no opportunity for Kemal to rise. Regardless of this interrelation between the military officer and the establishment of the modern Turkish nation state, "the creator of modern Turkey, has been one of the most controversial personalities of the Muslim world in the twentieth century. Some admire him while others despise him. In some quarters he is considered a role model for Muslim leaders and in others, the enemy of Islam."[23] Kemal's military success was initially not rewarded when the sultan acknowledged the achievements of the 27th and 57th regiments and decorated soldiers and officers in April 1916. Nor was he mentioned in official publications about the successful Ottoman defense of the Dardanelles.[24] The government was interested in documenting an important victory, and even sent "writers and journalists Ağaoğlu Ahmed, Ali Canip, Celal Sahir, Enis Behiç, Hakkı Süha, Hamdullah Suphi, Hıfzı Tevfik, Muhittin, Orhan Seyfi, Selahattin, Mehmed Emin, Yusuf Razi, Ömer Seyfettin, İbrahim Alaeddin, and Müfit Ratip; the musician Ahmed Yekta; and the painters İbrahim Çallı and

---

20 Umut Özkirimli, "The Changing Nature of Nationalism in Turkey: Actors, Discourses, and the Struggle for Hegemony," in *Symbiotic Antagonisms: Competing Nationalisms in Turkey*, ed. Ayse Kadioglu and Emin Fuat Keyman (Salt Lake City, UT: University of Utah Press, 2011), 90.
21 Ugut Ü. Üngör, *The Making of Modern Turkey: Nation and State in Eastern Anatolia, 1913–1950* (Oxford: Oxford University Press, 2011), 218.
22 Harold Courtenay Armstrong, *Gray Wolf, Mustafa Kemal: An Intimate Study of a Dictator* (Freeport, NY: Books for Libraries Press, 1972 [1932]), 80.
23 Khalid Sohail, *Prophets of Violence – Prophets of Peace: Understanding the Roots of Contemporary Political Violence* (Toronto: White Knight Publication, 2005), 133.
24 Macleod, *Gallipoli*, 157.

Nazmi Ziya"[25] to the battlefield in July 1915, just six months after the Allied troops had been evacuated from the peninsula. It is therefore worth noting, as MacLeod emphasizes, that "Kemal's role at Gallipoli became significantly more acclaimed after he attained power. Prior to that, it was the humble soldier who was primarily celebrated for his heroism at Gallipoli."[26] This is important, as the victory at Gallipoli was later more heavily emphasized to construct a line of Turkish nationalism that began with a victory against invading foreign forces, a victory that had been made possible by the man who would also unite Turkey during its fight for national sovereignty between 1918 and 1922, and it was thus an essential element of the War of Independence as well. Although Kemal was mentioned as a hero in some Ottoman reports about Gallipoli, his role would be more and more central in later narratives. A tradition of nationalist defense was consequently invented[27] to match the necessities of Kemal's later rule as Atatürk.

In some ways, Kemal's life story was very typical of a military officer who was part of the Young Turks movement,[28] but his experience of the First World War in general, and the Gallipoli campaign in particular, as well as the War of Independence, also provided him with a chance to create an "imagined community"[29] for all Turkish soldiers who shared similar experiences, and his national program would naturally exploit references to this shared past. The Turkish nation could be built due to the struggle against foreign occupation, which is why, as Andrew Mango outlined, "[t]he emergence of a fully independent, stable Turkish national state within the community of civilised nations was a fortunate, if unintended, consequence of the policies of the victors of the [First World] War."[30] Before further elaborating on Kemal's nationalist interpretation of Ottoman and Turkish history, a short description of his career and achievements seems to be in order here.

Born in Thessaloniki in 1880/81 as Mustafa Kemal, he undertook a military career that would eventually also change the way people referred to him. He achieved the rank of brigadier in the Ottoman Army by 1916, and he was thereafter

---

25 Ibid., 158.
26 Ibid., 155.
27 Eric Hobsbawm and Terence Ranger, *The Invention of Tradition* (Cambridge: Cambridge University Press, 1983).
28 Erik-Jan Zürcher, "In the Name of the Father, the Teacher and the Hero: The Atatürk Personality Cult in Turkey," in *Political Leadership, Nations and Charisma,* ed. Vivian Ibrahim and Margit Wunch (London: Routledge, 2012), 130.
29 Benedict Anderson, *Imagined Communities: Reflections on the Origin and Spread of Nationalism* (London: Verso, 1983).
30 Andrew Mango, *From the Sultan to Atatürk: Turkey* (London: Haus Publishing, 2010), 3.

referred to as Mustafa Kemal Pasha. After 1921, when his victory against the Greek Army at the Sakarya River turned him into a national hero and defender of Turkey, he was called Gazi, which could be translated either as "conquering hero" or "champion of Islam." In 1934, once he had established and secured the independent nation state of modern Turkey, the national assembly chose to award him with the name "Atatürk" and would thereby forever inscribe his history into that of the Turkish nation.[31] This rise to power was made possible by Kemal's military successes, and until the end of the First World War, his career was a purely military one. While Kemal had been trained according to Western standards during his time at military schools and the academy for future members of the general staff in Constantinople (today's Istanbul), he shared the idea of Turkish independence early on and therefore joined the Young Turks in 1908 and participated in their "revolution" during the same year.[32]

Sultan Abdülhamid II had intended to modernize his empire by establishing institutions that would provide Western-oriented education, but this also stimulated "the emergence of an enlightened intelligentsia within the ranks of the civil and military bureaucracy that adopted the principles of the French Revolution."[33] With an enlightened military elite, the sultan had also created his own enemies, who would demand political reforms to turn the Ottoman Empire into a constitutional monarchy to prevent its further decline. This was also a secular movement, as the Young Turks "despised Abdülhamid II's personal piety" and "blamed his attachment to Islam for his autocratic conservatism,"[34] although they shared the same enemy as the Muslim forces of the empire, namely Western imperialism. The Young Turks were consequently not a homogenous movement but divided into different factions, with the Committee of Union and Progress (CUP), the one Kemal had been a part of as well, being one of the more progressive forces.[35]

---

31 Zürcher, "In the Name of the Father," 130.
32 Bedross Der Matossian, *Shattered Dreams of Revolution: From Liberty to Violence in the Late Ottoman Empire* (Stanford: Stanford University Press, 2014); Şükrü M. Hanioğlu, *Preparation for a Revolution: The Young Turks, 1902–1908* (Oxford: Oxford University Press, 2001); Noémi Lévy-Aksu and François Georgeon, ed., *The Young Turk Revolution and the Ottoman Empire: The Aftermath of 1908* (London: Bloomsbury, 2017).
33 Sakir Dincsahin, *State and Intellectuals in Turkey: The Life and Times of Niyazi Berkes, 1908–1988* (Lanham, MD: Lexington Books, 2015), 9.
34 Michael A. Reynolds, *Shattering Empires: The Clash and Collapse of the Ottoman and Russian Empires 1908–1918* (Cambridge: Cambridge University Press, 2011), 83.
35 Dincsahin, *State and Intellectuals in Turkey*, 9.

The "revolution" of 1908 had shown that the diversity of the Young Turks movement would cause problems, especially since "non-Muslim communities sought opportunities to establish self-rule in their own nation-states rather than remaining subjects of the Sultan."[36] Kemal nevertheless continued his military life for the next few years and in 1911 organized guerilla warfare against Italy in Tripolitania before serving during the Balkan Wars. He continued to be active and influential in the CUP, although he was not one of its political leaders. During the July Crisis, Kemal, at that time a lieutenant colonel, served as the Ottoman military attaché in Sofia for the Balkan states, namely Bulgaria, Montenegro, and Serbia.[37] While he was negotiating with Bulgarian authorities to join the war on the side of Germany and the Ottoman Empire, Kemal realized that he would prefer an assignment of combat duty instead, and in November 1914, when war had officially been declared, he approached Enver Pasha with the request to be transferred. His anti-German position, as he had criticized the German military mission in the Ottoman Empire before, as well as his activities with regard to the CUP prevented such an assignment at that time. However, in January 1915, as the war had continued and demanded capable officers, "Mustafa Kemal finally left Sofia to take command of an Ottoman division that as yet existed only on paper."[38] In February 1915, Kemal was in Thrace to recruit and train his division, but a British attack, passing through the Dardanelles with a fleet, alarmed the military leadership and commanded him to head for Gallipoli. Hanioğlu has emphasized how the war created a window of opportunity for Kemal, whose rise was now made possible, and although "[s]eated at an embassy desk scarcely one month before, he now found himself in the midst of one of the greatest battles of modern times. At last he would have the chance to command an offensive operation within the context of a defensive campaign and win thereby a place in history."[39]

After the armistice in 1918, the Ottoman Empire was occupied by the Allied powers, whose political representatives had already discussed plans on how to divide it among themselves. The fear that caused the Ottoman leaders to join the alliance with Germany in the first place would now, four years later, become a reality. In this situation, Kemal began to rise up as a prominent figure and eventually the leading man of the nationalist liberation movement (*Kuva-i Milliye*), as he "managed to pull together a coalition of diverse

---

36 Ibid.
37 Ahmet Tetik, ed. *Sofya Askerî Ataşesi Mustafa Kemal'in Raporları, Kasım 1913–Kasım 1914* (Ankara: ATASE Yayin-Iari, 2007).
38 Şükrü M. Hanioğlu, *Ataturk: An Intellectual Biography* (Princeton, NJ: Princeton University Press, 2011), 73.
39 Ibid., 74.

constituencies, which, despite profound differences of opinion and allegiance, were unified in their opposition to the foreign takeover of Anatolia."[40] Considering the new situation and the end of the Ottoman Empire, Kemal attempted to establish a modern nation state of Turkey instead of returning to the status quo ante. As a Young Turk, he had demanded reforms, but now he would long for a clear discontinuum, i.e. a new start.[41]

Although the state, due to the necessities of military mobilization, had begun to centralize its power in the war years,[42] there had been side effects, namely "new alliances between the state and the Anatolian Muslim population"[43] as well as more state control on the local level. The wartime mobilization, as Besikçi emphasizes, consequently "achieved certain objectives and played a major role in reshaping Anatolia's social infrastructure in the years immediately preceding the Turkish National Struggle of 1919–1922."[44] Kemal could consequently base his efforts to secure a new and modern Turkish nation state on some aspects that had already been developed during the war. He could also channel a strong sense of nationalism, which had been directed toward minorities within Turkey, namely the Armenian population, who would become the victims of genocide during the war, but Kemal would now use and direct these nationalist sentiments against external enemies.

In May 1919, Kemal was appointed as the new inspector of the Ninth Army at Samsun, and he was supposed to help the British occupation forces to suppress banditry in the Black Sea region. Regardless of his appointment, Kemal began to forge an alliance for national resistance with other army officers, namely Kâzım Karabekir and Ali Fuat (Cebesoy). Between June and September, several meetings and congresses in Amasya, Erzurum, and Sivas led to the formation of a Turkish nationalist principle and the alliance that was supposed to defend it against the foreign invaders. A National Pact (*Misak-ı Milli*) was ratified in the soon-to-be new capital, Ankara, and the government by the sultan Mehmet VI was declared illegitimate, while Kemal and his supporters claimed to represent the Turkish nation. Constantinople was therefore sacked again by British occupation forces, who would rule the city by martial law.[45] Due to these events, "outraged parliamentary

---

40 Zeynep Kezer, *Building Modern Turkey: State, Space, and Ideology in the Early Republic* (Pittsburgh: University of Pittsburgh Press, 2015), 4.
41 Ibid., 5.
42 Mehmet Besikçi, *The Ottoman Mobilization of Manpower in the First World War: Between Voluntarism and Resistance* (Leiden: Brill, 2012), 1.
43 Ibid., 2.
44 Ibid., 314.
45 McMeekin, "World War I and the Establishment of the Republic," 41.

deputies fled to Ankara to convene the Turkish Grand National Assembly (Türkiye Büyük Millet Meclisi) on 23 April 1920, promptly electing Kemal its president."[46] The Grand National Assembly acted as the new government of Turkey so that, politically, the separation from the Ottoman past had been completed, but the peace treaty of Sèvres in May 1920 had severe territorial consequences for the new nation, as Greece received almost all of Thrace and was authorized to gain the Izmir region, to be confirmed by a subsequent plebiscite. Eastern Turkey was supposed to be divided between Armenia and Kurdistan, while Italy and France would receive occupational zones between Antalya and Afyon and in Cilicia, respectively.[47] These terms would limit Turkey's national integrity and sovereignty for years, and the accord stimulated a nationalist reaction as it was considered to be a dictatorial and anti-Turkish treaty, especially since it favored former minorities. McMeekin's evaluation of the treaty's impact highlights the nationalist responses that played into Kemal's hands: "Sèvres was the best possible recruiting poster for Kemal's nationalist army, which, from its base in Ankara, began a multi-front war against now-independent Armenia in the Caucasus, the Greeks advancing inland from Izmir and Bursa, (in theory) the Italian and French troops to the south and southeast, and even the British, responsible for defending the Straits and the capital."[48]

The war that would follow between 1918 and 1922 was one in which Turkey had to fight alone against all, and the task seemed doomed, considering that no support could be expected from any other power with an interest in the region, especially since Russia faced its own civil war in the aftermath of the Russian Revolution. Since Kemal and the Soviet Russian government were under pressure, they at least agreed on a pragmatic alliance, formally established by the Treaty of Kars in October 1921. Territorial claims were exchanged and granted. Kemal could thereby pacify his eastern front, and without the threat of a two-front war, he could focus on his main enemy, the Greek forces. Initial Turkish successes were countered by a Greek offensive, leading to the decisive battle between the two armies at the Sakarya River, in which 90,000 Turks would make a stand against 100,000 Greeks. What started as a possible battle of annihilation, as a Turkish defeat would have left the capital Ankara, around 50 miles away, open to an attack by the enemy, would, regardless of the Greeks' superiority in firepower, become a victory that would even intensify the image of Kemal as a nationalist hero who not only had defended the Ottoman Empire

---

46 Ibid.
47 Ibid.
48 Ibid., 41.

at Gallipoli, but also the Turkish nation at the Sakarya River: "The victory at Sakarya heralded Turkey's national revival."[49] The British authorities were willing to revise the Treaty of Sèvres in favor of Turkey in March 1922, granting them the Aegean region, although Thrace was supposed to remain Greek. Kemal realized that the full extent of the Turkish nation could not only be secured by peace and opted for, in a kind of Bismarckian sense, "blood and iron" to solve the current issues of the post-war order. In June 1922, the attack on Greece began, and Izmir was finally taken back in September. The Turkish forces were eventually also successful in regaining eastern Thrace, and the British had to accept these realities, while David Lloyd George, the "mastermind of Sèvres," resigned in October, "never to return to public office."[50]

The Treaty of Lausanne in 1923 would eventually secure the new Republic of Turkey territorially, and not only had the nation thereby "won its independence under arms, which gave its new Republican government the international prestige and legitimacy,"[51] but Kemal had also laid the ground for his dominant role within the new nation state in the years until his death. As its first president, he would turn his military success into political power and influence, making him the main winner of the Turkish War of Independence.[52] He would use this power to strengthen his position even further when conflicts with his former allies erupted once the foreign enemies had been defeated. In November 1924, Kazim Karabekir, Rauf Orbay, Ali Fuad Cebesoy, and Refet Bele, who had been important during the War of Independence as well, founded an opposition party in 1924, but Kemal used emergency laws to counter the menace to his uncontested position as the first man of the Turkish nation state. Until 1926, "all of the former leaders of the independence struggle had been purged in a spectacular political trial in which they were accused of involvement in a plot to assassinate the President,"[53] and Kemal was free to continue his political course as he alone saw fit.

Vogel referred to the following period as one of Kemal's "transformative leadership"[54] as the latter began to secularize and modernize Turkey in the years that

---

49 Ibid., 42.
50 Ibid.
51 Ibid., 43.
52 Zürcher, "In the Name of the Father," 131.
53 Ibid., 132.
54 Ezra F. Vogel, "Nation Rebuilders: Mustafa Kemal Atatürk, Lee Kuan Yew, Deng Xiaoping, and Park Chung Hee," in *The Park Chung Hee Era*, ed. Byung-Kook Kim and Ezra F. Vogel (Cambridge, MA: Harvard University Press, 2011), 513.

followed the establishment of the new nation state.[55] Kemal, as Vogel further highlights, "took an ancient empire that was being dismembered, firmed up some of the remaining borders, and built new institutions to remake Turkey into a modern, Western-style and Western oriented nation."[56] Hanioğlu in this regard argues that Kemal's "new ideology, unsurprisingly, was a modified, scientifically sanctioned version of Turkish nationalism."[57] Kemal intended, as the new political leader of Turkey, to replace the religious bonds of his citizens with nationalist ones "through a radical reinterpretation of Islam from a Turkish nationalist perspective."[58] He needed to give his people a new national narrative, and when he spoke for more than 36 hours during the six days of the first Republican People's Party's congress in October 1927, he intended to create the narrative for Turkish nationalism and to further center the power within the new nation state around himself. In his lectures, he reinterpreted the previous year and ensured that he alone would be remembered as the savior of Turkey,[59] and this overemphasis also stimulated later reinterpretations and myths about his role at Gallipoli.[60] Stories about this campaign would now be more like a vaticinium ex eventu, as Kemal's eventual success stimulated the overemphasis of his role in the military campaign to defend the Dardanelles as well. Kemalism would consequently become a "prime example of a personality cult manufactured by the state,"[61] creating a semi-religious person-bound nationalist narrative.

That Kemal at the same time based his nationalist narrative on modernization and secularization was also a necessity in regards to his own self-representation, as the beliefs related to Sunni Islam prohibited the glorification and depiction of bodies, e.g. as statues. Although it caused possible problems with such religious traditions, statues of Kemal would be erected in many cities, especially in central spaces. Kemalist nationalism was consequently in some regards even anti-Islamic, as the messages represented by the personal cult of the military hero and political leader of Turkey went against existent religious rules.[62] Later, Atatürk became a central element of Turkish nationalism, as he

> has been depicted over and over again in a limited number of well-defined roles. The repertoire of visualisation seems to be limited in two senses: the number of roles in which

---

55 Hanioğlu, *Ataturk*, 160–161.
56 Vogel, "Nation Rebuilders," 513.
57 Hanioğlu, *Ataturk*, 161.
58 Ibid., 132.
59 Ibid.
60 Macleod, *Gallipoli*, 159.
61 Zürcher, "In the Name of the Father," 132.
62 Ibid., 132–133.

Atatürk is depicted and the freedom of artistic expression. Only four different roles can be clearly identified (military hero, teacher, father and emblem of modernity), and the vast majority of the paintings and statues, and even of the poses taken up by actors in the Atatürk films, go back to photographs that can be easily identified. There seems to be a strong reluctance to allow for artistic licence when depicting the leader.[63]

These different interpretations and images already show that it was hard to clearly identify Kemal/Atatürk, and the narrative seemed to offer a variety of ways to attach him to one's own wishes and ideas. Kemal seems to have supported this "flexibility" of his own image, considering that his own reports about the Gallipoli campaign were not published before the early 1940s.[64] The commemoration of the events of 1915/16 played a less important role in the nationalist agenda after 1922, but it was part of Kemal's personal story and therefore of some interest, although the memory of the First World War and the last years of the Ottoman Empire obviously did not arouse too much attention in the early years of the republic, and as Macleod emphasized, when "it was remembered, it was increasingly known for the role of Mustafa Kemal as well as for the devotion of the country's ordinary soldiers."[65]

It is interesting to note here, too, that the legend of the Turkish president in relation to his military service at Gallipoli was later prominently supported, e.g. when Winston Churchill called Kemal a "man of destiny."[66] The campaign would especially be remembered by British veterans and other visitors who would travel to Turkey for trips to the Gallipoli Peninsula, but there were also visitors from other countries who would, during a cruise through the Mediterranean Sea, use the opportunity to visit the famous battlefields.[67] Official commemorations had nevertheless come to a halt in the interwar years, as Kemal focused on the War of Independence as a source for and focus of the new national narrative. It is therefore quite ironic that he expressed the following thoughts about national history in 1931: "[W]riting history is just as important as making history: if the writers are not faithful to the makers, then the immutable truth will be altered in ways that can confound mankind."[68] Nevertheless, Kemal's nationalist approach was successful, and as Atatürk, the "Father of the Turks," he would remain an essential part of the country's national identity for decades.

---

63 Ibid., 136.
64 Macleod, *Gallipoli*, 160.
65 Ibid., 161.
66 Ibid., 162.
67 Ibid., 165.
68 Quoted in Kezer, *Building Modern Turkey*, 1.

Atatürk's Turkish Nationalism and the Commemoration of Gallipoli

Once in power, Atatürk "spent the latter part of his life secularizing and Westernizing state and society"[69] as it not only served the necessities to build up a strong and modernized nation state but also to secure his own image as some kind of enlightened leader, or national educator. For these purposes, "he organized a major transformation from a polity governed by Islamic law to one that strictly separated affairs of religion and state"[70] and, due to his achievements, was well remembered for the remaining decades of the 20th century. With regard to "so many other charismatic leaders in recent world history, . . . [it is] the very length of his symbolism, its all but unanimously positive nature, and its near universality, both in his own country and world wide,"[71] that make Kemal Atatürk a powerful symbol of 20th century Turkish nationalism, although his political agenda was quite an internationalist one at the same time.

The unity between the man and the nation was not only emblematized by the many statutes but also by his mausoleum (the Anıtkabir), which "is more than just the final resting place of Atatürk's body but also a national stage set and a representation of the hopes and ideals of the Republic of Turkey."[72] With regard to the semiotics of Turkish nationalism, Atatürk became a central aspect of the existent system of the nationalist narrative, both on the textual and the visual level. While sayings by him became winged expressions and were often cited, his face would be extremely prominent in the public sphere of Turkey. You could see or read Atatürk almost everywhere. More importantly, the "Kemalist elite that followed Ataturk envisaged a militantly secular, ethnically homogeneous republic ready to join the Western world. It banished Islam from school curricula, glorified Turkish history, and 'purified' the Turkish language in order to foster national pride and unity."[73] The course of secular Turkey would be continued in the

---

[69] Yael Navaro-Yashin, *Faces of the State: Secularism and Public Life in Turkey* (Princeton, NJ: Princeton University Press, 2002), 189.
[70] Ibid.
[71] Walter F. Weiker, "Atatürk as a National Symbol," *Turkish Studies Association Bulletin* 6, no. 2 (1982): 1.
[72] Christopher S. Wilson, "Representing National Identity and Memory in the Mausoleum of Mustafa Kemal Atatürk," *Journal of the Society of Architectural Historians* 68, no. 2 (2009): 225.
[73] Cengiz Çandar, "Atatürk's Ambiguous Legacy," *The Wilson Quarterly* 24, no. 4 (2000): 89.

following decades⁷⁴ until the 1980s, with Atatürk remaining "still far and away the most central single symbolic focus of his nation."⁷⁵

Since the 1990s, Turkey has begun to remember Gallipoli more thoroughly, as it helped to stimulate friendly international relations with the former Allied powers, probably Australia first and foremost. The references to the campaign, however, also changed in their wording, and nationalist pride was no longer focused only on Atatürk but also on the victory of a battle that had laid the foundations for his rise in later years.⁷⁶ The images of Atatürk at the same time were diversified once more and his prominence increased even more,⁷⁷ leading to some kind of omnipresence of the national hero, who in a way linked the history of the last roar of the Ottoman Empire with the nationalist rise of a new and strong Turkish nation state. However, there was also a change with regard to the role of Islam from the 1990s, as "the state stresse[d] the public role of Islam to ensure social harmony and to serve as an ultimate source of legitimization just as it did in Ottoman times."⁷⁸ This "neo-Ottoman turn," not only with regard to Turkey's foreign policy, was even strengthened after Recep Tayyip Erdoğan determined the political fate of Turkey, although Atatürk's personality cult remained strong in the early 2000s.⁷⁹ Consequently, Kemalism was one side of a dichotomic Turkish identity, and those who represent the secular part of it "suggest that Kemalism is the Turkish equivalent of the enlightenment; a guiding philosophy which brought Turks out of their dark age and onto the road to modernity."⁸⁰

The idea of a Western-oriented modernization has nevertheless been criticized as a form of intellectual concept that provided no clear definition for the Kemalist agenda and its predecessors, but was rather a tool to connect Turkey to a capitalist world system in which its national position should be as strong as possible. Somay argues with regard to this problem that

---

74 Macleod, *Gallipoli*, 60–62.
75 Weiker, "Atatürk as a National Symbol," 1.
76 Macleod, *Gallipoli*, 175–187.
77 Esra Özyürek, "Miniaturizing Atatürk: Privatization of State Imagery and Ideology in Turkey," *American Ethnologist* 31, no. 3 (2004): 374.
78 Hakan M. Yavuz, *Islamic Political Identity in Turkey* (Oxford: Oxford University Press, 2003), 79.
79 Nazli Ökten, "An Endless Death and Eternal Mourning," in *The Politics of Public Memory in Turkey,* ed. Esra Özyürek (Syracuse, NY: Syracuse University Press, 2007), 95–113; Esra Özyürek, *Nostalgia for the Modern: State Secularism and Everyday Politics in Turkey* (Durham, NC: Duke University Press, 2006).
80 Sinan Ciddi, *Kemalism in Turkish Politics: The Republican People's Party, Secularism and Nationalism* (London: Routledge, 2009).

> The hypothesis that "modernisation," "Westernisation," "Europeanisation" and "development" (economic or otherwise) were all used as euphemistic signifiers for the advancement of capitalism, also indicates that they have little to do with their root concepts "modern," "Western," "European" and "developed." Since all these terms entered Oriental cultural structures and intellectual life as external factors, conceptualised, defined and put into circulation by either colonial or patronising European powers, the Oriental cultures that are supposed to modernise, Westernise, Europeanise or "develop" had little say in what they were supposed to mean.[81]

Modernization meant different things for different people in different times, but the diverse ideas were in a way united with regard to the idea of a strong Turkish nation by the central authority of Kemal after 1922. Nevertheless, the system was only held together by his commemoration and dominance, as different people continued to want different things when they talked about modernization. While "[e]verybody wanted some of them, but never all of them, and combinations and permutations (depending on the priorities) that emerged were almost as varied as there were people,"[82] Kemal's authority provided the link for different interests and channeled them in the same direction for a long period of time. For a long time, his mausoleum would represent the idea of the Turkish nation like no other building or space in Turkey. "An essential component of nationalist projects that seek to institute a new sense of nationhood and define a new national subject is the construction of national space,"[83] and so, along with the mausoleum, other Atatürk memorials also played an important role to create a sense of national belonging, a sense of being part of the nation that had been created by the "Father of the Turks" himself. Çinar highlighted in this regard that "nationhood is not only about the collective imagination of a national community, but also about the imagination of national space."[84]

Atatürk was consequently an important factor of the Turkish nation from 1922, one that was also considered anti-imperialist in any sense of the word. In his early military career, he had opposed the German military mission, whose officers ran the Ottoman Army and were very influential,[85] and the Gallipoli-related operations were "a prime example of combined arms warfare. The battle proved an instructive experience for all combat parties involved. This was

---

[81] Bülent Somay, *The Psychopolitics of the Oriental Father: Between Omnipotence and Emasculation* (London: Palgrave Macmillan, 2014), 9.
[82] Ibid.
[83] Alev Çinar, *Modernity, Islam, and Secularism in Turkey: Bodies, Places, and Time* (Minneapolis: University of Minnesota Press, 2005), 99.
[84] Ibid.
[85] Gerhardt Grüßhaber, *The German Spirit in the Ottoman and Turkish Army, 1908–1938: A History of Military Knowledge* (Berlin: De Gruyter Oldenbourg, 2018), 26–102.

especially the case for the more than 3000 German soldiers that saw action during the campaign."[86] However, "members of the German mission not only advised the Ottomans but actually took over field commands during the First World War,"[87] something Kemal had not only criticized but maybe even considered when he turned out to be relatively reluctant to commemorate his own involvement in this important Ottoman victory. As mentioned earlier, German officers, like Otto Liman von Sanders, still considered Gallipoli to be a German victory,[88] and reports about Kemal in Nazi Germany actually depicted a much more positive image of the strong Turkish leader. In the category "men of the month," the *Zeitschrift für Politik* (Journal for Politics) published a feature that compared Kemal's role for Turkey with that of Hitler for Germany:

> The "sick man" [Turkey] has become healthy today, healthier than ever and takes the position in the political power play of Europe that is his due to his geopolitical situation determined by barren and harsh Anatolia, by a man who equals – if not even surpasses – this landscape in harshness and spartan unpretentiousness![89]

Since Atatürk did not run a democratic state after 1923 but rather an autocratic democracy in which an opposition was not free to express criticism, the parallels made Hitler even feel some kind of admiration for the Turkish statesman.[90] "Atatürk and his New Turkey were understood [by National Socialists] not only as 'one of us' in the Third Reich, but also as forerunners of the new kind of völkisch modernity,"[91] and criticisms of an overemphasis of Kemal's role at Gallipoli eventually disappeared.

The centennial would resemble the climax of interest in the campaign, as it had been developed in Turkey over the years, yet it came at a time when Atatürk's legacy had been contested by a new form of Turkish nationalism.[92] The history of the defense of the Gallipoli Peninsula had eventually "earned its prominent position in Turkish history only after a lengthy and arduous journey, having long remained solely of interest to Turkish military officers and a small

---

86 Ibid., 79.
87 Zürcher, "In the Name of the Father," 130.
88 Erich R. Prigge, *Gallipoli: Der Kampf um den Orient, von einem offizier aus dem Stabe des Marschalls Liman von Sanders* (Berlin: A. Scherl, 1916).
89 Wolf Heberlein, "Kemal Atatürk," *Zeitschrift für Politik* 27, no. 3 (1937): 168.
90 Stefan Ihrig, *Atatürk in the Nazi Imagination* (Cambridge, MA: Belknap Press of Harvard University Press, 2014), 109–110.
91 Ibid., 148.
92 Mesut Uyar, "Remembering the Gallipoli Campaign: Turkish Official Military Historiography, War Memorials and Contested Ground," *First World War Studies* 7, no. 2 (2016): 165.

group of enthusiasts."[93] For many years, there had only been local commemorative events, and the attention the battlefields received by Australian and British tourists had not been matched by Turkish visitors. The Ottoman leadership around Enver Pasha had already tried to use the victory of Gallipoli for political purposes, but after the War of Independence, Kemal would not pay too much attention to this issue when "[t]he glory and sacrifices of the Gallipoli war dead and the campaign's veterans faded in the glow of the newly established Turkish Republic."[94] In later years, however, the myth of Gallipoli was transformed, and new interest from people beyond the military ranks sparked "a new form [of myth] in which 'Turkish' soldiers replaced the more multinational Ottoman or Anatolian troops and Atatürk became the commander who led them to victory. Gallipoli, unlike other campaigns, became the first defence of the motherland, although it carried no more significance than that."[95] The Gallipoli myth was consequently transformed, "Turkified," so to speak, to match the new national narrative, and the events of the campaign were said to match the overtowering image of Atatürk as the first man of the new and strong nation of modern Turkey. The now "official" Gallipoli myth was fully developed in the 1960s, and only military historians would provide different evaluations of something that had already been interpreted within the public space of national memory.

In the early 1950s, a debate about the insufficient commemoration of the events in 1915/16 also finally led to a broader recognition of Gallipoli's role, and demands for proper memorials to the fallen soldiers were made. It would, however, not be until 21 August 1960 that the Dardanelles Martyrs' Memorial (Çanakkale Şehitler Abidesi) was finished and would address from then on the "sacrifice, victory and national pride"[96] of the Turkish nation under Kemal's leadership in relation to the last roar and victory of the Ottoman Empire. Further monuments would follow, and the area would eventually be turned into a national park, although the interest of the government in Gallipoli decreased for a while.

From Kemalist Nationalism to Neo-Ottomanism

Since the 2000s, Gallipoli has played a more important role again, especially with regard to the centennial in 2015, although it was used in a different context

---

93 Ibid.
94 Ibid., 168.
95 Ibid., 170.
96 Ibid., 173.

2 Turkish Nationalism: From Gallipoli to Contemporary Neo-Ottomanism — 33

and according to a new nationalist agenda. Kemal's commemorative strategies had also allowed for a reconciliation with the nation state's former enemies, whom he had invited back to visit the battlefields early on to remember their fallen heroes. His main interest had been a strong Turkey, but one that was internationally accepted and considered an equal nation among its former enemies as well. The nationalism Kemal represented was one that wanted to create national unity for a strong Turkish future. The fact that he had repressed alternative views should not be omitted here, however, particularly since Kemal suppressed especially those elements that would later back a different nationalist approach, namely the neo-Ottomanist one by Erdoğan, which eventually backed away from possibilities to internationalize Turkey as part of a transnational organization like the European Union (EU), but rather sought to emphasize the strength of Turkey as a great power in the region.[97] In 2011, the Turkish foreign minister, Dr. Ahmet Davutoğlu, declared with regard to the centennial of the Gallipoli campaign that "[w]e are going to introduce the year of 2015 to the whole world. We will do so not as the anniversary of a genocide as some people have claimed and slandered, but as the anniversary of the glorious resistance of a nation, the anniversary of the resistance at Çanakkale."[98] It is clear that no form of reconciliation could be expected and that Turkey and its government would instead consider Gallipoli as an event that resembled a Turkish success against imperialist powers that wanted to keep the empire in check. Considering that Turkish neo-Ottomanism has been preaching expansive goals, it is not surprising that the events have been reinterpreted again. The role of Kemal in particular is no longer a dominant part of the commemoration, as Kemalist nationalism had attempted to restrict the influence of Islam in modern Turkey, while Erdoğan's political course embraces Islamic elements of the state and uses them as the fundamental base of his political course. Therefore, the remembrance of Gallipoli, as well as of Atatürk, is problematic today. First of all, the former is connected to the history of the Ottoman Empire's participation in the First World War and the Armenian genocide. Secondly, the new religiously determined nationalism of Erdoğan is rather reluctant to acknowledge the success of Atatürk, who secularized Turkey and tried to modernize it according to more Western standards. Turkey's foreign policy in the Middle East is characterized by the struggle between a

---

97 Soner Cagaptay, *Erdogan's Empire: Turkey and the Politics of the Middle East* (London: I.B. Tauris, 2019).
98 Cited in Macleod, *Gallipoli*, 154.

Kemalist and a neo-Ottomanist interpretation, as Ömer Taspinar, among others, described the situation in 2008.[99] He argued that

> [t]here are two main factors behind Ankara's new activism in the Middle East: neo-Ottomanism and the Kurdish challenge. Ironically, these two drivers of Turkish foreign policy are often at odds. The Kurdish challenge is essentially defined by the Kemalist norms of the Turkish Republic which consider Kurdish nationalism to be an existential threat to Turkey's territorial integrity and regional security. Neo-Ottomanism, on the other hand, is less obsessed with the Kurdish question and more focused on Turkey's "soft power." In terms of its geo-strategic vision, neo-Ottomanism is void of imperialist expansionism but determined to promote a high profile diplomatic, political, and economic role for Turkey in the larger Middle East and Europe. At peace with Turkey's Muslim heritage and multiple identities, neo-Ottomanism is also much more ambitious and idealistic than Kemalism in projecting Turkey as a regional superpower.[100]

The struggle between the two nationalist concepts is nevertheless not only stimulated by different foreign policy aims but also by two different interpretations of the nation, i.e. the idea and the consensus the nation state is based upon. M. Hakan Yavuz highlighted that "[a]lthough Kemalist nation-building incorporated all means to suppress the Ottoman heritage, this imperial 'ghost' has haunted the state and society since the empire's collapse. As Turkey became more secular, thus moving closer to the West, the search for its lost soul has intensified. The Ottoman past offers a reservoir of experiences, lessons, and opportunities to shape the present and come to terms with the roots of Turkish identity."[101]

It can obviously be observed that there is a struggle over the nation in Turkey that had already begun in the 1980s and that Yilmaz Çolak characterized as a conflict between many different interest groups:

> In the late 1980s, Turkish politics was subject to a war of cultures which was caused by the rise of the separatist Kurdish movement, which had rejected the homogenous Turkish identity and turned to violent action, the Islamist groups that included severe critics of the official policy of secularism, together with the Alevis, which condemned the state's

---

99 Ömer Taspinar, "Turkey's Middle East Policies: Between Neo-Ottomanism and Kemalism," *Carnegie Papers* 10 (September 2008). See also Alexander Murinson, "The Strategic Depth Doctrine of Turkish Foreign Policy," *Middle Eastern Studies* 42, no. 6 (2006): 945–964; Gabriela Özel Volfová, "Turkey's Middle Eastern Endeavors: Discourses and Practices of Neo-Ottomanism under the AKP," *Die Welt des Islams* 56, no. 3/4 (2016): 489–510.
100 Taspinar, "Turkey's Middle East Policies," 1.
101 Hakan M. Yavuz, "Social and Intellectual Origins of Neo-Ottomanism: Searching for a Post-National Vision," *Die Welt des Islams* 56, no. 3/4 (2016): 440.

propagation for Sunni-based Islam. This war of cultures resulted in questioning the official definition of Turkish culture and its implications for political membership.[102]

Since Erdoğan relies more and more on religious hardliners, his nationalist agenda also turned away from transnational projects, like membership status within the EU, especially since the fulfillment of the demands for such membership would probably have eroded his own power base in Turkey.[103] In addition to a more ideological struggle over the future, the "refugee crisis" since 2015 has intensified the struggle between Turkish ultranationalism and the EU,[104] while the latter has itself been shaken by growing populist-driven nationalisms in its member states. All in all, it is obvious that a reframing of Turkish nationalism took place in the early 2000s, one that also ultimately left transnational ambitions behind and replaced them with a rather expansive strategy to secure Turkey's position as a leading power in the Middle Eastern region. Such a great power would also need its own post-Kemalist national narratives and as such tends to look further back to the Ottoman Empire, though not so much at its political structure as its territorial expansion.

Conclusion

Considering these developments in Turkey, it is no surprise that commemorations of Atatürk and his role during the Gallipoli campaign have been reconsidered and reframed since the 1990s and are being sacrificed to make space for a different form of nationalism. This new form has been quite strong since the beginning of the 21st century and is directed toward tradition and religious values rather than enlightenment and modernization, although it undoubtedly continued to keep the repressive elements of Kemalism, which should not be omitted here, alive. The new nationalist agenda, highly related to the foreign policy concept of neo-Ottomanism, eventually sacrificed all transnational ambitions and instead waged a turf war against the EU, taking refugees as political hostages and instrumentalizing their misery and sorrow. Since the political climate between

---

102 Yilmaz Çolak, "Ottomanism vs. Kemalism: Collective Memory and Cultural Pluralism in 1990s Turkey," *Middle Eastern Studies* 42, no. 4 (2006): 587.
103 Sezer İdil Göğüş and Matthias Dembinski, "Die Türkei und die EU: Der Bruch der europäisch-türkischen Beziehungen und Perspektiven für neue Wege," *PRIF Spotlight* (2017), accessed February 1, 2021, https://www.jstor.org/stable/resrep14332.
104 Helen Hintjens and Ali Bilgic, "The EU's Proxy War on Refugees," *State Crime Journal* 8, no. 1 (2019): 80–103.

Ankara and the EU has worsened due to conflicts in the region that created a neo-Ottomanist expansionism by the Turkish government and which were directed toward political enemies, ethnic minorities, and foreign states, where Turkish migrants in the diaspora are drawn into the political struggles at home,[105] the future of Turkish nationalism and the role Atatürk will play within it are currently being renegotiated. Time will eventually show which elements will be important for the reshaped nation of Turkey in the 21st century, but it is not yet clear which role the rise and impact of Kemal as well as the commemoration of Gallipoli are going to play in the recently redefined form of Turkish nationalism.

Works Cited

Ahmad, Feroz. *The Young Turks: The Committee of Union and Progress in Turkish Politics 1908–1914*. New York: Oxford University Press, 1969.
Aksakal, Mustafa. *The Ottoman Road to War in 1914: The Ottoman Empire and the First World War*. New York: Cambridge University Press, 2008.
Anderson, Benedict. *Imagined Communities: Reflections on the Origin and Spread of Nationalism*. London: Verso, 1983.
Armstrong, Harold Courtenay. *Gray Wolf, Mustafa Kemal: An Intimate Study of a Dictator*. Freeport, NY: Books for Libraries Press, 1972 [1932].
Baser, Bahar. "Gezi Spirit in the Diaspora: Diffusion of Turkish Politics to Europe." In *Everywhere Taksim: Sowing the Seeds for a New Turkey at Gezi*, edited by Isabel David and Kumru F. Toktamış, 251–266. Amsterdam: Amsterdam University Press, 2015.
Beşikçi, Mehmet. "Mobilizing Military Labor in the Age of Total War: Ottoman Conscription before and during the Great War." In *Fighting for a Living: A Comparative Study of Military Labour 1500–2000*, edited by Erik-Jan Zürcher, 547–580. Amsterdam: Amsterdam University Press, 2014.
Besikçi, Mehmet. *The Ottoman Mobilization of Manpower in the First World War: Between Voluntarism and Resistance*. Leiden: Brill, 2012.
Cagaptay, Soner. *Erdogan's Empire: Turkey and the Politics of the Middle East*. London: I.B. Tauris, 2019.
Çandar, Cengiz. "Atatürk's Ambiguous Legacy." *The Wilson Quarterly* 24, no. 4 (2000): 88–96.
Carlyon, Les A. *Gallipoli*. London: Bantam, 2003.
Ciddi, Sinan. *Kemalism in Turkish Politics: The Republican People's Party, Secularism and Nationalism*. London: Routledge, 2009.
Çinar, Alev. *Modernity, Islam, and Secularism in Turkey: Bodies, Places, and Time*. Minneapolis: University of Minnesota Press, 2005.

---

105 For an example of Turkish politics and their impact on Turkish communities in Europe, see Bahar Baser, "Gezi Spirit in the Diaspora: Diffusion of Turkish Politics to Europe," in *Everywhere Taksim: Sowing the Seeds for a New Turkey at Gezi*, ed. Isabel David and Kumru F. Toktamış (Amsterdam: Amsterdam University Press, 2015), 251–266.

Çolak, Yılmaz. "Ottomanism vs. Kemalism: Collective Memory and Cultural Pluralism in 1990s Turkey." *Middle Eastern Studies* 42, no. 4 (2006): 587–602.
Der Matossian, Bedross. *Shattered Dreams of Revolution: From Liberty to Violence in the Late Ottoman Empire*. Stanford: Stanford University Press, 2014.
Dincsahin, Sakir. *State and Intellectuals in Turkey: The Life and Times of Niyazi Berkes, 1908–1988*. Lanham, MD: Lexington Books, 2015.
Erickson, Edward J. *Gallipoli: Command under Fire*. London: Bloomsbury, 2015.
Erickson, Edward J. *Gallipoli: The Ottoman Campaign*. Barnsley: Pen & Sword, 2015.
Findley, Carter V. *Turkey, Islam, Nationalism, and Modernity: A History, 1789–2007*. New Haven, CT: Yale University Press, 2010.
Göğüş, Sezer İdil and Matthias Dembinski. "Die Türkei und die EU: Der Bruch der europäisch-türkischen Beziehungen und Perspektiven für neue Wege." *PRIF Spotlight* (2017). Accessed February 1, 2021. https://www.jstor.org/stable/resrep14332
Grüßhaber, Gerhardt. *The German Spirit in the Ottoman and Turkish Army, 1908–1938: A History of Military Knowledge*. Berlin: De Gruyter Oldenbourg, 2018.
Hanioğlu, Şükrü M. *Ataturk: An Intellectual Biography*. Princeton, NJ: Princeton University Press, 2011.
Hanioğlu, Şükrü M. *Preparation for a Revolution: The Young Turks, 1902–1908*. Oxford: Oxford University Press, 2001.
Hart, Peter. *Gallipoli*. Oxford: Oxford University Press, 2014.
Haythornthwaite, Philip J. *Gallipoli 1915: Frontal Assault on Turkey*. London: Osprey, 1991.
Heberlein, Wolf. "Kemal Atatürk." *Zeitschrift für Politik* 27, no. 3 (1937): 168–172.
Hintjens, Helen and Ali Bilgic. "The EU's Proxy War on Refugees." *State Crime Journal* 8, no. 1 (2019): 80–103.
Hobsbawm, Eric, and Terence Ranger. *The Invention of Tradition*. Cambridge: Cambridge University Press, 1983.
Hopkins-Weise, Jeff. *Blood Brothers: The ANZAC Genesis*. Auckland: Penguin, 2007.
Ihrig, Stefan. *Atatürk in the Nazi Imagination*. Cambridge, MA: Belknap Press of Harvard University Press, 2014.
Jacob, Frank. "China's Eruption after the First World War: Japanese Imperialism, Western Jingoism, and the Awakening of Chinese Nationalism." In *Zeiten des Aufruhrs (1916–1921): Globale Proteste, Streiks und Revolutionen gegen den Ersten Weltkrieg und seine Auswirkungen*, edited by Marcel Bois and Frank Jacob, 171–213. Berlin: Metropol, 2020.
Jacob, Frank. "The Construction of a Memorial Space: The Gallipoli Campaign and Spatial Remembrance." In *War and Memorials*, edited by Frank Jacob and Kenneth Pearl, 189–207. Paderborn: Schöning, 2019.
Jacob, Frank. *Gallipoli 1915/16: Britanniens bitterste Niederlage*. Berlin: De Gruyter Oldenbourg, 2020.
Kezer, Zeynep. *Building Modern Turkey: State, Space, and Ideology in the Early Republic*. Pittsburgh: University of Pittsburgh Press, 2015.
Lévy-Aksu, Noémi and François Georgeon, eds. *The Young Turk Revolution and the Ottoman Empire: The Aftermath of 1908*. London: Bloomsbury, 2017.
Liddle, Peter. *The Gallipoli Experience Reconsidered*. Barnsley: Pen & Sword, 2015.
Macleod, Jenny. *Gallipoli*. Oxford: Oxford University Press, 2015.
Mango, Andrew. *From the Sultan to Atatürk: Turkey*. London: Haus Publishing, 2010.

McMeekin, Sean. "World War I and the Establishment of the Republic." In *The Routledge Handbook of Modern Turkey*, edited by Metin Heper and Sabri Sayari, 35–43. London: Routledge, 2012.

Moorehead, Alan. *Gallipoli*. London: Hamish Hamilton, 1956.

Murinson, Alexander. "The Strategic Depth Doctrine of Turkish Foreign Policy." *Middle Eastern Studies* 42, no. 6 (2006): 945–964.

Navaro-Yashin, Yael. *Faces of the State: Secularism and Public Life in Turkey*. Princeton, NJ: Princeton University Press, 2002.

Ökten, Nazli. "An Endless Death and Eternal Mourning." In *The Politics of Public Memory in Turkey*, edited by Esra Özyürek, 95–113. Syracuse, NY: Syracuse University Press, 2007.

Ozdemir, Hikmet. *The Ottoman Army 1914–1918: Disease and Death on the Battlefield*. Salt Lake City, UT: University of Utah Press, 2008.

Özkirimli, Umut. "The Changing Nature of Nationalism in Turkey: Actors, Discourses, and the Struggle for Hegemony." In *Symbiotic Antagonisms: Competing Nationalisms in Turkey*, edited by Ayse Kadioglu and Emin Fuat Keyman, 82–100. Salt Lake City, UT: University of Utah Press, 2011.

Özyürek, Esra. "Miniaturizing Atatürk: Privatization of State Imagery and Ideology in Turkey." *American Ethnologist* 31, no. 3 (2004): 374–91.

Özyürek, Esra. *Nostalgia for the Modern: State Secularism and Everyday Politics in Turkey*. Durham, NC: Duke University Press, 2006.

Perk, Kadri. *Çanakkale Savaşları Tarihi*. 3 vols. İstanbul: Askeri Matbaa, 1940.

Prigge, Erich R. *Gallipoli: Der Kampf um den Orient, von einem offizier aus dem Stabe des Marschalls Liman von Sanders*. Berlin: A. Scherl, 1916.

Prior, Robin. *Gallipoli: The End of a Myth*. New Haven, CT: Yale University Press, 2015.

Reynolds, Michael A. *Shattering Empires: The Clash and Collapse of the Ottoman and Russian Empires 1908–1918*. Cambridge: Cambridge University Press, 2011.

Sohail, Khalid. *Prophets of Violence – Prophets of Peace: Understanding the Roots of Contemporary Political Violence*. Toronto: White Knight Publication, 2005.

Somay, Bülent. *The Psychopolitics of the Oriental Father: Between Omnipotence and Emasculation*. London: Palgrave Macmillan, 2014.

Taspinar, Ömer. "Turkey's Middle East Policies: Between Neo-Ottomanism and Kemalism." *Carnegie Papers* 10 (September 2008).

Tetik, Ahmet, ed. *Sofya Askerî Ataşesi Mustafa Kemal'in Raporları, Kasım 1913–Kasım 1914*. Ankara: ATASE Yayin-Iari, 2007.

Ulrichsen, Kristian C. *The First World War in the Middle East*. London: Oxford University Press, 2014.

Üngör, Ugut Ü. *The Making of Modern Turkey: Nation and State in Eastern Anatolia, 1913–1950*. Oxford: Oxford University Press, 2011.

Uyar, Mesut. "Remembering the Gallipoli Campaign: Turkish Official Military Historiography, War Memorials and Contested Ground." *First World War Studies* 7, no. 2 (2016): 165–191.

Vogel, Ezra F. "Nation Rebuilders: Mustafa Kemal Atatürk, Lee Kuan Yew, Deng Xiaoping, and Park Chung Hee." In *The Park Chung Hee Era*, edited by Byung-Kook Kim and Ezra F. Vogel, 513–541. Cambridge, MA: Harvard University Press, 2011.

Volfová, Gabriela Özel. "Turkey's Middle Eastern Endeavors: Discourses and Practices of Neo-Ottomanism under the AKP." *Die Welt des Islams* 56, no. 3/4 (2016): 489–510.

Weiker, Walter F. "Atatürk as a National Symbol." *Turkish Studies Association Bulletin* 6, no. 2 (1982): 1–6.

Wilson, Christopher S. "Representing National Identity and Memory in the Mausoleum of Mustafa Kemal Atatürk." *Journal of the Society of Architectural Historians* 68, no. 2 (2009): 224–253.

Yavuz, Hakan M. "Social and Intellectual Origins of Neo-Ottomanism: Searching for a Post-National Vision." *Die Welt des Islams* 56, no. 3/4 (2016): 438–465.

Yavuz, Hakan M. *Islamic Political Identity in Turkey*. Oxford: Oxford University Press, 2003.

Zürcher, Erik-Jan. "In the Name of the Father, the Teacher and the Hero: The Atatürk Personality Cult in Turkey." In *Political Leadership, Nations and Charisma*, edited by Vivian Ibrahim and Margit Wunch, 129–142. London: Routledge, 2012.

Sven Brajer and Johannes Schütz
3 Old Concepts in Changing Societies? Continuities and Transformation of Nationalism in East Germany, 1871–2019

Introduction

After the fall of the Iron Curtain and the end of real existing socialism, it was common to discuss the end of nation states and the era of a transnational order to come.[1] After a period of globalization and internationalization, nation states played only a minor role in processes of decision-making, economic integration as well as historical development in general. Referrals were repeatedly made to Europe, to name one example here, because the EU significantly represented this global trend.[2] Thus, when Eric Hobsbawm (1917–2012) wrote a new prologue to the German edition of his famous book *Nations and Nationalism since 1780* in 2005, he claimed that nations were disappearing, and that is the time for scientific research because exploring nationalism was possible as recently as the phenomenon had gone.[3]

This perception changed over a couple of years. Several states have re-nationalized and thus apparently interrupted this development. To describe this process, we only need to mention a few keywords: Brexit, "Make America great again," or border control, and everyone already knows that nationalism is still a vivid political concept. Last but not least, the consequences of the coronavirus as a nightmare for a totally globalized economy led to the complete isolation of individual countries in the northern hemisphere within a few days. The economic and political consequences are not yet foreseeable – a re-nationalization of states cannot be excluded.

---

[1] See, for instance, Rana Dasgupta, "The demise of the nation state," *The Guardian*, April 5, 2018, https://www.theguardian.com/news/2018/apr/05/demise-of-the-nation-state-rana-dasgupta.
[2] Etienne Francois, Hannes Siegrist and Jakob Vogel, "Die Nation. Vorstellungen, Inszenierungen, Emotionen," in *Nation und Emotion. Deutschland und Frankreich im Vergleich 19. und 20. Jahrhundert*, ed. Etienne Francois, Hannes Siegrist and Jakob Vogel (Göttingen: Vandenhoeck und Ruprecht, 1995), 13–14.
[3] Eric Hobsbawm, *Nationen und Nationalismus. Mythos und Realität seit 1780* (Frankfurt a.M./ New York: Campus, 2006), vii–xiii.

Open Access. © 2021 Sven Brajer et al., published by De Gruyter. This work is licensed under the Creative Commons Attribution-NonCommercial-NoDerivatives 4.0 International License.
https://doi.org/10.1515/9783110729290-003

Therefore, many observers remark that nationalism is coming back today – sociology, political sciences, and history assert that re-strengthened nationalism is currently occurring in many places all over the world. However, before we look at this perception, we would like to make some theoretical remarks about nationalism in general.

According to Christian Jansen and Henning Borggräfe, most historians differentiate between two particular manifestations under the term 'nationalism.' On the one hand, it is a "conglomerate of political ideas, feelings and symbols" that "can fit into a closed ideology," but does not necessarily have to.[4] On the other hand, there are the associated political movements adopting these ideas, emphasizing feelings, and creating new symbols. By demanding a consciousness of nationality, state unity, and sovereignty, ergo a nation state, nationalism socializes as a political movement. After the nation state is built, nationalist groups and movements strive to preserve and regularly also create further internal cohesion in what they consider as the nation.[5] By doing so, nationalism tries to tie together the different social groups and classes.[6]

Since its beginning, however, nationalism has been an ambivalent concept. Started as a project of emancipation, which was able to overcome stratified societies and to integrate common people into political power, it soon exaggerated and overemphasized ethnic homogeneity as a fundament of national integration and thus drifted off into an "age of extremes,"[7] an age of violence.[8] This development was made possible by the transformation of nationalistic movements into sacral communities, too. By combining several aspects which refer to the monotheistic religions – like the chosen people, the holy land, the enemy inside and outside as well as the historical mission – nationalism obtained, as Hans-Ulrich Wehler highlights, a quasi-religious character and almost became a "political religion."[9] Furthermore, nationalism creates

---

[4] Christian Jansen and Henning Borggräfe, *Nation – Nationalität – Nationalismus* (Frankfurt a.M./New York: Campus, 2007), 18. Still relevant and useful to define the concept: Benedict Anderson, *Imagined Communities: Reflections on the Origin and Spread of Nationalism* (London: Verso, 1983).

[5] Jansen and Borggräfe, *Nation*, 10–16

[6] Ibid., 18.

[7] Eric Hobsbawm, *The Age of Extremes: A History of the World, 1914–1991* (New York: Vintage Books, 1996).

[8] Andreas Fahrmeir, *Die Deutschen und ihre Nation: Geschichte einer Idee* (Stuttgart: Reclam, 2017), 11.

[9] Hans-Ulrich Wehler, *Nationalismus: Geschichte, Formen, Folgen* (Munich: C.H. Beck, 2001), 27–35.

emotional communities.¹⁰ As Borggräfe and Jansen emphasize, most empirical considerations, which focus on "in-groups," show that these communities include or exclude individuals according to their own scale, which creates an exaggerated emotionality.¹¹

This was the fundament of more militant developments of nationalist groups and actors. With a view to our subject, we would like to touch on the "völkisch" movement. Stefan Breuer, a sociologist with a special focus on the far right, defines it as "a conglomerate of middle-class ideology, radical nationalism and an ambivalent attitude towards modernity."¹² Despite the popular preference for the acceptance of the racial theory at that time, Breuer considers the "Völkischen," i.e. people within the "völkisch" movement, as nationalists because of their unconditional preference with regard to people and nation in their attempt to order society. Thus, he can "avoid corresponding semantics that can be found in word creations such as 'völkisch-rassistisch' or the translation of 'völkisch' with 'racist'."¹³ But we would like to emphasize that some representatives of the völkish movement were extremely racist. Being nationalist does not exclude being racist at the same time; on the contrary, nationalism and racism were congenial (in German: *wahlverwandt*), as the historian Christian Geulen convincingly shows.¹⁴ This discussion underlines that nationalism manifested itself in particular nationalist agents, and some of them acted radically; by overemphasizing the national and defining politics through their national and racial goal(s), radical nationalism became a social reality.

In this contribution, we will focus on the interaction of emotions, imaginations, and practices of nationalism in East Germany. Our main thesis is that East Germany did not reach the transnational age. Nationalism has had a vivid history in East Germany until now. Hence this nationalism changed, and as Geulen recently emphasized, the debate about the re-birth of nations is almost as old as conscious nationalism itself. Inhabitants of the German Empire and contemporary far-right politicians in Germany are united in dreaming of connecting to the glorious past and returning to national strength, which existed

---

10 For the theoretical background to this term we used: Barbara Rosenwein, *Emotional Communities in the Early Middle Ages* (Ithaca, NY: Cornell University Press, 2006).
11 Jansen and Borggräfe, *Nation*, 18.
12 Stefan Breuer, *Die Völkischen in Deutschland* (Darmstadt: WBG, 2008), 10. Translation by ourselves.
13 Ibid.
14 Christian Geulen, *Wahlverwandte. Rassendiskurs und Nationalismus im späten 19. Jahrhundert* (Hamburg: Hamburger Edition, 2006).

and exists only in their imaginations.¹⁵ Therefore, we will not speak about the return of nationalism. Instead, we would like to highlight a transformation of nationalist ideology, concepts, and discourses. Geulen argues that nationalism transformed continuously and permanently throughout the whole 20th century; the concept and idea of "nationalism" only work as concept and idea; in reality, the world is more complex, as always.¹⁶

This theoretical background structures our analysis. We would consequently like to give more of an insight into the different manifestations and particular differentiations of nationalism by looking at one example: nationalism in East Germany from 1871 until now; therefore, we focus especially on Saxony and its capital, Dresden. In this city, nationalistic actors and groups were and still are visible in a particular way. We will therefore trace the imaginations of nationhood back to the beginning of the German Empire in 1871. We refer to East Germany as the territories of the former German Democratic Republic (GDR) and less concretely as the region right of the river Elbe.¹⁷ We do so because several historical studies connect the regional history of East Germany with the rise of radical nationalist parties in Saxony, Thuringia, Saxony-Anhalt, Brandenburg, and Mecklenburg-Vorpommern nowadays, especially in the correlation between votes for the NSDAP in 1933 and the AfD in 2019.¹⁸

---

15 Christian Geulen, "Zur 'Wiederkehr' des Nationalismus," *Aus Politik und Zeitgeschichte* 68, no. 48 (2018): 4–8.
16 Ibid. Irene Goetz similarly argues that processes of de-nationalization and re-nationalization are ambivalently connected. Irene Goetz, *Deutsche Identitäten: Die Wiederentdeckung des Nationalen nach 1989* (Cologne/Weimar/Vienna: Böhlau, 2011).
17 Raj Kollmorgen, *Ostdeutschland: Beobachtungen einer Übergangs- und Teilgesellschaft* (Wiesbaden: Springer, 2005). See also Thomas Ahbe, "Die Konstruktion der Ostdeutschen: Diskursive Spannungen, Stereotype und Identitäten seit 1989," *Aus Politik und Zeitgeschichte* 41, no. 42 (2004): 12–22. More controversial is the denomination of Central Germany (*Mitteldeutschland*), because this term is as fluent as East Germany, and a clear and accepted definition of it does not exist. Furthermore, Central Germany was used as a historical argument to imagine a German Reich that did not exist yet. See Jürgen John, ed., *"Mitteldeutschland": Begriff – Geschichte – Konstrukt* (Rudolstadt/Jena: Hain-Verlag, 2001). A controversial discussion can be found in Michael Richter, Thomas Schaarschmidt and Mike Schmeitzner, eds., *Länder, Gaue und Bezirke: Mitteldeutschland im 20. Jahrhundert* (Dresden: Landeszentrale für politische Bildung, 2007).
18 James Hawes, *The Shortest History of Germany* (London: Old Street Publishing, 2017). Hawes speaks of *"Ostelbien,"* which means the area east of the Elbe. Davide Cantoni, Felix Hagemeister and Marc Westscott, "Persistence and Activation of Right-Wing Political Ideology," *Rationality and Competition, Discussion Paper No. 143* (2019). For Saxony in detail, see Uwe Backes and Steffen Kailitz, eds., *Sachsen – Eine Hochburg des Rechtsextremismus?* (Göttingen: Vandenhoeck und Ruprecht, 2020).

The question is: does East Germany have its own traditions and particular ideas of nationhood?[19]

Nationalism in Germany, 1871–1945

The German Empire: 1871–1918

Before the foundation of the Reich, the concept of nation or fatherland referred to its own immediate territory, for example, Saxony or Mecklenburg.[20] Besides Martin Luther (1483–1546), who was born in Eisleben (today's federal state of Saxony-Anhalt) and who was particularly influential in East and North Germany, it was especially Otto von Bismarck (1815–1898), who came from Schönhausen on the Elbe (also in today's Saxony-Anhalt), who became the national hero of German protestant nationalists after 1871.[21] From then on, the united German nation served as the founding myth of the Reich. Especially in East Germany, Otto von Bismarck was imagined and venerated as the founder of the Empire. This can also be seen from the following numbers: by around 1900, 240 towers had been built in honor of von Bismarck (so-called *Bismarcktürme*), some of which stood outside the German Empire, and 174 are still preserved today. Of these, the density is particularly high in eastern Germany; in the territory of the comparatively small state Thuringia, there were 24 of them, in Saxony 23, Saxony-Anhalt 16, Brandenburg 11, and in Mecklenburg-Western Pomerania 4, while in eastern Brandenburg, East Prussia, West Prussia, Pomerania, Poznan and Silesia, which today belong to Poland, there was a total of 40. In comparison, there were only 13 such monuments in the large German states of Bavaria and only 9 in Baden-Württemberg.[22] Bismarck and the specifically "German," unifying nationalism initiated in Prussia found its most loyal followers in East Germany, in contrast to South or Southwest Germany, and the Bismarck celebrations at these

---

19 This was recently argued by Ilko-Sascha Kowalczuk. See Ilko-Sascha Kowalczuk, *Die Übernahme. Wie Ostdeutschland Teil der Bundesrepublik wurde* (Munich: C.H. Beck, 2019), 215–233.
20 Fahrmeir, *Die Deutschen und ihre Nation*, 70–97.
21 Rainer Lächele, "Protestantismus und Völkische Religion im deutschen Kaiserreich" in *Handbuch zur "Völkischen Bewegung" 1871–1918*, ed. Uwe Puschner, Walter Schmitz and Justus H. Ulbricht (Munich: KG Saur, 1999), 149–163; Christopher König, *Zwischen Kulturprotestantismus und völkischer Bewegung: Arthur Bonus (1864–1941) als religiöser Schriftsteller im wilhelminischen Kaiserreich* (Tübingen: Mohr Siebeck, 2018), 26–61.
22 Jörg Bielefeld, "Bismarcktürme- und Bismarcksäulen. Das Infoportal Bismarcktürme," accessed July 7, 2020, https://www.bismarcktuerme.de/index.html.

memorials were often visited by numerous people – today, local activists "rediscover" them uncritically and build them up as destinations for excursions or locations for celebrations of various kinds.²³ Even the politicians of the AfD have a special affection for Bismarck, like the Thuringian state chairman Björn Höcke. His party referred to Bismarck on an election poster, which is subtitled with the slogan "His role model is our obligation."²⁴

In East Germany, Protestantism was a second unifying bond that stretched from the Baltic Sea to the Ore Mountains (Figure 1). In addition, an increasing heroization of ancient Greece in art and culture played a major role and had a big impact on cultural-imperial practices. For example, the biography of the Dresden völkish sculptor and painter Richard Guhr (1873–1956) is representative of conservative artists, politicians, scientists, doctors, civil servants, merchants, craftsmen – typical representatives from the old middle class. Guhr had become a nationalistic anti-Semite at the latest by 1918 with the decay of the empire founded by von Bismarck in 1871. He demonstrated this in various pamphlets, but above all in his paintings between 1912 and 1933.²⁵

Guhr was born in the town of Schwerin (Mecklenburg) and socialized there. He had a middle-class educational background and did his military service voluntarily. From the 1890s on, he lived in Berlin and Dresden, from 1914 until 1945 exclusively in the Saxon capital.²⁶ All these cities had a clear Protestant majority.

Guhr saw himself in the tradition of the ancient philosophers.²⁷ Even today in Dresden, the most famous sculpture of the demigod Heracles, erected in 1908

---

23 One of the authors was allowed to experience this in the contemplative Ebersbach-Neugersdorf, district Neugersdorf, Eastern Saxony; see Jenny Thümmler, "Heimatverein lädt zur Bismarckfeier," *Sächsische Zeitung GOS Görlitz Lokales*, March 31, 2015, https://www.saechsische.de/plus/heimatvereinlaedt-zur-bismarckfeier-3072675.html.
24 Ulrich M. Schmid, "Bismarck, eine Karriere – der «eiserne Kanzler» wird in Deutschland immer noch zu wenig kritisch gesehen," *Neue Zürcher Zeitung*, January 20, 2020, https://www.nzz.ch/meinung/bismarck-eine-karriere-der-eiserne-kanzler-wird-in-deutschland-immer-noch-zu-wenig-kritisch-gesehen-ld.1532085.
25 Richard Guhr, *Der Judenstil oder der Expressionismus* (Dresden: Max Emil Fischer, 1922); Richard Guhr, *Die Schuld am Verfall der Künste* (Dresden: Fischer, 1923). The most important pictures, which were largely destroyed in the bombing of Dresden on 13–14 February 1945, can be found in the illustrated book: Ernst Köhler-Hausen, ed., *Aus der Dresdner Wagner-Ehrung im Schloss Albrechtsberg* (Dresden: Stadtmuseum, 1939).
26 Ruth Stummann-Bowert, *Ein Leben für Richard Wagner: Richard Guhr: Maler und Bildhauer 1873–1956* (Fritzlar: Stiftung Museum Fritzlar, 1988), 209.
27 Barbara Stiewe, *Der "Dritte Humanismus": Aspekte deutscher Griechenrezeption vom George-Kreis bis zum Nationalsozialismus* (Berlin/Boston: De Gruyter, 2011), 88–123, 159–163, 185–188, 198–200, 223–232.

Figure 1: AfD Bundestagswahlplakat, Weimar, Thüringen 2017 (Andreas Werner).

by Guhr, the so-called "Golden Town Hall Man" on the tower of the New Town Hall, stands out impressively from Guhr's great creative period (Figure 2). For Guhr, Heracles was symbolically considered a demigod and, inspired by Friedrich Nietzsche, as an *Übermensch*. The art historian Ruth Stummann-Bowert interprets the demigod on the one hand as a völkish manifestation and on the other as an educational theme, which was particularly suited to the Dresden court; he was supposed to symbolize the protection of the population of the city.[28]

---

[28] Stummann-Bowert, *Ein Leben für Richard Wagner*, 12, 172. See also Johann Chapoutot, *Greeks, Romans, Germans: How the Nazis Usurped Europe's Classical Past* (Berkeley: University of California Press, 2016), 165.

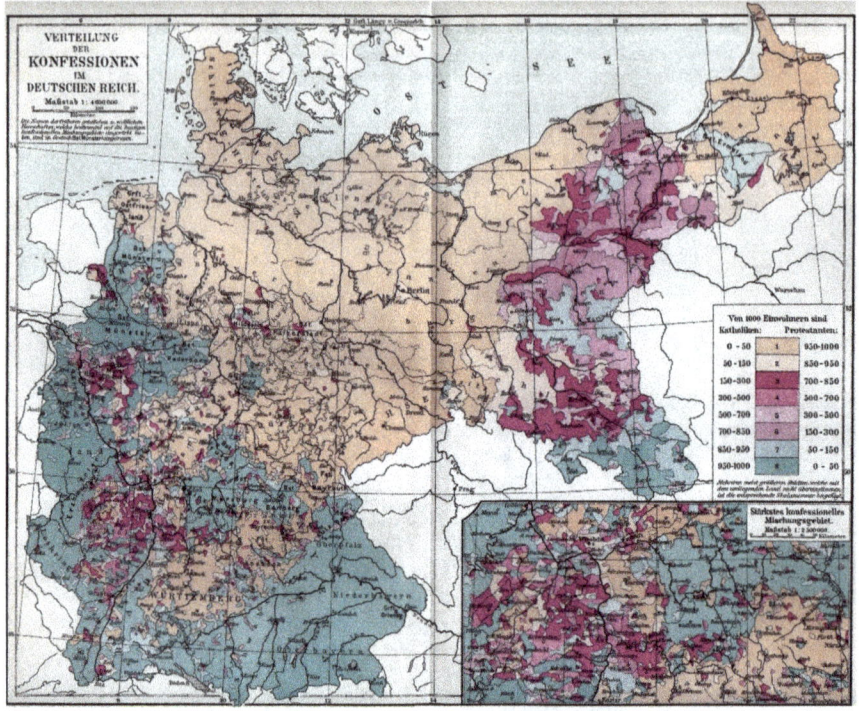

Figure 2: The spread of confessional denominations in the German Empire (*Meyers Konversationslexikon*, 5th ed., 1897).

A few years later, in 1911/12, Guhr made an esoteric fasting cure,[29] which ended with a trip to the grave of the famous composer Richard Wagner (1813–1883) in Bayreuth.[30] Shortly afterward in 1912/13, he built the biggest Richard Wagner monument worldwide, which was erected and inaugurated in 1933 in the Liebethaler Grund in Saxon Switzerland by the Nazis (Figure 3).

---

29 For the "crisis year" of 1912 for the völkish, see Frank Jacob, *Die Thule-Gesellschaft und die Kokuryûkai: Geheimgesellschaften im global-historischen Vergleich* (Würzburg: Königshausen & Neumann, 2013), 103.
30 Richard Guhr, *Das Problem der erotischen Regeneration* (1912) in Stummann-Bowert, *Ein Leben für Richard Wagner,* 220–224, quotation 220.

Figure 3: "Goldener Rathausmann" (1908–1910; R. Guhr) after restoration, standing on the green area in front of the New Town Hall, Dresden. Photo by Siegfried Bregulla, 2006 (Deutsche Fotothek).

Wagner's Bayreuth acted as a German(ic) "*Sehnsuchtsort*" (place of longing) for many people, such as Houston Stewart Chamberlain (1855–1927) and Adolf Hitler (1889–1945).[31] Alongside Luther's and Bismarck's influences, Wagner's "*Weltanschauung*"[32] (worldview) served as a further pillar in the national-protestant cosmos. Guhr regarded Wagner's Scriptures as a key to a supposed "Aryan regeneration,"[33] a völkish-teleological ideology. For Guhr, Wagner, and numerous other

---

[31] Udo Bermbach, *Richard Wagner in Deutschland: Rezeption – Verfälschungen* (Stuttgart/Weimar: Metzler, 2011), 429–470.
[32] Rudolf Louis, *Die Weltanschauung Richard Wagners* (Leipzig: Breitkopf & Härtel, 1898); see also Josef Lehmkuhl, *Der Kunst-Messias: Richard Wagners Vermächtnis in seinen Schriften* (Würzburg: Königshausen & Neumann, 2009), especially 187–220.
[33] On this term and its origin see Solveig Weber, *Das Bild Richard Wagners: Ikonographische Bestandsaufnahme eines Künstlerkults*, vol. 1: *Text* (Mainz: Schott, 1993), 171, 250.

conservative nationalists, who often lived in the protestant regions of East Germany,[34] the German himself was considered as the rebirth of the Aryan. He above all was to break away from the supposed embrace of the so-called golden international banking and financial capital on the one hand and the red international social democrats, communists, and anarchists on the other, which, according to the interpretation of the völkish movement, was clearly dominated by Jews.[35] With the exception of the area of Posen, Berlin, Leipzig, and some cities in Silesia, the proportion of the Jewish population in eastern Germany was significantly lower than in the German Empire on the left side of the Elbe.[36] The barely visible enemy image of the "Jew," especially contrasted to the "German," was suitable for the paranoia of an entire generation.[37]

As a result, numerous nationalist and völkish clubs, associations, and cultural institutions were founded in East Germany: in 1881 the "Deutsche Reformpartei,"[38] in 1885 the "Allgemeine Deutsche Sprachverein,"[39] in 1920 the "Deutsche Kunstgesellschaft,"[40] and finally in Hellerau (near Dresden), almost simultaneously in 1919/20, the "Deutsche Bauernhochschule" under the guidance of Bruno Tanzmann (1878–1939).[41] The last one in particular emerged as an antiurban völkisch movement.

Theodor Fritsch (1852–1933), probably the most well-known and journalistically active anti-Semite of the German Empire, lived in Leipzig. He acted as an initiator of the journal *Der Hammer: Blätter für deutschen Sinn* (The Hammer: Sheets for the German Sense, 1902–1940), the "Germanenorden" (Germanic Order) in 1912,[42]

---

34 Hawes, *The Shortest History*, 193–194.
35 This is the antisemitic sound of the *Deutsche Wacht: Organ für nationale Politik; Publikationsorgan der völkischen Vereine Sachsens* (Dresden: Verlag der Deutschen Wacht Volumes, 1879–1933).
36 Steven M. Lowenstein et al., *Deutsch-jüdische Geschichte in der Neuzeit: Umstrittene Integration 1871–1918* (Munich: C.H. Beck, 1996), 29–32.
37 Max Bewer, *Der Rembrandtdeutsche. Von einem Wahrheitsfreund* (Dresden: Glöß, 1892), 97.
38 Founded as anti-Semitic Reform association in 1879, the party quickly spread to Eastern Saxony and Silesia. Matthias Piefel, *Antisemitismus und völkische Bewegung im Königreich Sachsen* (Göttingen: V&R Unipress 2004), 37; Sven Brajer, "Angst vor dem Fremden in Zeiten des Umbruchs? Aspekte von Antisemitismus und Rassismus im Kaiserreich in der Oberlausitz," *Neues Lausitzisches Magazin* 141 (2019): 81–92.
39 Deutschen Sprachverein Dresden and Hermann Dunger, eds., *Satzungen des Deutschen Sprachvereins. Neue Fassung von dem Beschlusse vom 17. Januar 1889* (Dresden: Teich, 1889).
40 A central pioneer of the concept of national socialistic art. Bettina Feistel-Rohmeder, "Kurzer Rückblick auf die Entstehung und Entwicklung der Deutschen Kunstgesellschaft," in *Im Terror des Kunstbolschewismus. Urkundensammlung des "Deutschen Kunstberichtes" aus den Jahren 1927–33* ed. Bettina Feistel-Rohmeder (Karlsruhe: Müller, 1938), 211–217.
41 Bruno Tanzmann, "Zur Einleitung. Aus meinem Leben als völkischer Vorkämpfer," in *Plan des Hochstiftes für Deutsche Art in Hellerau*, vol. 1, ed. Deutsche Bauernhochschule (1926), 5.
42 Frank Jacob, *Die Thule-Gesellschaft* (Berlin: uni-edition, 2010), 27–32; Jacob, *Die Thule-Gesellschaft und die Kokuryûkai*, 105–110, Damien Guillaume, "Vers 'l'agitation antisémitique'

and the "Sächsische Mittelstandsvereinigung" (Saxon Middle-Class Association) in 1905. The "Harzer Bergtheater," the first outdoor theatre in the Reich, originated in the Harz region, in Thale in 1903, initiated by the anti-Semite Ernst Wachler.[43] In 1924 the Artamans were founded in Limbach, Western Saxony, and were deeply involved with Tanzmann's Bauernhochschule. The exclusive and ideologically leading "Deutschbund" (German Federation) had its headquarters in Berlin, just like the nationalist "Deutsche Kolonialgesellschaft" (German Colonial Society)[44] and the Deutschnationale Volkspartei (DNVP, German National People's Party), founded in 1918.[45] In Posen (Poznań), the anti-Polish "Ostmarkenverein" (Eastern Border Association) had existed since 1894.[46] In addition to the anti-Semitism described above, all these groups more or less vituperated against the Slavs, who were equated with primitive, "inferior" peasants, against Rome (the Catholic Church), against the French (especially the arts), and more or less against English liberalism and mercantilism ("Manchestertum").[47] All these clubs and organizations, the artists and their benefactors, the media and the public opinion represent the widespread dissemination of radical nationalism crossed with aggressive racism in Eastern Germany during the Empire: all of them imagined Germany as a nationally and racially homogenous nation state under threat from inner and outer enemies, and they were more than willing to defend their nation, no doubt even with violence.

---

comme phénomène transnational: hostilité antijuive, équivoques libérales et solidarité juive internationale de l'Affaire Mortara au Congrès de Berlin (1858–1878)," in *Antisemitismus im 19. Jahrhundert aus internationaler Perspektive: Nineteenth Century Anti-Semitism in International Perspective*, ed. Mareike König and Oliver Schulz (Göttingen: V&R Unipress, 2019), 313.
43 Uwe Puschner, "Deutsche Reformbühne und völkische Kultstätte. Ernst Wachler und das Harzer Bergtheater," in *Handbuch zur "Völkischen Bewegung" 1871–1918*, ed. Uwe Puschner, Walter Schmitz and Justus H. Ulbricht (München: Saur 1996), 762–796.
44 Reiner Fenske, *Imperiale Verbände im Deutschland der Zwischenkriegszeit im Vergleich. Die Beispiele des "Deutschen Ostbundes" und der "Deutschen Kolonialgesellschaft"* (Dresden: Diss, 2018).
45 Maik Ohnezeit, *Zwischen "schärfster Opposition" und dem "Willen zur Macht" – Die Deutschnationale Volkspartei (DNVP) in der Weimarer Republik 1918–1928* (Düsseldorf: Droste, 2011); Thomas Mergel, "Das Scheitern des deutschen Tory-Konservatismus. Die Umformung der DNVP zu einer rechtsradikalen Partei 1928–1932," *Historische Zeitschrift* 276 (2003): 323–368.
46 Christoph Kienemann, *Der koloniale Blick gen Osten. Osteuropa im Diskurs des Deutschen Kaiserreiches von 1871* (Paderborn: Schöningh, 2018).
47 For Dresden in particular, see the powerful local group of the Alldeutscher Verband who fought all these enemy images: Gerald Kolditz, "Rolle und Wirksamkeit des Alldeutschen Verbandes in Dresden zwischen 1895 und 1918: ein Beitrag zum bürgerlichen Vereinsleben der nationalistischen Kräfte in der wilhelminischen Ära des deutschen Kaiserreiches" (PhD diss., TU Dresden, 1994).

Weimar and Beyond: 1918–1945

The years 1933 and beyond were the peak of the nationalistic dream. And they kept their dreams alive during the Weimar years. Again, Richard Guhr witnesses that the nationalist movement thought of the German community as a united *ethnos*, as a community of people, as the German *"Völksgemeinschaft."*[48] This picture, "Germania 1918/Ultima ratio," (Figure 4) was painted by Guhr in 1919 or 1920. Ernst Köhler-Hausens, a journalist and friend of Guhr who also lived in Dresden, gave the following description in the year 1938:

Figure 4: Richard-Wagner-Monument at Liebethaler Grund, Saxony. Photo by Walter Möbius, 1933 (Deutsche Fotothek).

---

48 For the latest on this crucial historical term, see Michael Wildt, *Volk, Volksgemeinschaft, AfD* (Hamburg: Hamburger Edition, 2017).

Our feet in chains, we see Germany collapsing in despair on a hill on the Rhine plain. The Jewish star [sic!] with Jehovah's sign threatens to rule over it; terrified ravens[49] flutter around it. Only one has remained: the blue flower, which represents faith in the powers of the heart and the soul, no matter whether we see in it the blue flower of romanticism or a parable for the Aryan-Germanic quality of loyalty to one's own being. From the German landscape, the forest on the mountain, a torrent of fog streams down, which forms itself into a white snake, the symbol of blessed, secret powers; it is crowned by a new temple, a parable for the fact that a new faith of mankind can regain salvation from the Aryan being.[50]

This description sounds strongly like an arrangement with the artist, Guhr: Germany, as the mother Germania in black with a mourning veil on a hill in the Madonna position, shows the much-described shocked rigidity of nationalist and völkish forces after the lost war. The chained feet, the wreath of thorns, and the Star of David with the inscription "Yahweh," which was removed after 1945 by Guhr's widow, Hedwig, clearly name Judaism as the guilty party for the defeat. At the same time (1918/19), according to Guhr, Jewry had also become the new master in Germany. Presumably, the gentian, as the flower of loyalty, and the legendary snake, possibly to be interpreted as the Rhine (*the* German river par excellence), show the way to the supposed Aryan regeneration of Germany.

The Weimar Republic, symbolically disparaged here by Guhr, was considered a catastrophe by a large part of the German population, from the center to the far right. With the lost war and the revolution of 9 November 1918, which was mainly formed by workers and soldiers, this perception led to a briefly shocked rigidity for those people. And also, from the center to the far right, the Treaty of Versailles was rejected and attacked as a product of an international conspiracy by which Germany was solely to blame for the war. By inventing this master narrative, the heterogeneous nationalistic groups and actors united and formed a resistance. Thus, the DNVP was founded in Berlin in 1918, with bastions mainly in East Prussia, Mecklenburg, Pomerania, and Saxony. In a poster of the party from the Reichstag elections in 1920 (Figure 5), the DNVP is depicted as a submarine from the First World War with the flag of the empire torpedoing the merchant ship of the Weimar Republic with the black-red-gold flag. The torpedo represents the Reichstag election. The phrase means: "It must hit." The Weimar Republic is embodied by "*Schiebertum*" (racketeerdom, representing the "Golden International" and liberalism) and Bolshevism (representing the "Red International" and communism); both terms were used with explicit anti-Semitic connotations.

---

[49] Ravens were the messengers of fate of the old Germanic god Wotan.
[50] Köhler-Hausen, *Aus der Dresdner Wagner-Ehrung im Schloss Albrechtsberg*, 6.

Figure 5: "Germania 1918/Ultima ratio" by Richard Guhr.

The Nationalsozialistische Deutsche Arbeiterpartei (NSDAP, National Socialist German Workers' Party), founded in Munich in 1920, had its first success outside Bavaria in the early 1920s. In Saxony, especially in the area in the southwest around Zwickau and Plauen, lots of unemployed craftsmen and factory workers were hit by the economic crises after the First World War.[51] From

---

[51] Andreas Wagner, *"Machtergreifung" in Sachsen: NSDAP und staatliche Verwaltung 1930–1935* (Cologne: Böhlau, 2004), 31–39 Also see: Günther Heydemann, Jan Erik Schulte and Francesca Weil, "Sachsen und der Nationalsozialismus: Zur Vielfalt gesellschaftlicher Teilhabe – Einführung," in *Sachsen und der Nationalsozialismus*, eds. idem (Göttingen: Vandenhoeck & Ruprecht, 2014), 9–19.

Figure 6: DNVP poster on the Reichstag election, 1920, © Deutsches Historisches Museum, Berlin Inv. No.: P 57/98.

there on, the party had more and more success in East and North Germany, increasingly displacing the less radical DNVP. It had important centers in Mecklenburg-Schwerin, Pomerania, (East) Prussia, Anhalt, Saxony, and Thuringia (Figure 6). In the latter, with the formation of the "Baum-Frick government" at the beginning of 1930, the NSDAP provided two government posts in a federal state government for the first time in the Weimar Republic. Wilhelm Frick (1877–1946), who later became Reichsminister of the Interior, was appointed Minister of the Interior and Education in Thuringia.[52] This first-ever participation in a government by the National Socialists was expressly praised by Adolf Hitler as a great success and represented a field of experimentation for him. In the years after, the national socialistic "*Machtergreifung*," the socialization and general implementation of the

---

[52] Alexandra Esche, *Hitlers "völkische Vorkämpfer". Die Entwicklung nationalsozialistischer Kultur- und Rassenpolitik in der Baum-Frick-Regierung 1930–1931* (Berlin/New York: Peter Lang), 2017.

national socialist worldview into German society, the war, and the Holocaust were the most extreme manifestations of the aspiration for a homogenous and ethnically "pure" nation in conjuncture with the imagination of the nation being attacked by different domestic and foreign enemies.

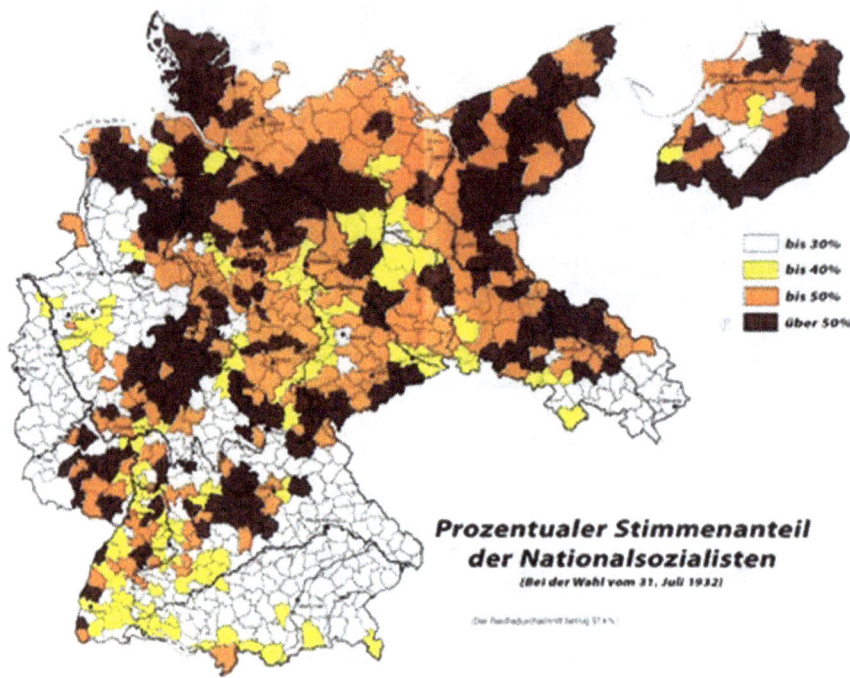

Figure 7: Percentage of National Socialist votes in the Reichstag elections on 31 July 1932.

While their personnel and followers had still formed from the numerous associations of the fatherland associations of the empire (military associations, Alldeutscher Verband, etc.), the Nazis had much younger personnel,[53] who were surprisingly often allowed to indulge in their authoritarian worldviews even in the Sowjet Occupational Zone and the later GDR, despite the strict denazification by the Soviets. Three prominent examples from different generations are referred to here. Willy Gehler (1876–1953), Professor of Civil Engineering at the Technical University of Dresden, who had been a member of the NSDAP and SS since 1933,

---

[53] Ulrike Jureit, "Ein Rhythmus der Geschichte? Generationsgeschichtliche Deutungsmuster zum 20. Jahrhundert," in *Detlev Peukert und die NS-Forschung*, ed. Rüdiger Hachtmann and Sven Reichardt (Göttingen: Wallstein, 2015), 88–94.

was able to continue his research there after 1945, although in a less high position.[54] Bodo Uhse (1904–1963) was active on the völkish scene in Southern Germany from 1921, and was a member of the NSDAP from 1927 to 1930, and later of the KPD, and in 1949 he joined the SED. From 1950 to 1954, Uhse was, among other positions, a member of the SED in the Völkskammer and from 1950 to 1952 first chairman of the German Writers' Association in the Cultural Association for the Democratic Renewal of Germany.[55] Finally, Hans Bentzien (1927–2015) joined the NSDAP in 1944 and was later the first district secretary of the SED in Jena, Gera, and Halle and was to rise to the position of Minister of Culture of the GDR.[56] These three, as well as all the unnamed exponents of the nationalistic movement that later became part of the NSDAP, connect the pre- and postwar eras. They transferred and transformed, in a more or less hidden way, ideas about the nation and embedded them into the "new society." Thus, nationalism nowadays has its one tradition rooted in the GDR as well as in the nationalistic movements and parties before 1945.

Hidden and Open Nationalism from 1945 until the Present

Nationalism was not dismissed in some German regions that are congruent with the GDR. Instead, the idea of the nation has always been a powerful political resource. However, the question is: what is different from the years before 1945?

In 1945, the German Empire was defeated and divided into different parts, from which emerged two states: the Federal Republic of Germany (FRG) in the western zones and the German Democratic Republic in the eastern zone. In the

---

54 Manfred Curbach, Thomas Hänseroth and Oliver Steinbock, "Willy Gehler in der Triade aus Wissenschaft, Industrie und Verwaltung," in *Mit den wohlfeilsten Mitteln dauerhaft, feuersicher und bequem. Sparsamkeit als Prinzip, Rationalität als Weltsicht,* ed. Gesellschaft für Bautechnikgeschichte (Dresden: Thelem, 2019), 245–261.
55 Wolfgang Bauer, "Nachdenken über Bodo Uhse," *Das Blättchen,* 16, no. 14 (July 2013), accessed July 7, 2020, https://das-blaettchen.de/2013/07/nachdenken-ueber-bodo-uhse-25720.html.
56 Sandra Meenzen, "'Gutes Klassenbewusstsein, Parteiverbundenheit und Prinzipienfestigkeit': SED-Sekretäre mit NSDAP-Vergangenheit in Thüringen" ["Class consciousness, party alignment and adherence to Principles": Thuringian SED party secretaries with a NSDAP past], *Historical Social Research* 35, no. 3 (2010): 59–63.

SBZ/later GDR, a socialist Germany would be created.[57] The claim of the communist leaders was clear. They emphasized loudly that after the National Socialists had taken the Germans hostage and plunged Europe into a destructive war, they would establish a self-determined government of the German people under anti-fascist and socialist auspices.[58] Nevertheless, the "nation" continued to form a self-evident and unquestioned reference point of their policy.

The SED, however, changed its conception of the nation several times by emphasizing different aspects of nationhood. Therefore, the discussion about the national character of the socialist country, the GDR, was correspondingly complex.[59] Immediately after the founding of the socialist state and during the early 1950s, leading representatives of the SED addressed the nationalist worldviews among the population. They heard that after Hitler's fascism, it was now US imperialism that wanted to subject Germany. The SED resolutely opposed this and offered the entire German people a life of freedom, peace, and unity. The party tried to work for a national unity in a socialist order and did not shy away from using explicitly nationalistic language.[60]

Thus, the SED staged itself as the only legitimate representative of the interests of the German people at the beginning of the GDR. In 1969, the references to the nation changed, and this was due to what historians call the "German-German" relationship and negotiations of the so-called "*Nationale Frage*" (national question). Politicians, especially those from the FRG, attacked the German division and strove for German unification. Challenged by the Federal Republic's propaganda that a uniformly German "*Kulturnation*" (cultural nation) would outlast the German division, the East German leaders started to construct and spread a new notion of the nation.[61]

---

57 Ulrich Herbert, *Geschichte Deutschlands im 20. Jahrhundert* (Munich: C.H. Beck, 2014).
58 Sigrid Meuschel, *Legitimation und Parteiherrschaft: Zum Paradox von Stabilität und Revolution in der DDR, 1945–1989* (Frankfurt: Suhrkamp, 1992); Aleida Assmann and Ute Frevert, *Geschichtsvergessenheit–Geschichtsversessenheit: Vom Umgang mit deutschen Vergangenheiten* (Stuttgart: Deutsche Verlagsanstalt, 1999).
59 Joanna McKay, *The Official Concept of the Nation in the Former GDR: Theory, Pragmatism and the Search for Legitimacy* (Aldershot: Ashgate, 1998). In a nutshell: Reinhart Koselleck, "Volk, Nation. XV. Ausblick 1945–1991," in *Geschichtliche Grundbegriffe: Historisches Lexikon zur politisch-sozialen Sprache in Deutschland*, vol. 7, ed. Otto Brunner (Stuttgart: Klett-Cotta, 2004), 420–430.
60 Michael Lemke, "Nationalismus im Deutschlandkonzept der SED 1949–1955," in *Nationalismus in Europa nach 1945*, ed. Heiner Timmermann (Berlin: Duncker und Humblot, 2001), 41–58.
61 Heike Amos, *Die SED-Deutschlandpolitik 1961–1989: Ziele, Aktivitäten und Konflikte* (Göttingen: Vandenhoeck & Ruprecht, 2015); Gunther Mai, "Sozialistische Nation und Nationalkultur,"

The leading party in the GDR party broke away from the idea of an indivisible German nation and proclaimed the development of two separate nations. Numerous social theorists defined a new national order for the GDR and FRG.[62] The state division of the German Empire not only produced two German states, but also split the formerly uniform nation into a capitalist nation in the west and a socialist nation in the east. Not only were the ethnic, linguistic, and cultural similarities seen as decisive for the national character, but the socio-economic order or, materialistically speaking, the social formation (in its Marxist meaning) had also become the decisive criterion of nationality. This new concept challenged widespread beliefs and incorporated national identities that were based on traditional nationalism. Historians have not yet sufficiently researched the adherence to the imagination of a united German nation in the GDR, but in 1989, when the people stood up and reclaimed their liberal rights, they soon imagined themselves as one, undividable people. First, they proclaimed "We are the people" then "We are one people."[63] Following other sources and findings, we argue that many in the GDR still imagined Germany as a national union; for them, it was an ethnic community that could not be separated by the claims of the socialist leaders.[64]

Nevertheless, none of the official parties or institutions stood for this understanding of a nation. The SED neutralized any form of opposition by forcing all other parties into the anti-fascist democratic bloc. Even the National Democratic Party of Germany (NDPD) did not gather a national opposition. Although the NDPD addressed former National Socialists above all, the SED soon incorporated this party into the bloc system, too. In the GDR, there was simply no institutional framework for nationalist politics.[65]

---

in *Weimarer Klassik in der Ära Honecker*, ed. Gunther Mai and Lother Ehrlich (Cologne/Weimar/Vienna: Böhlau, 2001), 29–76.
62 Alfred Kosing, *Nation in Geschichte und Gegenwart: Studien zur historisch-materialistischen Theorie der Nation* (Berlin: Dietz, 1976); Alfred Kosing and Walter Schmidt, "Zur Herausbildung der sozialistischen Nation in der DDR," Einheit 29 (1974): 179–188.
63 Konrad J. Jarausch, *Die unverhoffte Einheit: 1989–1990* (Frankfurt: Suhrkamp, 1995); Andreas Rödder, *Deutschland, einig Vaterland: Eine Geschichte der Wiedervereinigung* (Munich: C.H. Beck, 2009).
64 As one example: Johannes Schütz, "Dresden bleibt deutsch?! Vorstellungen von nationaler Gemeinschaft im Bezirk Dresden, 1969–1990," in *Freiheit, Angst und Provokation: Zum gesellschaftlichen Zusammenhalt in der postdiktatorischen Gesellschaft*, ed. Joachim Klose and Walter Schmitz (Dresden: Thelem, 2016), 48–57.
65 Christoph Wunnicke, *Die Blockparteien der DDR. Kontinuitäten und Transformation 1945–1990* (Berlin: Der Berliner Landesbeauftragte für die Unterlagen des Staatssicherheitsdienstes der ehem. DDR, 2014); Christoph Schreiber, *"Deutsche, auf die wir stolz sind": Untersuchungen zur NPDP* (Hamburg: Dr. Kovac, 2018); Bernd Wagner, "Rechtsradikalismus in der Spät-DDR," in Backes and Kailitz, *Hochburg*, 23.

Aside from this official policy, several groups – or rather, most of the people in the GDR – still imagined themselves as German and still imagined Germany as a united community. They tried to transform the old nationalism into a new one, with greater or lesser degrees of success. The most effective way of identifying with the German nation was not by talking but by doing – and that was possible by creating the GDR as "*Heimat*" (home). Already in the 19th century, *Heimat* became the most important driver to translate the abstract imagery of a national community into local contexts. *Heimat* thus became a prerequisite for national integration by being the most important representation of the nation: *Heimat* was the hinge between the local area and the existing state. The numerous "*Heimaten*" made it possible, on the one hand, to be connected to the local area, but at the same time to create a community of all Germans. The nation was seen as a community of Bavarians, Wuerttemberger, and Saxons. It was only in this multitude of particular histories, dialects, and traditions that the German nation was constituted, and through the connection with the *Heimat*, a specifically German national consciousness was internalized. The *Heimat* movement then translated these images, narratives, and metaphors into concrete practices designing the respective *Heimaten*.[66] Again, Saxony was at the core of this development. The Bund Heimatschutz was founded in Dresden in 1904, and the majority of clubs devoted to maintaining regional characteristics and traditions emerged in Saxony.[67]

The SED and the official politics of the GDR adopted this tradition of *Heimat* and transformed it for their purposes: from the 1960s, most of the *Heimat* practices in the GDR were only possible if they could be related to the development of socialism and the work of the party. Local chronologists, history teachers, and brigade leaders had to adhere to the linguistic order and the hierarchy of pictures in their activities; they had to be positive about the role of the SED, and in different extents, to the ideal overhang.[68] But for the agents, *Heimat* was more than the socialist community – *Heimat* was the idea of keeping in touch with German history, German culture, and German traditions. Future research may show that, through the construction of their *Heimat*, many people in the GDR constructed a unified

---

[66] Celia Applegate, *A Nation of Provincials: The German Idea of Heimat* (Berkeley: University of California Press, 1990); Alon Confino, *The Nation as Local Metaphor: Württemberg, Imperial Germany and National Memory, 1871–1918* (Chapel Hill, NC/London: University of North Carolina Press, 1997).
[67] Thomas Schaarschmidt, *Regionalkultur und Diktatur. Sächsische Heimatbewegung und Heimat-Propaganda im Dritten Reich und in der SBZ/DDR* (Cologne/Weimar/Vienna: Böhlau, 2004).
[68] Jan Palmowski, *Inventing a Socialist Nation: Heimat and the Politics of Everyday Life in the GDR, 1945–1990* (Cambridge: Cambridge University Press, 2013).

German identity themselves. This room for imagination was unlocked at the beginning of the 1990s and is still open today.[69]

In addition, and in contrast to the officially legitimated discourse of *Heimat*, some individuals or small groups cultivated the National Socialist heritage. We have to notice here that there were some very active right-wing movements in the GDR who represented a radical nationalism. A comprehensive chronicle of right-wing extremist actions details how verbal and physical violence spread throughout the GDR in the 1980s. There were numerous attacks against "contract workers" from Vietnam, Mozambique, or Algeria, with violence and arson attacks on their homes and the direct use of force against them as well as against "punks" and "goths" in the GDR. Officially banned by the anti-fascist dogma of the GDR, anti-Semitism did not dominate the radical nationalistic worldview anymore. But from the top of the party down to the right-wing groups, we can trace anti-Semitic speeches and actions.[70]

Although it is well known that there were possibilities of violence from the far right in the GDR, how these groups organized themselves in the GDR, which dynamics configured these processes, and which constellations determined the escalation have hardly been explored.[71] We hypothesize that since these actors could not organize themselves in any institutional form, neither parties nor associations nor campaigns, they met primarily in groups who separated themselves from the West German parties by their explicit will to use violence.[72]

With the collapse of state power in the GDR, the right-wing street struggle escalated visibly and met those identified as foreign or political opponents almost daily. Hoyerswerda and Rostock-Lichtenhagen, for instance, are two East German cities that are well-known and connected to events in this series. Naming the cities

---

[69] Johannes Schütz works in this field of research; his project at the University of Dresden is entitled "Polyphonie der Heimat. Konstruktionen von Gemeinschaft durch Imagination, Praktiken und Gefühle in Sachsen, 1969–2000."

[70] Heike Radvan, *"Das hat's bei uns nicht gegeben!" Antisemitismus in der DDR. Das Buch zur Ausstellung der Amadeu-Antonio-Stiftung* (Berlin: Amadeu-Antonio-Stiftung, 2010); Harry Waibel, *Die braune Saat. Antisemitismus und Neonazismus in der DDR* (Stuttgart: Schmetterling, 2017); Wolfgang Benz, ed., *Antisemitismus in der DDR. Manifestationen und Folgen des Feindbildes Israel* (Berlin: Metropol-Verlag, 2018).

[71] Yves Müller and Dominik Rigoll, "Rechtsextremismus als Gegenstand der Zeitgeschichte," *Zeitgeschichte-Online*, accessed February 6, 2020, https://zeitgeschichte-online.de/themen/rechtsextremismus-als-gegenstand-der-zeitgeschichte.

[72] Not to mention the violent neo-Nazi groups that existed even in the FRG. Barbara Manthe, "On the Pathway to Violence. West German Right-Wing Terrorism in the 1970s," *Terrorism and Political Violence* 12 (2019): 1–22; Barbara Manthe, "Racism and Violence in Germany since 1980," *Global Humanities: Studies in Histories, Cultures, and Societies* 4 (2017): 35–53.

serves to set markers in the national narrative of "reunification." Furthermore, and not included in this master narrative, East Germany became a place of violence in the years after 1990, and Dresden had its own role in this process: it was seen as the new capital of the movement (*Hauptstadt der Bewegung*). The most significant impact was the new confidence of the right political spectrum. In the 1990s and early 2000s, right-wing extremists demonstrated in Dresden on February 13, the day of the destruction of the city in World War II. By referring explicitly to the national socialist term *Hauptstadt der Bewegung*, some far-right politicians tried to unite the German nationalist groups of East and West in one party and thus regain discursive and practical influence. The most extreme consequence was the violation of everyday life in unified Germany. Nationalists, patriots, or "*Heimatschützer*" (homeland protectors), as they called themselves, created violent nightmares and formed underground terrorist cells. Again, the homogeneous community was made the core of politics. Even if young radicals executed these politics, the ideas of national unity, sovereignty, and distinction, interpreted as ethnic homogeneity, were rooted in many different groups and actors of East Germany. Nationalism in this notion seeks to protect the "*Heimat*" and legitimizes violence.[73] In 2011, the so-called NSU, the national socialist underground, revealed itself. These young East Germans were socialized in the disappearing GDR and transforming East Germany.[74] They became part of the violent right-wing specter and, while hiding, conducted the program of leaderless resistance by murdering several Germans whom they regarded as migrants. This was the most extreme manifestation of radical nationalism in recent decades.

In the common politics and communication of everyday life, nationalism became stronger again. In different fields of public discourse, the nation took on a significant role in narrating the new unity of the states. What was German and how Germans defined themselves were part of vivid discussions, which infiltrated everyday life to a greater or lesser extent.[75]

This is one reason why nationalist parties had success in Saxony, Thuringia, and Brandenburg. Since the German unification in 1990, nationalist parties have infiltrated the political discourse with national phrases, and over the

---

[73] Christian Schüle, *Heimat. Ein Phantomschmerz* (Munich: Droemer, 2017), 85–117.
[74] Michael Lausberg, *Die extreme Rechte in Ostdeutschland 1990–1998* (Marburg: Tectum-Verlag, 2012); Stefan Aust and Dirk Laabs, *Heimatschutz: Der Staat und die Mordserie des NSU* (Munich: Pantheon, 2014); Matthias Quent, *Rassismus, Radikalisierung, Rechtsterrorismus: Wie der NSU entstand und was er über die Gesellschaft verrät* (Basel: Beltz Juventa, 2019).
[75] Konrad J. Jarausch, ed., *After Unity: Reconfiguring German Identities* (Providence/Oxford: Berghahn Books, 1997); Goetz, *Deutsche Identitäten*.

years, they became more and more attractive to people in these regions, who were hardly met by local or global transformations. After the National Democratic Party of Germany (NPD) emerged, especially in some regions of Mecklenburg-Vorpommern, Saxony, and Thuringia, and obtained many seats in communal and regional parliaments,[76] now the Alternative for Germany (AfD) is proclaiming nationalistic discourse loudly and emphatically. Again, the nation is a socially relevant image for many Germans.[77] They claim politics for Germans alone; they want to reserve social assurance for Germans alone, and – most importantly – they aim to preserve "German culture," as they call it. All this by striving to make Germany homogenously white and German again. In summary, let us refer here to Christian Geulen again, who describes how the transformed nationalism unites in defence against anything foreign, but has no idea of what the nation has in common: "Die Nation, für die hier geworben und protestiert wird, ist eigentlich keine gegebene Partikularität mehr, sondern ein diffuses, aber umso flexibleres Programm der Stiftung von Gemeinschaftlichkeit durch Ausgrenzung und Anfeindung von allem, was irgendwie fremd erscheint."[78]

Conclusion

To sum up, we would like to make some concluding remarks on what these different forms of nationalism have in common. The presented nationalisms are united in their will to regard the nation as a homogenous group, often believed to be founded by the German people. They imagine this nation as threatened by enemies from outside and within; these could be the so-called Jewish world conspiracy, the Bolshevik revolution, Soviet puppets in the SED, or foreign workers in their community. In this way, these simple constructions of reality react to what we are all used to calling "modernity."

The example of Richard Guhr, who was conservatively socialized during the Empire, showed the authoritarian and anti-modern attitude of large parts of the population of Northeastern Germany, most of whom were Protestants. With the fall of the Empire in 1918, a supposedly intact world perished for them. For Guhr, the

---

[76] Toralf Staud, *Moderne Nazis: Die neuen Rechten und der Aufstieg der NPD*, (Cologne: KiWi, 2006); Norbert Frei, Franka Maubach, Christina Morina and Maik Tändler, *Zur rechten Zeit: Wider die Rückkehr des Nationalismus* (Berlin: Ullstein, 2019).
[77] Jay Julian Rosellini, *German New Right: Afd, Pegida and the Re-Imagining of National Identity* (London: Hurst & Company, 2019).
[78] Geulen, "Wiederkehr," 7.

DNVP, and not least for the Nazis, the democracy of the Weimar Republic stood as an artificial construct dominated by Jews and external enemies through liberalism and communism. Thus, many non-democrats hoped that the so-called Third Reich would provide them with an ideological link to the Second Reich (1871–1918).

Nationalism was not dismissed after World War II in some German regions that are congruent with the former GDR. Instead, over the years, the nation has been transformed and become a powerful political resource that has deeply rooted itself in the GDR. Explicitly anti-Semitic notions were banned, though they were probably still held under the surface; the threat to the German people, however, was still a vivid phantasm of nationalistic discourse. After reunification in 1990, this nationalism unleashed itself in the East, and images of old and new enemies such as foreigners in general, Judaism, the EU, or Islam were presented.

Works Cited

Ahbe, Thomas. "Die Konstruktion der Ostdeutschen: Diskursive Spannungen, Stereotype und Identitäten seit 1989." *Aus Politik und Zeitgeschichte* 41, no. 42 (October 2004): 12–22.
Amos, Heike. *Die SED-Deutschlandpolitik 1961–1989. Ziele, Aktivitäten und Konflikte.* Göttingen: Vandenhoeck & Ruprecht, 2015.
Anderson, Benedict. *Imagined Communities: Reflections on the Origin and Spread of Nationalism.* London: Verso, 1983.
Applegate, Celia. *A Nation of Provincials: The German Idea of Heimat.* Berkeley: University of California Press, 1990.
Assmann, Aleida and Ute Frevert. *Geschichtsvergessenheit–Geschichtsversessenheit: Vom Umgang mit deutschen Vergangenheiten.* Stuttgart: Deutsche Verlagsanstalt, 1999.
Aust, Stefan and Dirk Laabs. *Heimatschutz: Der Staat und die Mordserie des NSU.* Munich: Pantheon, 2014.
Backes, Uwe and Steffen Kailitz, eds. *Sachsen – Eine Hochburg des Rechtsextremismus?* Göttingen: Vandenhoeck und Ruprecht, 2020.
Bauer, Wolfgang. "Nachdenken über Bodo Uhse." *Das Blättchen* 16, no. 14 (July 2013), accessed July 7, 2020, https://das-blaettchen.de/2013/07/nachdenken-ueber-bodo-uhse-25720.html.
Benz, Wolfgang, ed. *Antisemitismus in der DDR. Manifestationen und Folgen des Feindbildes Israel.* Berlin: Metropol-Verlag, 2018.
Bermbach, Udo. *Richard Wagner in Deutschland: Rezeption – Verfälschungen.* Stuttgart/Weimar: Metzler, 2011.
Bewer, Max. *Der Rembrandtdeutsche. Von einem Wahrheitsfreund.* Dresden: Glöß, 1892.
Bielefeld, Jörg. "Bismarcktürme- und Bismarcksäulen. Das Infoportal Bismarcktürme." Accessed July 7, 2020. https://www.bismarcktuerme.de/index.html.
Brajer, Sven. "Angst vor dem Fremden in Zeiten des Umbruchs? Aspekte von Antisemitismus und Rassismus im Kaiserreich in der Oberlausitz." *Neues Lausitzisches Magazin* 141 (2019): 81–92.

Breuer, Stefan. *Die Völkischen in Deutschland*. Darmstadt: WBG, 2008.
Cantoni, Davide, Felix Hagemeister and Marc Westcott. "Persistence and Activation of Right-Wing Political Ideology." Rationality and Competition, Discussion Paper No. 143 (February 2019): 1–44.
Chapoutot, Johann. *Greeks, Romans, Germans: How the Nazis Usurped Europe's Classical Past*. Berkeley: University of California Press, 2016.
Confino, Alon. *The Nation as Local Metaphor: Württemberg, Imperial Germany and National Memory, 1871–1918*. Chapel Hill, NC/London: University of North Carolina Press, 1997.
Curbach, Manfred, Thomas Hänseroth and Oliver Steinbock. "Willy Gehler in der Triade aus Wissenschaft, Industrie und Verwaltung." In *Mit den wohlfeilsten Mitteln dauerhaft, feuersicher und bequem". Sparsamkeit als Prinzip, Rationalität als Weltsicht?* (Schriftenreihe der Gesellschaft für Bautechnikgeschichte, vol. 2.), edited by Gesellschaft für Bautechnikgeschichte, 245–261. Dresden: Thelem, 2019.
Dasgupta, Rana. "The demise of the nation state." *The Guardian*, April 5, 2018. https://www.theguardian.com/news/2018/apr/05/demise-of-the-nation-state-rana-dasgupta.
Deutsche Wacht: Organ für nationale Politik; Publikationsorgan der völkischen Vereine Sachsens. Dresden: Verlag der Deutschen Wacht Volumes, 1879–1933.
Deutschen Sprachverein Dresden and Hermann Dunger, eds. *Satzungen des Deutschen Sprachvereins. Neue Fassung von dem Beschlusse vom 17. Januar 1889*. Dresden: Teich, 1889.
Esche, Alexandra. *Hitlers "völkische Vorkämpfer". Die Entwicklung nationalsozialistischer Kultur- und Rassenpolitik in der Baum-Frick-Regierung 1930–1931* (Zivilisationen & Geschichte, vol. 47). Berlin/New York: Peter Lang, 2017.
Fahrmeir, Andreas. *Die Deutschen und ihre Nation: Geschichte einer Idee*. Stuttgart: Reclam, 2017.
Feistel-Rohmeder, Bettina. "Kurzer Rückblick auf die Entstehung und Entwicklung der Deutschen Kunstgesellschaft." In *Im Terror des Kunstbolschewismus. Urkundensammlung des "Deutschen Kunstberichtes" aus den Jahren 1927–33*, edited by Bettina Feistel-Rohmeder. Karlsruhe: Müller, 1938.
Fenske, Reiner. *Imperiale Verbände im Deutschland der Zwischenkriegszeit im Vergleich. Die Beispiele des "Deutschen Ostbundes" und der "Deutschen Kolonialgesellschaft"*. Dresden: Diss, 2018.
Francois, Etienne, Hannes Siegrist and Jakob Vogel. "Die Nation. Vorstellungen, Inszenierungen, Emotionen." In *Nation und Emotion. Deutschland und Frankreich im Vergleich 19. und 20. Jahrhundert*, edited by Etienne Francois, Hannes Siegrist and Jakob Vogel, 13–35. Göttingen: Vandenhoeck und Ruprecht, 1995.
Frei, Norbert, Franka Maubach, Christina Morina and Maik Tändler. *Zur rechten Zeit: Wider die Rückkehr des Nationalismus*. Berlin: Ullstein, 2019.
Geulen, Christian. "Zur 'Wiederkehr' des Nationalismus." *Aus Politik und Zeitgeschichte* 68, no. 48 (November 2018): 4–8.
Geulen, Christian. *Wahlverwandte. Rassendiskurs und Nationalismus im späten 19. Jahrhundert*. Hamburg: Hamburger Edition, 2006.
Goetz, Irene. *Deutsche Identitäten: Die Wiederentdeckung des Nationalen nach 1989*. Cologne/Weimar/Vienna: Böhlau, 2011.
Guhr, Richard. *Der Judenstil oder der Expressionismus*. Dresden: Max Emil Fischer, 1922.
Guhr, Richard. *Die Schuld am Verfall der Künste*. Dresden: Fischer, 1923.
Guillaume, Damien. "Vers 'l'agitation antisémitique' comme phénomène transnational: hostilité antijuive, équivoques libérales et solidarité juive internationale de l'Affaire

Mortara au Congrès de Berlin (1858–1878)." In *Antisemitismus im 19. Jahrhundert aus internationaler Perspektive: Nineteenth Century Anti-Semitism in International Perspective*, edited by Mareike König and Oliver Schulz. Göttingen: V&R Unipress, 2019.

Hawes, James. *The Shortest History of Germany*. London: Old Street Publishing, 2017.

Herbert, Ulrich. *Geschichte Deutschlands im 20. Jahrhundert*. Munich: C.H. Beck, 2014.

Günther Heydemann, Jan Erik Schulte and Francesca Weil, "Sachsen und der Nationalsozialismus: Zur Vielfalt gesellschaftlicher Teilhabe – Einführung," in *Sachsen und der Nationalsozialismus*, eds. idem (Göttingen: Vandenhoeck & Ruprecht, 2014), 9–19.

Hobsbawm, Eric. *Nationen und Nationalismus: Mythos und Realität seit 1780*. Frankfurt a.M./New York: Campus, 2006.

Hobsbawm, Eric. *The Age of Extremes. A History of the World, 1914–1991*. New York: Vintage Books, 1996.

Jacob, Frank. *Die Thule-Gesellschaft*. Berlin: uni-edition, 2010.

Jacob, Frank. *Die Thule-Gesellschaft und die Kokuryûkai: Geheimgesellschaften im globalhistorischen Vergleich*. Würzburg: Königshausen & Neumann, 2013.

Jansen, Christian and Henning Borggräfe. *Nation. Nationalität. Nationalismus*. Frankfurt a.M./New York: Campus, 2007.

Jarausch, Konrad J. *Die unverhoffte Einheit: 1989–1990*. Frankfurt: Suhrkamp, 1995.

Jarausch, Konrad J., ed. *After Unity: Reconfiguring German Identities*. Providence/Oxford: Berghahn Books, 1997.

John, Jürgen, ed. *"Mitteldeutschland". Begriff – Geschichte – Konstrukt*. Rudolstadt/Jena: Hain-Verlag, 2001.

Jureit, Ulrike. "Ein Rhythmus der Geschichte? Generationsgeschichtliche Deutungsmuster zum 20. Jahrhundert." In *Detlev Peukert und die NS-Forschung*, ed. Rüdiger Hachtmann and Sven Reichardt, 88–94. Göttingen: Wallstein, 2015.

Kienemann, Christoph. *Der koloniale Blick gen Osten. Osteuropa im Diskurs des Deutschen Kaiserreiches von 1871*. Paderborn: Schöningh, 2018.

Köhler-Hausen, Ernst. *Aus der Dresdner Wagner-Ehrung im Schloss Albrechtsberg*. Dresden: Stadtmuseum, 1939.

Kolditz, Gerald. "Rolle und Wirksamkeit des Alldeutschen Verbandes in Dresden zwischen 1895 und 1918: ein Beitrag zum bürgerlichen Vereinsleben der nationalistischen Kräfte in der wilhelminischen Ära des deutschen Kaiserreiches." PhD diss., TU Dresden, 1994.

Kollmorgen, Raj. *Ostdeutschland: Beobachtungen einer Übergangs- und Teilgesellschaft*. Wiesbaden: Springer, 2005.

König, Christopher. *Zwischen Kulturprotestantismus und völkischer Bewegung: Arthur Bonus (1864–1941) als religiöser Schriftsteller im wilhelminischen Kaiserreich*. Tübingen: Mohr Siebeck, 2018.

Koselleck, Reinhart. "Volk, Nation. XV. Ausblick 1945–1991." In *Geschichtliche Grundbegriffe: Historisches Lexikon zur politisch-sozialen Sprache in Deutschland, vol. 7*, edited by Otto Brunner, 420–430. Stuttgart: Klett-Cotta, 2004.

Kosing, Alfred and Walter Schmidt. "Zur Herausbildung der sozialistischen Nation in der DDR." *Einheit* 29 (Autumn 1974): 179–188.

Kosing, Alfred. *Nation in Geschichte und Gegenwart: Studien zur historisch-materialistischen Theorie der Nation*. Berlin: Dietz, 1976.

Kowalczuk, Ilko-Sascha. *Die Übernahme. Wie Ostdeutschland Teil der Bundesrepublik wurde*. Munich: C.H. Beck, 2019.

Lächele, Rainer. "Protestantismus und Völkische Religion im deutschen Kaiserreich." In *Handbuch zur »Völkischen Bewegung« 1871–1918*, edited by Uwe Puschner, Walter Schmitz and Justus H. Ulbricht. Munich: KG Saur, 1999.

Lausberg, Michael. *Die extreme Rechte in Ostdeutschland 1990–1998*. Marburg: Tectum-Verlag, 2012.

Lehmkuhl, Josef. *Der Kunst-Messias: Richard Wagners Vermächtnis in seinen Schriften*. Würzburg: Königshausen und Neumann, 2009.

Lemke, Michael. "Nationalismus im Deutschlandkonzept der SED 1949–1955." In *Nationalismus in Europa nach 1945*, edited by Heiner Timmermann, 41–58. Berlin: Duncker und Humblot, 2001.

Louis, Rudolf. *Die Weltanschauung Richard Wagners*. Leipzig: Breitkopf & Härtel, 1898.

Lowenstein, Steven M. et al. *Deutsch-jüdische Geschichte in der Neuzeit: Umstrittene Integration 1871–1918*. Munich: C.H. Beck, 1996.

Mai, Gunther. "Sozialistische Nation und Nationalkultur." In *Weimarer Klassik in der Ära Honecker*, edited by Gunther Mai and Lother Ehrlich, 29–76. Köln/Weimar/Wien: Böhlau, 2001.

Manthe, Barbara. "On the Pathway to Violence. West German Right-Wing Terrorism in the 1970s." *Terrorism and Political Violence* 12 (February 2019): 1–22.

Manthe, Barbara. "Racism and Violence in Germany since 1980." *Global Humanities. Studies in Histories, Cultures, and Societies* 4 (2017): 35–53.

McKay, Joanna. *The Official Concept of the Nation in the Former GDR: Theory, Pragmatism and the Search for Legitimacy*. Aldershot: Ashgate, 1998.

Meenzen, Sandra. "'Gutes Klassenbewusstsein, Parteiverbundenheit und Prinzipienfestigkeit': SED-Sekretäre mit NSDAP-Vergangenheit in Thüringen" ["Class consciousness, party alignment and adherence to Principles": Thuringian SED party secretaries with a NSDAP past]. *Historical Social Research* 35, no. 3 (2010): 59–63

Mergel, Thomas. "Das Scheitern des deutschen Tory-Konservatismus. Die Umformung der DNVP zu einer rechtsradikalen Partei 1928–1932." *Historische Zeitschrift* 276 (2003): 323–368.

Meuschel, Sigrid. *Legitimation und Parteiherrschaft: Zum Paradox von Stabilität und Revolution in der DDR, 1945–1989*. Frankfurt: Suhrkamp, 1992.

Müller, Yves and Dominik Rigoll. "Rechtsextremismus als Gegenstand der Zeitgeschichte." *Zeitgeschichte-Online*, accessed February 6, 2020. https://zeitgeschichte-online.de/themen/rechtsextremismus-als-gegenstand-der-zeitgeschichte.

Ohnezeit, Maik. *Zwischen "schärfster Opposition" und dem "Willen zur Macht" – Die Deutschnationale Volkspartei (DNVP) in der Weimarer Republik 1918–1928*. Düsseldorf: Droste, 2011.

Palmowski, Jan. *Inventing a Socialist Nation: Heimat and the Politics of Everyday Life in the GDR, 1945–1990*. Cambridge: Cambridge University Press, 2013.

Piefel, Matthias. *Antisemitismus und völkische Bewegung im Königreich Sachsen*. Göttingen: V&R Unipress, 2004.

Puschner, Uwe. "Deutsche Reformbühne und völkische Kultstätte. Ernst Wachler und das Harzer Bergtheater." In *Handbuch zur "Völkischen Bewegung" 1871 – 1918*, edited by Uwe Puschner, Walter Schmitz and Justus H. Ulbricht, 762–796. München: Saur, 1996.

Quent, Matthias. *Rassismus, Radikalisierung, Rechtsterrorismus: Wie der NSU entstand und was er über die Gesellschaft verrät*. Basel: Beltz Juventa, 2019.

Radvan, Heike. *"Das hat's bei uns nicht gegeben!" Antisemitismus in der DDR. Das Buch zur Ausstellung der Amadeu-Antonio-Stiftung*. Berlin: Amadeu-Antonio-Stiftung, 2010.

Richter, Michael, Thomas Schaarschmidt and Mike Schmeitzner, eds. *Länder, Gaue und Bezirke: Mitteldeutschland im 20. Jahrhundert*. Dresden: Landeszentrale für politische Bildung, 2007.

Rödder, Andreas. *Deutschland, einig Vaterland: Eine Geschichte der Wiedervereinigung*. Munich: C.H. Beck, 2009.

Rosellini, Jay Julian. *German New Right: AfD, Pegida and the Re-Imagining of National Identity*. London: Hurst & Company, 2019.

Rosenwein, Barbara. *Emotional Communities in the Early Middle Ages*. Ithaca, NY: Cornell University Press, 2006.

Schaarschmidt, Thomas. *Regionalkultur und Diktatur. Sächsische Heimatbewegung und Heimat-Propaganda im Dritten Reich und in der SBZ/DDR*. Cologne/Weimar/Vienna: Böhlau, 2004.

Schmid, Ulrich M. "Bismarck, eine Karriere – der «eiserne Kanzler» wird in Deutschland immer noch zu wenig kritisch gesehen." *Neue Zürcher Zeitung*, January 20, 2020. https://www.nzz.ch/meinung/bismarck-eine-karriere-der-eiserne-kanzler-wird-in-deutschland-immer-noch-zu-wenig-kritisch-gesehen-ld.1532085.

Schreiber, Christoph. *"Deutsche, auf die wir stolz sind": Untersuchungen zur NPDP*. Hamburg: Dr. Kovac, 2018.

Schüle, Christian. *Heimat. Ein Phantomschmerz*. Munich: Droemer, 2017.

Schütz, Johannes. "Dresden bleibt deutsch?! Vorstellungen von nationaler Gemeinschaft im Bezirk Dresden, 1969–1990." In *Freiheit, Angst und Provokation: Zum gesellschaftlichen Zusammenhalt in der postdiktatorischen Gesellschaft*, edited by Joachim Klose and Walter Schmitz, 48–57. Dresden: Thelem, 2016.

Staud, Toralf. *Moderne Nazis: Die neuen Rechten und der Aufstieg der NPD*. Köln: KiWi, 2006.

Stiewe, Barbara. *Der "Dritte Humanismus": Aspekte deutscher Griechenrezeption vom George-Kreis bis zum Nationalsozialismus*. Berlin, Boston: De Gruyter, 2011.

Stummann-Bowert, Ruth. *Ein Leben für Richard Wagner. Richard Guhr. Maler und Bildhauer 1873–1956*. Fritzlar: Stiftung Museum Fritzlar, 1988.

Tanzmann, Bruno. "Zur Einleitung. Aus meinem Leben als völkischer Vorkämpfer." In *Plan des Hochstiftes für Deutsche Art in Hellerau* (Deutsche Bauernhochschule vol. 1), 1–2. 1926.

Thümmler, Jenny. "Heimatverein lädt zur Bismarckfeier." *Sächsische Zeitung GOS Görlitz Lokales*, March 31, 2015. https://www.saechsische.de/plus/heimatvereinlaedt-zur-bismarckfeier-3072675.html.

Wagner, Andreas. *"Machtergreifung" in Sachsen: NSDAP und staatliche Verwaltung 1930 – 1935*. Cologne: Böhlau, 2004.

Wagner, Bernd. "Rechtsradikalismus in der Spät-DDR." In *Sachsen – Eine Hochburg des Rechtsextremismus?*, edited by Uwe Backes and Steffen Kailitz, 21–43. Göttingen: Vandenhoeck und Ruprecht, 2020.

Waibel, Harry. *Die braune Saat. Antisemitismus und Neonazismus in der DDR*. Stuttgart: Schmetterling, 2017.

Weber, Solveig. *Das Bild Richard Wagners. Ikonographische Bestandsaufnahme eines Künstlerkults. Volume I: Text*. Schott: Mainz, 1993.

Wehler, Hans-Ulrich. *Nationalismus: Geschichte, Formen, Folgen*. Munich: C.H. Beck, 2001.

Wildt, Michael. *Volk, Volksgemeinschaft, AfD*. Hamburg: Hamburger Edition, 2017.

Wunnicke, Christoph. *Die Blockparteien der DDR. Kontinuitäten und Transformation 1945–1990*. Berlin: Der Berliner Landesbeauftragte für die Unterlagen des Staatssicherheitsdienstes der ehem. DDR, 2014.

Alicja Curanović
4 The Phantomic Nature of Missionary Nationalism in a Former Empire: The Case of Russia

Introduction

Only in the 20th century did empires give away their dominant position in the international arena to self-determined national states. Many celebrated the fall of the empires, but there were also a few who felt bereaved. Among the latter were members of the imperial nations, i.e. groups who identified with the imperial project the most. Empires are gone (at least for the time being), but what happened to the missionary nationalism that, in the opinion of some scholars,[1] was characteristic of the imperial nations? The key feature of missionary nationalism, as defined by Krishan Kumar, is "the attachment of a dominant or core ethnic group to a state entity that conceives itself as dedicated to some large course or purpose, religious, cultural or political."[2] Hence the central category of missionary imperialism is the sense of mission.

The goal of this contribution is to trace and describe the continuation of missionary imperialism in former empires, using post-Soviet Russia as the case study. While approaching Russian contemporary missionary nationalism, I focus on its crucial component, i.e. the mission. I use a broad notion of mission which combines components of different variations of messianism (e.g. missionism). I argue that mission is a conviction that a certain community (state/nation) believes is exceptional and that this exceptionality manifests itself in its special destiny. I

---

[1] Krishan Kumar, *The Making of English National Identity* (Cambridge: Cambridge University Press, 2003); Herfried Münkler, *Empires: The Logic of World Domination from Ancient Rome to the United States* (Cambridge: Polity Press, 2007); Emil Pain, "The Imperial Syndrome and Its Influence on Russian Nationalism," in *The New Russian Nationalism: Imperialism, Ethnicity and Authoritarianism 2000–2015*, ed. Pål Kolstø and Helge Blakkisrud (Edinburgh: Edinburgh University Press, 2016).
[2] Kumar, *The Making of English National Identity*, 34.

Notes: This research has been conducted as part of SONATA project no. 2015/19/D/HS5/03149, financed by the National Science Centre, Poland. The material for this article was selected and analyzed during the author's stay as a Fulbright Visiting Fellow at the Davis Center, Harvard University in 2018.

Open Access. © 2021 Alicja Curanović, published by De Gruyter. This work is licensed under the Creative Commons Attribution-NonCommercial-NoDerivatives 4.0 International License.
https://doi.org/10.1515/9783110729290-004

discern three distinctive but interconnected features of the 'mission': 1) the conviction of having a special destiny, 2) a sense of moral superiority, and 3) the conviction that the state's activity is motivated not only by its own particular interest but also by the 'common cause.' I recover mission as expressed in a narrative. The 'mission narrative' is thus a narrative that features direct references to mission or to any of its three features mentioned above.

In the process of the self-identification of imperial nations, mission served as a meta-idea that brings together people of different backgrounds and gives them a sense of common purpose. Moreover, within this process, mission became the ideational foundation of imperial nations' identity. At the same time, mission was an attribute of an empire. It is one of the criteria which allow a hegemonic power to be distinguished from an empire; the latter does not limit its actions to the implementation of national interests but pursues a higher ideal.[3] Hence the idea of mission does not just integrate members of an imperial nation and the peoples ruled by it. It is also a part of the image of a state. Additionally, since mission builds a constitutive feature of an empire, it functions as a status marker as well. For this reason, the sense of mission is evoked most often in imperial foreign policy even though the mission narrative targets the domestic audience first and foremost.[4] A mission narrative is a narrative with messianic overtones. It contains direct references to the mission or to any of its three features as defined above. In my research on missionary nationalism, I focus on the mission narrative that is present in official foreign policy discourse of Russia (2000–2018).

The sense of mission was an essential feature within the foreign policy of the Russian Empire as well as its Soviet successor. So far, scholars have not, however, reached a consensus on the role of mission narrative in modern Russia's foreign policy.[5] My findings show that it is neither the dominant motif nor is it completely gone. It is a narrative routine/habit, as defined by Ted Hopf, which is a derivative of the master narrative of "Russia as a great power." I argue that today's references to missions in the official discourse on foreign policy are phantomic. They owe their existence to the inertia of the imperial legacy. The mission narrative is an example of a routine/habit which was formed during

---

[3] Ibid., 30–32.
[4] Münkler, *Empires*, 84–85.
[5] Stephen Kotkin, "Vechnaya geopolitika Rossii," *Rossiya v Global'noy politike* 14, no. 4 (2016): 46–57; Vakhtang Surguladze, *Grani rossiyskogo samosoznaniya: Imperiya, natsional'noye soznaniye, messianizm i vizantizm Rossii* (Moscow: W. Bafing, 2010); Marcel H. Van Herpen, *Putin's Propaganda Machine: Soft Power and Russian Foreign Policy* (Lanham, MD: Rowman & Littlefield, 2016).

the times of the Empire and still lingers even though the Empire is gone. I call this "phantom messianism."

As for the method, I discuss the existing materials and sociological polls. I group this data with the results of the content analysis of official Russian foreign policy discourse. In order to assess the mission narrative, I, together with my research team,[6] analyzed public statements, interviews, and articles authored by the creators of Russia's foreign policy – president, prime minister, minister of foreign affairs, permanent representatives of Russia to the selected international organizations, regular diplomats – within the time period 2000–2018. All in all, we read approximately 25,000 texts.

I see the contribution of the present chapter in three areas. Firstly, it provides the reader with an original concept of mission and reveals the often missed connection between mission narrative, foreign policy, and ontological security. Secondly, it discusses rich empirical material that allows insights into the self-identification process of contemporary Russia. Thirdly, it highlights the persistence of post-imperial routines (habits) as well as their dynamic nature as a base for post-imperial nationalism. Hence, it contributes to the debate about continuity and change in post-Soviet Russia. The notion of "phantom messianism" captures the complexity of this phenomenon well.

The text starts by introducing the main notions and conceptualizing the link between mission narrative and the identity-building process of an empire. The following two sections are dedicated to the Russian Federation. First, I discuss the demand for mission argumentation in Russian society and group my observations with the findings from the analysis of the official foreign policy discourse documents, which supports the presentation of the mission narrative as a particular routine. In the closing section, I will sum up the conclusions with the notion of "phantom messianism."

Empire, Sense of Mission and Ontological Security

There are numerous books dedicated to the empire phenomenon. And although there is no single definition of which all scholars approve, most of them emphasize

---

[6] The members of my research team were Katarzyna Biersztańska, Irmina Ołowska-Szymańska, Piotr Szymański, and Grzegorz Szymanowski.

the significance of the dynamics between the center and the peripheries.⁷ Empire is the structure of power exercised by the center over the peripheries, where the former uses various instruments to sustain its dominance over the latter. In Bruce Parrot's words, an empire is "the dominant society's control of the effective sovereignty of two or more subordinate societies that are substantially concentrated in particular regions or homelands in the empire."⁸ In simple words, the center rules over a multi-ethnic and multi-religious population living in a vast territory. This observation signals difficulties within an empire concerning providing a sense of community to a population of diverse ethnicities, religions, languages, etc. Students of empires have juxtaposed them with nation states and nationalism.⁹ However, more and more evidence has shown that by presenting nationalism and empire as two opposite poles, we miss important phenomena related to the identity-building process.¹⁰ One of these phenomena is "imperial nationalism." This notion can be found in the works of Pål Kolstø or Krishan Kumar. Kolstø distinguishes two kinds of "imperial nationalism" depending on the type of empire. He writes about "nation-building imperialism" and "ethnocratic imperialism." The first case is characteristic of colonial empires overseas, and the second of continental empires. As he explains, "In the first case, the imperialists want to turn the empire into a homogenous state in which one culture dominates throughout; in the second case, the defenders of the imperial state want it to be controlled by a specific nation or ethnic group, without combining this with any desire to spread their national culture to the entire population of the state."¹¹

Kumar's research allows us to see a common denominator of identity-building processes, regardless of the type of empire, namely the sense of mission. Kumar

---

7 Münkler, *Empires*, 6–8. See also Dominic Lieven, *Empire. The Russian Empire and Its Rivals* (New Haven, CT: Yale University Press, 2002); Anthony Pagden, *Lords of All the World* (New Haven, CT: Yale University Press, 1995).
8 Bruce Parrot, "Analyzing the Transformation of the Soviet Union in Comparative Perspective," in *End of Empire? The Transformation of the USSR in Comparative Perspective*, ed. Karen Dawisha and Bruce Parrott (Armonk, NY: M.A. Sharpe, 1997), 7.
9 Alexander Motyl, *Revolutions, Nations, Empires: Conceptual Limits and Theoretical Possibilities* (New York: Columbia University Press, 1999); David G. Rowley, "Imperial Versus National Discourse: The Case of Russia," *Nations and Nationalism* 6, no. 1 (2000): 23–42.
10 Stefan Berger and Alexei Miller, "Introduction: Building Nations in and with Empires – A Re-assessment," in *Nationalizing Empires*, ed. Stefan Berger and Alexei Miller (Budapest/New York: Central European University Press, 2015).
11 Pål Kolstø, "Is imperialist nationalism an oxymoron?" *Nations and Nationalism* 25, no. 1 (2019): 40; Aleksey Miller, *Imperiya Romanovykh i natsionalizm. Esse po metodologii istoricheskogo issledovaniya* (Moscow: Novoye literaturnoye obozreniye, 2010).

comes up with the notion of "'missionary' or 'imperial' nationalism," which "rests not so much on the nature of empire as a general political form as on the perceptions of particular groups within it."[12] In the case of this particular group, i.e. members of the imperial nation, they understand that "[b]eyond the sense of their own uniqueness lies the conviction of a global purpose that prompts them to play down mere national pride or the cultivation of national culture. More is at stake than the making of a nation-state."[13] This thought is also expressed by Herfried Münkler:

> The mission of an empire binds its protagonists by oath to a project which, if only because of its long-term nature, greatly exceeds the limited horizon of individual interests. For this reason, the mission may also be conceived a means whereby an empire intended to last for thousands of years imposes its action logic on people who have power and influence within it for only a limited period of time. It requires them to set aside their own interests if they wish to pursue the imperial policy [. . .].[14]

In other words, the sense of global purpose/mission provides the basic ideational framework for the self-understanding of the group which identifies with the imperial project the most.

Mission as a central category of the identity-building process within an empire also appears in the works of David G. Rowley even though he sees empire in opposition to the nation state and ideas of nationalism. The American historian argues that the sense of universal mission is a meta-idea necessary to provide peoples of an empire with a sense of community. Unlike exclusivist nationalism, this meta-idea is inclusive and universal. According to Rowley, mission is forward-looking and legitimates the existence of the empire, which is said to pursue a higher ideal. Peoples of an empire are encouraged to think in terms of more general ideals than just their own particular interests.[15] The mission is pursued by the empire, and only the empire can achieve it.

It should be emphasized that "missionary nationalism" is not identical with "national messianism," i.e. the idea of the chosen/elected nation that was entrusted by providence with a special mission in the history of humankind. The Polish theologian Dymitr Romanowski defined "national messianism" as a religious dimension of the national idea which serves to "define the exceptional nature of a given nation, to distinguish it among others and draw attention to

---

12 Kumar, *The Making of English National Identity*, 30.
13 Ibid., 32.
14 Münkler, *Empires*, 84–85.
15 David G. Rowley, "'Redeemer Empire': Russian Millenarism," *American Historical Review* 104, no. 5 (1999): 1591.

its specific mission in the history of the world."[16] References to "national messianism" can also be found in the works of Andrzej Walicki[17] and James Class.[18] Judith Wolfe instead uses the term "messianic nationalism."[19] They all focus on the nation and its exceptionalism expressed in a messianic manner. Kumar, on the other hand, advances "missionary nationalism" with the purpose of emphasizing the connection between the self-identification of an imperial nation and the structure of an empire.[20]

This variety of notions can be confusing. Therefore, taking Kumar's definition as a starting point, I concentrate in my research on the category which features all the definitions, i.e. sense of mission. I go beyond the numerous typologies of messianism whose ancient tradition embraced by the Roman Empire is the reason for entwining a sense of mission with imperial policies.[21] In my research, I use a broad notion of mission which combines components of different variations of messianism (e.g. missionism).[22] I assume that mission is a conviction that a certain community (state/nation) is exceptional and that this exceptionality manifests itself in its special destiny. I discern three distinctive but interconnected features of the 'mission': 1) the conviction of having a special destiny, 2) a sense of moral superiority, and 3) the conviction that the state's activity is motivated not only by its own particular interest but also by the 'common cause.' The third component is rooted in the universalistic assumption that the mission must not be pursued exclusively for the sake of the 'chosen one' but for the benefit of all humankind.

---

16 Dymitr Romanowski, "Na bezdrożach rosyjskiej tożsamości. Od Trzeciego Rzymu do Trzeciej Międzynarodowówki: Mikołaj Bierdiajew i Gierogij Fiedotow," *Slavia Orientalis* 62, no. 3 (2013): 367.
17 Andrzej Walicki, *Filozofia a mesjanizm: Studia z dziejów filozofii i myśli społeczno-religijnej romantyzmu polskiego* (Warsaw: PIW, 1968), 14.
18 James Class, "Defending the Enlightenment from Napoleon: Russian Messianism in 1814," *Slovo* 23, no. 1 (2011): 48.
19 Judith Wolfe, "Messianism," in *The Oxford Handbook of Theology and Modern European Thought*, ed. Nicholas Adams, George Pattison and Graham Ward (Oxford: Oxford University Press, 2013), 301–324.
20 Kumar, *The Making of English National Identity*, 30. Reinhold Niebuhr, who feels that messianism is an intrinsic part of identity and imperial legitimacy, wrote about "nationalistic messianism" when referring to Russia. Reinhold Niebuhr, *The Structure of Nations and Empires* (New York: Charles Scribner's Sons, 1959), 167.
21 Pagden, *Lords of All the World*, 8–10.
22 Conversation of Marek A. Cichocki with Andrzej Walicki, "Między polskim mesjanizmem a misjonizmem," *Teologia Polityczna* 4 (2006/7): 30; Mikhail V. Filatov, "Messianstvo i missionizm v russkoy religioznoy filosofii nachala XX veka," *Lesnoy Vestnik* 3 (2002): 156–161.

As has already been said, within the process of nation-building, mission functions as a meta-idea that provides a population of diverse ethnicities with a sense of common purpose. With time, it also becomes a cornerstone idea of the imperial nation (as imperial nations Kumar names i.a. Englishmen within the British Empire, Germans in the Habsburg Monarchy, and Russians in the Russian Empire). At the same time, referring to mission in foreign policy becomes an attribute of a true empire; hence it is one of the constitutive features of an imperial state. Kumar admits that "it's difficult to think of any empire, ancient or modern, that was not possessed of some sense of its mission in the world, some conviction that its rule existed in the service of the higher ideal than mere power and advantage."[23] Münkler also advances this argument: "All empires that have lasted any length of time have chosen as their self-justifying objective a world-historical task or mission that confers cosmological or redemptive meaning on their activity."[24] For the German political scientist, the sense of mission is the criterion that allows empires to be distinguished from other polities. He argues: "Hegemonic powers do not need a mission, but empires cannot do without one."[25] It is important to note that while writing about mission as an attribute of an empire, Münkler does not lose sight of its role in shaping the self-understanding of the imperial nation. He explains: "The imperial mission . . . is directed at people within the empire, especially at those in the imperial centre. It is from auto-suggestion more than anything else, however, that the political elites draw the conviction and energy to press on with the imperial project."[26]

In the case of an empire, the sense of mission is linked to both the particular status of a country (a leading power) and the identity of the people. This connection welcomes the analysis of mission in the self-identification process of imperial nations in regard to ontological security. The latter refers to the need for social collectives to envision themselves as unchangeable, eternal entities. In Jennifer Mitzen's understanding, ontological security refers to "the need to experience oneself as a whole, continuous person in time rather than constantly changing – in order to realise the sense of agency."[27] For Brent J. Steele "[o]ntological security, as opposed to security as survival, is security as being."[28]

---

23 Kumar, *The Making of English National Identity*, 32.
24 Münkler, *Empires*, 84.
25 Ibid.
26 Ibid.
27 Jennifer Mitzen, "Ontological Security in World Politics: State Identity and the Security Dilemma," *European Journal of International Relations* 12, no. 3 (2006): 342.
28 Brent J. Steele "Ontological Security and the Power of Self-Identity: British Neutrality and the American Civil War," *Review of International Studies* 31, no. 3 (2005): 526.

The sense of existential continuity is achieved by a coherent biographical narrative about the past, present, and future of the particular agent. Students of ontological security accept this as a common premise but differ in their evaluations of whose ontological security we should talk about: that of a state (Mitzen) or that of society (Steele, Chernobrov).[29] In the case of the mission narrative, I would answer this question in the following manner. The mission narrative addresses the needs of the ontological security of the people living in the empire. However, since mission is also an attribute of a particular status of a state, the story about the empire's special destiny and its role in the history of humankind is told by the state. Official foreign policy discourse is the "space" where the sense of mission is expressed (discourse/narrative) and can be implemented (actions). The needs of an imperial nation in regard to its ontological security cannot be satisfied without the state's actual performance.

The mission narrative's capacity to strengthen ontological security is connected to the fact that it links past, present, and future into a single coherent, collective, biographical narrative of the empire.[30] Pursuing the universal mission is presented as a timeless quality of the imperial political entity. As Münkler correctly noted, "the imperial mission converts self-legitimation into self-sacralization. Its quasi-religious sense of purpose means that empire is no longer in thrall to the random decisions of the politically powerful and culturally influential. . . . [T]he imperial mission must be given a solemnity that raises it far above humdrum political affairs."[31]

Mission is a crucial component of a biographical narrative of imperial nations and, as such, it functions as a mechanism that provides ontological security. Once the empire is gone, however, ways to create a sense of community (and ontological security) in a multi-ethnic and multi-religious population might present a challenge. One of the possible alternatives is the concept of citizenship which makes an individual a member of a national community, regardless of the individual's background. But in the case of former imperial nation states, is it enough to make the good old mechanism of mission narrative obsolete? In other words, can the former imperial nations sustain their biographical narratives without mission? In order to answer this question, I introduce the Russian case by describing expectations of contemporary Russian society and dynamics of the political discourse.

---

29 Ibid.; Dmitry Chernobrov, "Ontological Security and Public (Mis)Recognition of International Crises: Uncertainty, Political Imaging and the Self," *Political Psychology* 37, no. 5 (2016): 581–596.
30 Eduard Batalov, *Russkaya ideya i amerikanskaya mechta* (Moscow: Progress-Traditsiya, 2009).
31 Münkler, *Empires*, 85.

A Sense of Mission in Contemporary Russia?

Russia makes an exemplary case of an imperial nation. According to Emil Pain, the noticeable imperial nationalism is a consequence of merging Russian nationalism with "imperial consciousness," which turned the preservation of the empire come what may into the crucial component of ethnic Russians' identity.[32] As Rowley explains, "Until well after the Second World War, Russian political and intellectual elites organised their understanding of the world according to a conceptual apparatus that had more in common with the universal, absolute religious categories of medieval Christendom than with the particularistic, relative and secular categories of modern Europe."[33] The Soviet Union preserved to a significant extent the imperial logic of the center and the peripheries as well as the sense of mission in its foreign policy.[34] The fall of the USSR was often perceived as the end of the last true empire. In post-Soviet Russia, finding a new formula for national identity has become one of the national priorities. There are numerous books that analyze the debates about this issue, the formation of various intellectual camps, the impact of the mass media, the stance of the ruling elite, or the new dynamics within Russian nationalism.[35] Authors emphasize the conflictual tendencies in contemporary discourse. On the one hand, the ruling elite talk about the civic nation and citizenship as the central category. On the other hand, they do not shy away from highlighting the special role of ethnic Russians in the state-building of the nation.[36] For reasons of space and due

---

[32] As a result, three features are characteristic of Russian imperial nationalism, i.e. essentialism, defensive imperial character, and the principle of the political domination of ethnic Russians. Essentialism – the idea that there are special unchangeable mental and cultural qualities of the Russian people, especially in contrast to the West. Defensive imperial character – service to the ruler in order to preserve the empire; political domination – merging the protection of the empire with the preferential right for ethnic Russians. Pain, "The Imperial Syndrome," 51; Emil Pain, "Imperskiy natsionalizm (Vozniknoveniye, evolyutsiya i politicheskiye perspektivy v Rossii," *Obshchestvennyye nauki i sovremennost'* 2 (2015): 54–71.
[33] Rowley, "Imperial Versus National Discourse," 24.
[34] Niebuhr, *The Structure of Nations and Empires*, 167; Pål Kolstø, "The Concept of 'Patriotic Internationalism': A Contribution to the Understanding of Soviet Ideology," *Nordic Journal of Soviet and East European Studies* 1, no. 4 (1984): 1–29.
[35] Vera Tolz, *Russia (Inventing the Nation)* (London: Bloomsbury Academic, 2001); Pål Kolstø and Helge Blakkisrud, eds., *The New Russian Nationalism. Imperialism, Ethnicity and Authoritarianism 2000–2015* (Edinburgh: Edinburgh University Press, 2016); Marlene Laurelle, *Russian Nationalism: Imaginaries, Doctrines and Political Battlefields* (London: Routledge, 2018); Anne L. Clunan, *The Social Construction of Russia's Resurgence: Aspirations, Identity, and Security Interests* (Washington, DC: Johns Hopkins University Press, 2009).
[36] Vladimir Putin, "Rossiya: natsional'nyy vopros," *Nezavisimaya Gazeta*, January 23, 2012.

to the quality and number of existing materials discussing these problems in detail, I will move straight on to the analysis of the mission narrative.

Today's Russia is a former empire. To be more precise, it is a post-imperial country which, nevertheless, keeps certain routines that are characteristic of an empire.[37] As an example of such a routine, Andrei Makarychev points to imperial discourse,[38] while Emil Pain writes about "imperial syndrome," which consists of imperial "regime," "body," and "consciousness."[39] As one of the most significant manifestations of the post-imperial legacy, I would indicate Russians' attachment to the understanding of their country as a great power. This is the crucial master narrative of contemporary Russian public debate.[40] Mikhail Gorshkov and Vladimir Petukhov argue that "the issue of Russia's international status as a major power plays the main role in Russia's political self-identification."[41] The status of being a major player joins all historical embodiments of Russia, i.e. Muscovy, the Russian Empire, and the USSR. Hence it allows for creating and sustaining a coherent biographical narrative despite all the abrupt shifts and state collapses that marked Russian history in the 20th century. More importantly, the connection between the particular status of Russia and its citizens' self-esteem testifies to the role of the master narrative of "Russia as a great power" in providing a sense of ontological security. As an example, Anne Clunan points to the fate of Boris Yeltsin's team.[42] She convincingly argues that the main reason for the decrease in the popularity of the ruling elite in the mid-1990s was not so much the difficult reforms as the fact

---

37 Andrei Makarychev, "Imperial Discourse in Post-Imperial Russia: Where Will it Float to?" in *Empire and International Order*, ed. Noel Parker (Farnham: Ashgate, 2013), 113–115.
38 Ibid.
39 As defined by Emil Pain, the *imperial order* is the political regime of the empire, i.e. power over many people without their consent. The *imperial body* refers to "the territory of the country, divided into regions that are not culturally integrated with one another and have preserved historical traces of colonial conquest." The *imperial consciousness* includes a "complex of traditional stereotypes of popular imaginary . . . that preserves stable statist values, hopes for 'a wise tsar' and 'a firm hand,' and also imperial ambitions." Pain, "The Imperial Syndrome," 59–60.
40 David Cadier and Margot Light, eds., *Russia's Foreign Policy: Ideas, Domestic Politics and External Relations* (London: Palgrave Macmillan, 2015); Valeria Kasamara and Anna Sorokina, "Imperial Ambitions of Russians," *Post-Communist Studies* 45, no. 3–4 (2012): 279–288.
41 Mikhail Gorshkov and Vladimir Petukhov, "Vneshnepoliticheskiye oriyentatsii rossiyan na novom perelome," *POLIS: Politicheskoye issledovaniya* 2 (2015): 22; Eduard Ponarin and Boris Sokolov, "Global'naya politika glazami rossiyskoy elity," *Rossiya v global'noy politike* 12, no. 5 (2014): 110.
42 The first president of the Russian Federation (1991–1999).

that the minister of foreign affairs, Andrei Kozyrev, resigned from hegemonic policies in the post-Soviet era.[43] This dynamic shows that the state's performance in the international arena is relevant to society's ontological anxiety. In addition, the failure of the ruling elite to preserve or regain the desired status may have led to weakening its own legitimacy.

The connection between the state's status, the people's ontological security, and the legitimacy of the government is well illustrated by the change in social postures after the annexation of Crimea in 2014. The sociological polls conducted a year later showed that this particular event, despite all its costly consequences (e.g. sanctions), boosted the citizens' self-esteem: 70% of respondents felt proud about the fact that their country had proved to be a great power that was respected and feared in the world.[44] At the same time, the annexation elevated Vladimir Putin's popularity well above 80%.[45] According to the surveys conducted by the Levada Center in 2018, 88% of respondents thought that Russia should strive to preserve its status as a major power, while only for 10% was there no need for their country to aspire to the top position in the international hierarchy.[46] It is important to note that rebuilding Russia's status was perceived by more than half of respondents to be the most important priority of the president's actions since 1999 (hence it has a direct influence on the president's legitimacy).[47] Attachment to this status still functions in a way as a meta-idea that joins Russian citizens together, regardless of their ethnicity, religion, or, in most cases, political worldview (figure 1).

Sociologist Denis Volkov from the Levada Center states that the attachment to the image of Russia as a great power does not mean that Russian citizens would support restoring the empire. As the main reason for this, he names the visible lack of readiness to bear the costs of the expansion and assimilation of the peripheries. Volkov argues that the majority of Russians "have developed certain patterns of nationalism-patriotism [Russian: *natsionalizm-patriotizm*]: we shouldn't provide for 'all the other' [Russian: *vsekh etikh*]. Let's take care of our own interests

---

43 Anne L. Clunan, "Historical Aspiration and the Domestic Politics of Russia's Pursuit of International Status," *Communist and Post-Communist Studies* 47, no. 3–4 (2014): 281–290.
44 Levada.ru, "Istoriya rossiyskogo antiamerikanizma: pochemu v Rossii stali schitat' SSHA vragom," last modified June 9, 2015, http://www.levada.ru/2015/06/09/istoriya-rossijskogo-antiamerikanizma-pochemu-v-rossii-stali-schitat-ssha-vragom/.
45 Levada.ru, "Odobreniye deyatel'nosti Vladimira Putina," last modified December 16, 2019, https://www.levada.ru/indikatory/.
46 Levada.ru, "Natsional'naya identichnost' i gordost'," last modified January 17, 2019, https://www.levada.ru/2019/01/17/natsionalnaya-identichnost-i-gordost/.
47 Levada.ru, "Za kokogo politika gotovy progolosovat' rossiyane i chego ozhidayut ot vyborov," last modified February 2, 2012, https://www.levada.ru/2012/02/02/za-kakogo-politika-gotovy-progolosovat-rossiyane-i-chego-ozhidayut-ot-vyborov/.

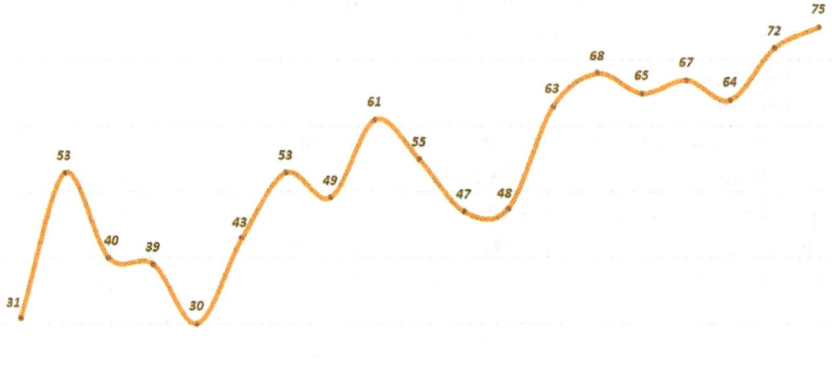

Figure 1: The number of Russians who consider Russia a major power (1999–2018), https://www.levada.ru/2019/01/17/natsionalnaya-identichnost-i-gordost/.

first. This does not mean, however, that we should not get involved."[48] As Volkov explains, "Another logic works here: we can and we should get involved, because this is what major powers do. If Americans can, so can we. This is of great importance, and hence there is no alternative."[49] It is worth noting that for most ordinary Russians, the desired status should be achieved due to domestic reforms. In this regard, in 2015 (hence after the annexation), 58% of the questioned group named "modernization of economy" and 53% an improvement in the standard of living. Therefore, as Gorshkov and Petukhov sum up, "the grandeur of the homeland should be forged within Russia and not in the international arena."[50]

This data, grouped together with the remarks of Volkov, could indicate that today there is no demand among ordinary Russians for a mission narrative. Indeed, such conclusions are drawn by some sociologists. Vladimir Petukhov and Raisa Barash state that a "messianic idea of the great power doesn't correspond

---

[48] Levada.ru, "Pochemu rossiyanam nravitsya ideya velikoy derzhavy i chto oni dumayut o stranakh Baltii?", last modified November 14, 2019, https://www.levada.ru/2019/11/14/pochemu-rossiyanam-nravitsya-ideya-velikoj-derzhavy-i-chto-oni-dumayut-o-stranah-baltii/.
[49] Ibid.
[50] Gorshkov and Petukhov, "Vneshnepoliticheskiye oriyentatsii rossiyan," 28.

to the expectations of many of our citizens . . . the majority of Russians are not ready to pay for great power status with belt-tightening. Showing enthusiasm about reunification with Crimea – that's one thing, while less than one-third of Russians are ready to sacrifice their own prosperity (or even life)."[51] In another article written together with Mikhail Gorshkov, Petukhov repeated this thought, though in a slightly different manner: "only a few Russians (in contrast to the representatives of the ruling class) are attracted by the 'messianic' attribute of a major power."[52] The observation that the elite are more "mission-oriented" than ordinary Russians is intriguing and should not be overlooked. This is also reflected in the interviews conducted by Mikhail Tarusin's team in 2007 with 326 individuals representing the elites of business, church, culture, mass media, opposition groups, and NGOs as well as regional and federal authorities.[53] It turned out that 78% of all respondents believed that Russia was destined for greatness and grand historical tasks. This inclination of the Russian elite was labeled by sociologists as a "secretive messianic spirit."[54] The results of my analysis of the official foreign policy discourse shaped by the ruling elites show that a mission narrative, although officially denied, is still present. It resembles an old habit so deeply rooted in discursive practice that it resurfaces almost automatically.

Mission Narrative as a Routine of Russian Foreign Policy's Official Discourse

Before presenting the main findings about the contemporary mission narrative, I will briefly explain the method. I performed a content analysis which is suitable for reconstructing motifs of a particular narrative. Together with my team, I analyzed public appearances of the main creators of Russian foreign policy – i.e. president, prime minister, minister of foreign affairs, minister of defense, permanent representatives of Russia to the selected international organizations, regular diplomats – as well as the State Duma's and the Security Council's stenographic records for the time period 2000–2018.

---

51 Vladimir Petukhov and Raisa Barash, "Russkiye i russkiy mir: istoricheskiy kontekst i sovremennoye prochteniye," *POLIS: Politicheskiye issledovaniya*, no. 6 (2014): 93.
52 Ibid., 30.
53 Mikhail Tarusin, *Summa ideologii: Mirovozzreniye i ideologiya sovremennoy rossiyskoy elity* (Moscow: Institut obshchestvennogo proyektivnaya, 2008), 24–51.
54 Ibid.

We looked for "mission texts" using keywords (56 of them) and particular kinds of public appearances. In the latter case, we read all interviews, articles, and ritual ceremonial speeches (e.g. addresses to the Federal Assembly, commemorative speeches on state holidays – Russia Day, Victory Day, Unity Day, Slavic Writing and Culture Day, New Year –, the president's annual conferences for journalists, meetings of the Valdai Club, and speeches at the UN). We used these keywords and kinds of appearances in order to identify a "mission text." This is a text where there is a direct reference to the mission or to one of its three features (unique destiny, moral superiority, universalism). Bearing in mind the specifics of the contemporary use of diplomatic language – which is highly formalized and, importantly when discussing mission, also highly secularized – I decided to introduce a further way of identifying a "mission text." I searched for a definition of mission that would be both as abstract as possible and also expressed in the spirit of the terminology of foreign policy. Hence I also accept the use of the term "mission role" (i.e. "mission") for the cases where a country claims to pursue a special role and justifies this by its own identity. For example, there is a certain connotation to providence in the statement that a country's unique culture means that it is the one that needs to moderate intercivilizational dialogue; this connotation is missing in demands to strengthen a country's energy security, for example. Therefore, identifying a self-attributed role justified by a country's identity was the third way of finding "mission texts." Once we found a mission text, we coded it manually, i.e. we registered it in a table. It was necessary to step away from the computer program and return to doing things by hand in order to correctly identify "mission texts." For example, the word "mission" appears 461 times in Duma texts in 2000–2018, but only 26 times within a messianic context. The vast majority of "missions" appeared in a "non-messianic" context. While coding, we always entered a relevant quotation, its description, and a label. Apart from inserting data into the table, we developed the practice of team members having notepads to make observations and write quotations that had mission connotations but which were incomplete, which significantly hampered the process of entering them into the table, and at times made this impossible. Furthermore, the table itself had a column for "comments" in which each team member signaled new contexts, suggested making labels more nuanced, flagged divergences, etc. Having found a "mission text," a coder looked for particular pieces of information: references to mission, its content and function; mentions of Russia's identity, status, or threat; visions of international order and history; religious connotations; the figure of the one entrusted with the mission (e.g. state, nation, Church); the source of the messianic call (e.g. God, history, fate), etc.

All in all we read approximately 25,000 texts, 4% of which contained mission-related motifs. This finding shows that the mission narrative does not occupy the dominant position in the official discourse on foreign policy but rather lingers on its margins. This is an important observation for it questions the thesis about the renewal of Russian political messianism after the annexation of Crimea.[55] The mission narrative, although marginal in today's discourse, is surprisingly persistent. It can be traced in politicians' speeches even though all the leading figures officially reject messianic zeal. President Putin or Foreign Minister Sergey Lavrov have on many occasions praised pragmatism as the new guiding principle of Russia's foreign policy.[56] They condemn "*messiyanstvo*" as being associated with Soviet foreign policy and blame it for the collapse of the USSR. They argue that it was mission-driven international activity that broke the Soviet economy and brought the superpower to an end. Lavrov said, "Russia is the successor of the Soviet Union and also the continuer of the tradition of the era of Dostoyevsky. It is clearly aware of the counterproductive nature of messianism, of the disastrous attempts to impose one's own developmental method and values onto others."[57]

This reluctance to pay for satisfying aspirations of status with one's own prosperity is similar to the views of many ordinary Russians. Hence it would seem that both the elite and the citizens prioritize pragmatism and national wealth over pursuing higher ideals. But before we make this our final conclusion, let us recall the paradox noticed by Volkov – the absence of the readiness for self-sacrifice is accompanied by expectations that Russia should act in the international arena as "major powers do," which is, more often than not, costly. It is this attachment to Russia's status as a major power that does not allow the mission narrative to go completely out of date. It rather functions as a derivative of the master narrative of "Russia as a great power." It is a consequence of perceiving mission as an attribute of a country that occupies a leading position in the international hierarchy. This is well illustrated in a fragment of an article by Sergey Lavrov when he refers to Russian philosopher Ivan Ilyin (1883–1954): "Ilyin, thinking about Russia as a major power in the world, emphasized that the status of a major power is not determined by the size of its territory or the

---

55 Van Herpen, *Putin's Propaganda Machine*.
56 Sergey Lavrov, "Vneshnepoliticheskaya filosofiya Rossii." *Mezhdunarodnaya zhizn'*, no. 3 (2013), accessed May 1, 2020, https://interaffairs.ru/jauthor/material/826.
57 Sergey Lavrov, "Vystupleniye Ministra inostrannykh del Rossii S.V.Lavrova na vstreche s kollektivom Diplomaticheskoy akademii MID Rossii," last modified March 25, 2016, http://www.mid.ru/web/guest/meropriyatiya_s_uchastiem_ministra/-/asset_publisher/xK1BhB2bUjd3/content/id/2189906.

population, but by the readiness of the government and its people to take upon themselves the burden of grand international tasks."[58] Lavrov ends his argument by stating that a true major power can be recognized by the fact that it cares about the well-being of other countries while implementing its own national interests. This understanding is in line with the interpretation of universalism presented in my concept – in order for mission to have a universal character, it does not have to mean self-sacrifice; it is sufficient to implement tasks that are beneficial not just for Russia but for other countries as well.[59]

I see the tendency to disconnect the sense of mission from the necessity to self-sacrifice as a manifestation of the post-Soviet trauma, i.e. the reaction to losing the status of the Cold War superpower. The analysis of the official discourse, like the sociological polls quoted earlier, shows that Russians want to live in a country which is a great power, but they would like to achieve it while putting their own interests first. Hence, we can observe a reformulation of one of the key features of the mission, namely universalism. Universalism in this post-Soviet interpretation does not require self-sacrifice for the sake of others. It is just one of the possible scenarios. To pass as a "mission pursuing major power," it is enough if a country, while implementing its own foreign policy, considers the prosperity of other nations as well. When comparing today's mission narrative with the tradition of Russian messianism, we can also observe some other changes (e.g. minimal presence of religious connotations). In general, however, the set of mission roles ascribed to Russia by intellectuals from the 19th to the 21st centuries is surprisingly stable. Just like almost two hundred years ago, today Russia by nationalists is still considered the *global balance bringer*, the *defender of faith and values*, the *guardian of justice*, the *intercivilizational bridge*, or the *shield* protecting the world from evil – to name just a few examples.[60] The historical stability and coherence of the mission narrative allow a sense of continuity to be sustained and hence contributions to ontological security to be made. The stability of the narrative whose framework and main ideas were formulated in different historical circumstances could indicate that referring to mission has become a routine, repeated by interlocutors sometimes unreflexively. The

---

58 Sergey Lavrov, "Istoricheskaya perspektiva vneshney politiki Rossii," *Russia in Global Affairs*, March 3, 2016, https://globalaffairs.ru/global-processes/Istoricheskaya-perspektiva-vneshnei-politiki-Rossii-18017.
59 Ibid.
60 See Vladimir Storchak, *Fenomen rossiyskogo messianizma v obshchestvenno-politicheskoy i filosofskoy mysli Rossii (vtoraya polovina XIX – pervaya tret' XX v.)* (Moscow: RAGS, 2005); Andrzej Walicki, *The Flow of Ideas: Russian Thought from the Enlightenment to the Religious-Philosophical Renaissance* (Frankfurt am Main: Peter Lang, 2015).

analysis of the official foreign policy discourse reveals that politicians tend to talk about Russia's mission in connection with particular contexts, e.g. the Second World War, the imperial past, or the tradition of Russian Orthodoxy.

My research also shows that in the case of the mission narrative, it is not just about simple manipulation, i.e. the elite consciously reacting to anxiety expressed by the citizens. The creators of Russia's foreign policy officially reject mission and see it as an archaic, harmful idea. Additionally, most of the citizens, although attached to Russia's status as a major power, would like it to be achieved by domestic reforms and not by chasing higher ideals in the international arena. These circumstances should work against preserving the mission narrative. This fact, juxtaposed with the narrative's persistence, encourages us to perceive references to mission as a particular narrative habit. Moreover, I argue that talking about a mission in foreign politics reflects the foremost anxiety of the elite leading a country that is struggling to keep its status as a major power. The analysis of the official discourse reveals that references to mission appear most often in the statements addressed to the establishment of today's Russia, i.e. representatives not only of political parties but also of business, culture, and religious institutions. The mission narrative functions as a self-reassuring mechanism helping to consolidate the elite. It is true that the elite do not represent the whole of society but, as Tanya Narozhna showed, it is this group which, since the 2000s, has dominated the production of identity discourse in the Russian Federation.[61] The analysis of the contemporary mission narrative brings one more argument to the discussion about the condition of imperial nationalism and its carriers, i.e. imperial nations. Mission has stopped playing the role of the main meta-idea but, nevertheless, it is still too early to consign it to the dustbin of history.

Concluding Remarks: "Phantom Messianism"

The detailed analysis of mission-related motifs in the Russian official discourse brings us to the conclusion that we are dealing with a narrative that nobody officially cares for but which, nevertheless, keeps appearing in public statements. The narrative is still present because it is anchored in the image of "Russia as a major power." The strong conviction shared by the elite and the majority of ordinary Russians that their country cannot be anything else but a great power is,

---

[61] Tanya Narozhna, "State-Society Complexes in Ontological Security-Seeking in IR," *Journal of International Relations and Development* 23 (2018): 559–583.

in turn, part of the imperial legacy and indicates that imperial nationalism is still relevant to Russians' self-identification process.

I argue that referring today to mission is a particular routine or habit. Ted Hopf emphasized the significance of habits to reproduce identities. The American political scientist defined habits as "the unreflective reactions we have to the world around us: our perceptions, attitudes, emotions, and practices. They simplify the world, short-circuiting rational reflection."[62] Hopf also stressed that habits are "unintentional, unconscious, involuntary, and effortless, that is, they do not consume limited cognitive processing capacity."[63] Furthermore, habits "imply actions by giving us ready-made responses to the world that we execute without thinking."[64] The mission narrative fits this description, for instance when used to describe Russia's victory in the Second World War or its special responsibilities in the immediate neighborhood in the spirit of civilizational mission. Putin, for example, declared that it is also certain "that Russia should continue its civilising mission on the Eurasian continent. This mission consists in ensuring that democratic values, combined with national interests, enrich and strengthen our historic community."[65]

Hopf points to the social structure as the primary source of habits. Individuals learn about them in different ways (e.g. socialization, cost-benefit calculation, imitation). Later on, these learned habits underpin the actions of a state in the international environment. The mission narrative feeds on the imperial legacy, which is also the source of Russian current status ambitions. Approaching the mission narrative as a habit allows us to explain its persistence since habits are maintained "through use, utility, the absence of challenges, and the physiology of the brain."[66] As Hopf concludes, "[t]he more dominant a particular discourse of identity, the more widely and deeply shared within the state, between the state and its society, and between the two states as they interact, the more unlikely habitual perceptions, attitudes, and practices will ever be challenged to the extent that necessary reflection will occur."[67]

The attachment to a status of great power brings together Russian citizens and the elite. Apart from the first three years of the 1990s, the major power

---

[62] Ted Hopf, "The Logic of Habit in International Relations," *European Journal of International Relations* 16, no. 4 (2010): 544.
[63] Ibid., 541.
[64] Ibid.
[65] Vladimir Putin, "Poslaniye Federal'nomu Sobraniyu Rossiyskoy Federatsii," last modified April 25, 2005, http://kremlin.ru/events/president/transcripts/22931.
[66] Hopf, "The Logic of Habit in International Relations," 544.
[67] Ibid., 555.

status was not questioned, which provided fertile ground for the habit to survive. In the times of the Empire, mission was a meta-idea and a cornerstone idea of the imperial nation. The Empire is gone, but the narrative routine is still present. To address this new nature of mission-related motifs in foreign policy, I use the notion of "phantom messianism." Today's references to mission resemble phantomic reflexes, which remain for a long time after a limb has been removed. They are not the main ideational drive behind Russia's foreign policy. The mission narrative is also far from being an effective ideological tool of the government since ordinary Russians really do not yearn for a grand mission. It is rather a habit which resurfaces in passing. The language has changed; talking directly about a mission in the world seems archaic even to politicians. Moreover, after the fall of the USSR, there has not been even a handful who would openly call for sacrifice in the name of higher ideals of foreign policy. Nevertheless, the Russian elite are more attached than ordinary citizens to formulating foreign policy in terms of mission. On the other hand, the end of the USSR triggered reflections upon messianic zeal and resulted in attaching negative associations to mission.

The stability of the mission narrative with its traditional patterns allows it to play a part in constructing a coherent biographical narrative that highlights Russia's historical continuity and strengthens its ontological security. Within an empire, missionary nationalism connected the self-identification process of its peoples with the idea of a global mission. Today, the mission narrative is a derivative of a status of great power. As discussed on many occasions, Russians' fixation on this particular issue[68] today plays the role of an integrative meta-idea. Although almost three decades have passed since the fall of the USSR, the Russian Federation is still in a transition from an imperial structure to a nation state. Many routines rooted in the imperial legacy are still present. The fate of old habits depends on the level of reflexivity stimulated by changes both in the international environment as well as in the domestic debate. The absence of an open and free discussion in today's Russia gives the mission narrative habit a chance to stay for longer. The years to come and the dynamics within the Russian self-identification process will be decisive for the prospect of the mission narrative. The main challenge for those who openly reject mission is to frame the idea of great power with no references to its unique role in the world.

---

[68] Regina Heller, Tuomas Forsberg and Reinhard Wolf, eds., "Status and Emotions in Russian Foreign Policy," special issue, *Communist and Post-Communist Studies* 47, no. 3–4 (2014).

Works Cited

Batalov, Eduard. *Russkaya ideya i amerikanskaya mechta*. Moscow: Progress-Traditsiya, 2009.
Berger, Stefan and Alexei Miller, eds. *Nationalizing Empires*. Budapest/New York: Central European University Press, 2015.
Chernobrov, Dmitry. "Ontological Security and Public (Mis)Recognition of International Crises: Uncertainty, Political Imaging and the Self." *Political Psychology* 37, no. 5 (2016): 581–596.
Cadier, David and Margot Light, eds. *Russia's Foreign Policy: Ideas, Domestic Politics and External Relations*. London: Palgrave Macmillan, 2015.
Class, James. "Defending the Enlightenment from Napoleon: Russian Messianism in 1814." *Slovo* 23, no. 1 (Spring 2011): 48–64.
Clunan, Anne L. *The Social Construction of Russia's Resurgence: Aspirations, Identity, and Security Interests*, Washington, DC: Johns Hopkins University Press, 2009.
Clunan, Anne L. "Historical aspiration and the domestic politics of Russia's pursuit of international status." *Communist and Post-Communist Studies* 47, no. 3–4 (2014): 281–290.
Conversation of Marek A. Cichocki with Andrzej Walicki. "Między polskim mesjanizmem a misjonizmem." *Teologia Polityczna* 4 (2006–2007): 30–41.
Filatov, Mikhail V. "Messianstvo i missionizm v russkoy religioznoy filosofii nachala XX veka." *Lesnoy Vestnik* no. 3 (2002): 156–161.
Gorshkov, Mikhail and Vladimir Petukhov. "Vneshnepoliticheskiye oriyentatsii rossiyan na novom perelome." *POLIS. Politicheskoye issledovaniya*, no. 2 (2015): 10–34.
Heller, Regina, Tuomas Forsberg and Reinhard Wolf, eds. "Status and Emotions in Russian Foreign Policy." Special edition, *Communist and Post-Communist Studies* 47, no. 3–4 (2014), vol. 30.
Hopf, Ted. "The Logic of Habit in International Relations." *European Journal of International Relations* 16, no. 4 (2010): 539–561.
Kasamara, Valeria and Anna Sorokina. "Imperial ambitions of Russians." *Post-Communist Studies* 45, no. 3–4 (2012): 279–288.
Kolstø, Pål. "Is imperialist nationalism an oxymoron?" *Nations and Nationalism* 25, no. 1 (2019): 18–44.
Kolstø, Pål. "The Concept of 'Patriotic Internationalism'. A Contribution to the Understanding of Soviet Ideology." *Nordic Journal of Soviet and East European Studies* 1, no. 4 (1984): 1–29.
Kolstø, Pål and Helge Blakkisrud, eds. *The New Russian Nationalism. Imperialism, Ethnicity and Authoritarianism 2000–2015*. Edinburgh: Edinburgh University Press, 2016.
Kotkin, Stephen. "Vechnaya geopolitika Rossii." *Rossiya v Global'noy politike* 14, no. 4 (2016): 46–57.
Kumar, Krishan. *The Making of English National Identity*. Cambridge: Cambridge University Press, 2003.
Laurelle, Marlene. *Russian Nationalism. Imaginaries, Doctrines and Political Battlefields*. London: Routledge, 2018.
Lavrov, Sergei. "Vneshnepoliticheskaya filosofiya Rossii." *Mezhdunarodnaya zhizn'* no. 3 (2013), https://interaffairs.ru/jauthor/material/826.

Lavrov, Sergei. "Vystupleniye Ministra inostrannykh del Rossii S.V.Lavrova na vstreche s kollektivom Diplomaticheskoy akademii MID Rossii." Last modified March 25, 2016, http://www.mid.ru/web/guest/meropriyatiya_s_uchastiem_ministra/-/asset_publisher/xK1BhB2bUjd3/content/id/2189906.

Lavrov, Sergei. "Istoricheskaya perspektiva vneshney politiki Rossii." *Russia in Global Affairs*, March 3, 2016. https://globalaffairs.ru/global-processes/Istoricheskaya-perspektiva-vneshnei-politiki-Rossii-18017.

Levada.ru. "Istoriya rossiyskogo antiamerikanizma: pochemu v Rossii stali schitat' SSHA vragom." Last modified June 9, 2015. http://www.levada.ru/2015/06/09/istoriya-rossijskogo-antiamerikanizma-pochemu-v-rossii-stali-schitat-ssha-vragom/.

Levada.ru. "Odobreniye deyatel'nosti Vladimira Putina." Last modified December 16, 2019. https://www.levada.ru/indikatory/.

Levada.ru. "Natsional'naya identichnost' i gordost'." Last modified January 17, 2019. https://www.levada.ru/2019/01/17/natsionalnaya-identichnost-i-gordost/.

Levada.ru. "Za kokogo politika gotovy progolosovat' rossiyane i chego ozhidayut ot vyborov." Last modified February 2, 2012. https://www.levada.ru/2012/02/02/za-kakogo-politika-gotovy-progolosovat-rossiyane-i-chego-ozhidayut-ot-vyborov/.

Levada.ru. "Pochemu rossiyanam nravitsya ideya velikoy derzhavy i chto oni dumayut o stranakh Baltii?" Last modified November 14, 2019. https://www.levada.ru/2019/11/14/pochemu-rossiyanam-nravitsya-ideya-velikoj-derzhavy-i-chto-oni-dumayut-o-stranah-baltii/.

Lieven, Dominic. *Empire. The Russian Empire and Its Rivals*. New Haven/London: Yale University Press, 2002.

Makarychev, Andrei. "Imperial Discourse in Post-Imperial Russia: Where Will it Float to?" In *Empire and International Order*, edited by Noel Parker. Farnham: Ashgate, 2013.

Miller, Aleksey. *Imperiya Romanovykh i natsionalizm. Esse po metodologii istoricheskogo issledovaniya*. Moscow: Novoye literaturnoye obozreniye, 2010.

Mitzen, Jennifer. "Ontological Security in World Politics: State Identity and the Security Dilemma." *European Journal of International Relations* 12, no. 3 (2006): 341–370.

Motyl, Alexander. *Revolutions, Nations, Empires: Conceptual Limits and Theoretical Possibilities*. New York: Columbia University Press, 1999.

Münkler, Herfried. *Empires. The Logic of World Domination from Ancient Rome to the United States*. Cambridge/Malden: Polity Press, 2007.

Narozhna, Tanya. "State-society complexes in ontological security-seeking in IR", *Journal of International Relations and Development* 23 (2018): 559–583.

Niebuhr, Reinhold. *The Structure of Nations and Empires*. New York: Charles Scribner's Sons, 1959.

Pagden, Anthony. *Lords of All the World*. New Haven/London: Yale University Press, 1995.

Pain, Emil. "Imperskiy natsionalizm (Vozniknoveniye, evolyutsiya i politicheskiye perspektivy v Rossii." *Obshchestvennyye nauki i sovremennost'*, no. 2 (2015): 54–71.

Pain, Emil. "The imperial syndrome and its influence on Russian nationalism." In *The New Russian Nationalism. Imperialism, Ethnicity and Authoritarianism 2000–2015*, edited by Pål Kolstø and Helge Blakkisrud, 46–74. Edinburgh: Edinburgh University Press, 2016.

Parrot, Bruce. "Analyzing the transformation of the Soviet Union in comparative perspective." In *End of Empire? The Transformation of the USSR in Comparative Perspective*, edited by Karen Dawisha and Bruce Parrott, 3–28. Armonk, NY: M.A. Sharpe, 1997.

Petukhov, Vladimir and Raisa Barash. "Russkiye i russkiy mir: istoricheskiy kontekst i sovremennoye prochteniye." *POLIS. Politicheskiye issledovaniya*, no. 6 (2014): 83–101.

Ponarin, Eduard and Boris Sokolov. "Global'naya politika glazami rossiyskoy elity", *Rossiya v global'noy politike* 12, no. 5 (2014), https://globalaffairs.ru/number/Globalnaya-politika-glazami-rossiiskoi-elity-17106.

Putin, Vladimir. "Rossiya: natsional'nyy vopros." *Nezavisimaya Gazeta* January 23, 2012.

Putin, Vladimir. "Poslaniye Federal'nomu Sobraniyu Rossiyskoy Federatsii." Last modified April 25, 2005. http://kremlin.ru/events/president/transcripts/22931.

Romanowski, Dymitr. "Na bezdrożach rosyjskiej tożsamości. Od Trzeciego Rzymu do Trzeciej Międzynarodowówki. Mikołaj Bierdiajew i Gierogij Fiedotow." *Slavia Orientalis* LXII, no. 3 (2013): 351–368.

Rowley, David G. "Imperial versus national discourse: the case of Russia." *Nations and Nationalism* 6, no. 1 (2000): 23–42.

Rowley, David G. "'Redeemer Empire': Russian Millenarism." *American Historical Review* 104, no. 5 (1999): 1582–1602.

Steele Brent J. "Ontological security and the power of self-identity: British neutrality and the American Civil War." *Review of International Studies* 31, no. 3 (2005): 519–540.

Storchak, Vladimir. *Fenomen rossiyskogo messianizma v obshchestvenno-politicheskoy i filosofskoy mysli Rossii (vtoraya polovina XIX – pervaya tret' XX v.)*. Moscow: RAGS, 2005.

Surguladze, Vakhtang. *Grani rossiyskogo samosoznaniya. Imperiya, natsional'noye soznaniye, messianizm i vizantizm Rossii*. Moscow: W. Bafing, 2010.

Tarusin, Mikhail. *Summa ideologii. Mirovozzreniye i ideologiya sovremennoy rossiyskoy elity*. Moscow: Institut obshchestvennogo proyektivnaya, 2008.

Tolz, Vera. *Russia (Inventing the Nation)*. London: Bloomsbury Academic, 2001.

Van Herpen, Marcel H. *Putin's Propaganda Machine. Soft Power and Russian Foreign Policy*. Lanham, MD/ Boulder,CO/New York/London: Rowman & Littlefield, 2016.

Walicki, Andrzej. *Filozofia a mesjanizm. Studia z dziejów filozofii i myśli społeczno-religijnej romantyzmu polskiego*. Warszawa: PIW, 1968.

Walicki, Andrzej. *The Flow of Ideas: Russian Thought from the Enlightenment to the Religious-Philosophical Renaissance*. Frankfurt am Main: Peter Lang, 2015.

Wolfe, Judith. "Messianism." In *The Oxford Handbook of Theology and Modern European Thought* (Oxford Handbooks Online Series), edited by Nicholas Adams, George Pattison and Graham Ward. Oxford: Oxford University Press, 2013.

James Okolie-Osemene
5 New Transnational Pan-Africanism and Its Nationalist Limitations

Introduction

Adequate knowledge of the past remains critical for understanding the present era and the future in order to appreciate the evolution of events. Pan-Africanism is highly relevant to the discourse on nationalism and internationalism considering the involvement of different groups of people across nation state borders. This is because the issues generated by Pan-African initiatives offer more insight into how continental developments became globalized and entrenched attributes of the black people wherever they find themselves. Every issue concerning Pan-Africanism offers an opportunity for a reflection on the past and how to forge a new identity for Africans in this 21st century that has rather become highly contested across the world. Having a classed world in terms of culture, race, technology, and development indicates that nationalism at the continental level achievable through transnational Pan-Africanism is inevitable and must be prioritized for the expected outcome to be realized.

The transnational nature of nationalism in this context shows how Pan-Africanism is a collaborative endeavor that brings people from African ancestry together. Pan-Africanism has given birth to clichés like the African dream, African personality, neo-Africanism, black consciousness, black pride, dignity of blacks, and blacks in the diaspora. Africanization as a development now transcends the political independence of the states in Africa to the extent that the much-championed unity is dependent on the ability of people to come under one umbrella of ideas to forge an ethnic African identity.

Transnational Pan-Africanism has become a new pathway to the realization of an African dream of unity, cooperation, and development in this globalized world where identity now matters and remains significant to the actualization of many African-centered interests.[1] Pan-Africanism and the ideas that promote Africanness have given scholars a platform to study and engage in the discussion of issues or affairs concerning the continent.

Historically, the term Pan-Africanism was first used by Henry Sylvester Williams (1867–1911), who was a barrister from Trinidad, then the West Indies, and

---

[1] Ernest T. Aniche, "From Pan-Africanism to African Regionalism: A Chronicle," *African Studies* 79, no. 1 (2020): 3.

while in England, he received complaints from African chiefs and other dignitaries, and this culminated in the first Pan-African conference in 1900 held in London.² A conference that recorded the participation of over thirty delegates can be described as impactful as it charted a new course for African solidarity, with commendations from London's Lord Bishop and Queen Victoria. Pan-Africanism was categorized into four periods by historian and political scientist Vernon McKay, namely, 1900–1945 and 1945–1957, the period when Kwame Nkrumah (1909–1972) became Ghana's president (1957), and was characterized by disunity, as well as the years since 1970.³

The All-African Peoples' Conference (AAPC) is traceable to Pan-Africanist ideas, which informed the movement that metamorphosed into an intellectual gathering of all people of African descent whose effort remains sustaining the discussion and exchange of ideas at the individual, subgroup, and group levels.

A corpus of literature exists on Pan-Africanism. These works examine Pan-Africanist citizenship, political Pan-Africanism, black solidarity, Nkrumah's vision of Pan-Africanism, Pan-Africanist protagonists,⁴ Pan-African youth, Ubuntu as a Pan-African revolutionary ideology, the idea and movement of Pan-Africanism,⁵ the unfinished project of Pan-Africanism, and decolonization.⁶ Despite the potentials of using the platform of new Pan-Africanism to promote the African dream, most scholarly works have not focused on the transnational nature of the AAPC, especially as it concerns the future of nationalism, which is expected to impact the political reality in Africa.

This contribution examines the new transnational Pan-Africanism and its nationalist limitations with the aim of establishing the functionality of the All-African Peoples' Conference in reinforcing new Pan-Africanism, thereby reviving black consciousness. The study explores how the new Pan-African nationalism can address Africa's leadership question, using constructivist theory as its framework of analysis. This work is divided into seven sections, namely, introduction, Pan-African ideas: meaning and evolution, theoretical framework, the contemporary significance of Pan-African congress resolutions in Paris, nationalism-oriented

---

2 William J. Middleton, "Pan-Africanism: A Historical Analysis and Critique," *The Black Scholar: Journal of Black Studies and Research* 1, no. 3–4 (1970): 58.
3 Middleton, "Pan-Africanism" 58.
4 Vanessa Van den Boogaard, "Modern Post-Colonial Approaches to Citizenship: Kwame Nkrumah's Political thought on Pan-Africanism," *Citizenship Studies* 21, no. 1 (2017): 5–8.
5 Albert Kasanda, "Exploring Pan-Africanism's theories: From race-based solidarity to political unity and beyond," *Journal of African Cultural Studies* 28, no. 2 (2016): 179–195.
6 Kurt B. Young, "Towards a holistic review of Pan-Africanism: Linking the idea and the movement," *Nationalism and Ethnic Politics* 16, no. 2 (2010): 141–163.

aspects of the Pan-African idea, nationalist limitations of the new Pan-Africanism, and conclusion and recommendations. In terms of methodology, the study is qualitative. It combines both primary and secondary sources of data, including participant observation of the 2018 AAPC in Ghana, where the author interacted with participants and some of those who were part of the 1958 event in Accra, Ghana. It also combines a historical analytical approach with a theme mapping.

Pan-African Ideas: Meaning and Evolution

What Pan-Africanism means has gone a long way toward shaping the pattern and evolution of the idea and movement, which greatly determined the efforts of individuals and groups. Pan-Africanism encourages the running of African institutions for the interest and benefit of Africa as championed by Kwame Nkrumah, who was the first President of Ghana and an advocate of African transnationalism and integration.[7] The significance of Pan-Africanism has been demonstrated by various political parties across the continent which endeavor to have African-related names. For instance, two political parties in Togo have "Africa" in their party names: the Parti Démocratique Panafricain (PDP) and the Convergence Patriotique Panafricaine (CPP). This is an indication that Africa or Pan-Africa has become an identity for some institutions within the continent.

Nigerian historian Godfrey Uzoigwe identified "the chequered history of the Pan-African Movement as well as the epistemological problems associated with the Pan-African ideology."[8] From the activities and publications of the Pan-Africanists, Pan-Africanism has been classified into an idea and a movement, both portraying two phases of development.[9] Similarly, in terms of conceptual significance, Pan-Africanism refers to "a political and cultural phenomenon which in the early stages, regarded Africa, Africans and Persons of African stock as a unit, with the aim of generating the African solidarity among the people."[10] Such solidarity is premised on the need to demonstrate the richness of African socio-economic and political values. Africa has remained a center

---

7 Boogaard, "Modern Post-Colonial Approaches to Citizenship," 6.
8 Godfrey N. Uzoigwe, "A Matter of Identity: Africa and Its Diaspora in America Since 1900, Continuity and Change," *African and Asian Studies* 7 (2008): 260.
9 Peter Olisanwuche Esedebe, "The Emergence of Pan African Ideas," in *Themes in African Social and Political Thought*, ed. Onigu Otite (Enugu: Fourth Dimension Publishing, 1978), 75.
10 Esedebe, "The Emergence of Pan African Ideas," 75.

of attention since the pre-colonial era when the slave trade and the scramble for Africa troubled the continent. To show the strategic nature of Africa in world politics, great power politics also revolve around the continent as a majority of great powers in history had to focus their foreign policy objectives toward Africa.

Pan-Africanism is generally regarded as an intervention of African peoples over what they view as a Eurocentric conspiracy targeting blacks and aimed at sustaining the dependence of Africa on the developed world and the continuous exploitation of its people by those in the Western world.[11] So, this intervention is centered on advocacy for equity in the interest of Africa. According to Ndlovu-Gatsheni, Pan-Africanism, which recognizes the contemporary international system as a racially hierarchized, partial, imperial, colonial, and capitalist global social order, is a movement that emerged as a result of black racial consciousness and sought to challenge the domination of Africa by a Eurocentric-centered world system. The latter's existence gives little opportunity to the less privileged race to actualize their potentials through what is generally perceived as the oppression, abuse, and exploitation of black identity by white racial groups who desire continuous economic, technological, etc. dependences on the West.[12]

Bunting states that

> Pan Africanism is an ideology and an objective informed by the culture values, beliefs and customs of African peoples and their experiences that have developed over the past six centuries of the modern era. The experiences of African peoples and states have, over this epoch, been as both resisters to, and victims of, the systems, policies and practices of dehumanization and commodification of their bodies, lands and culture in capitalist relations within an imperialist framework.[13]

Pan-Africanism is traceable to the efforts of the people of Africa who crossed the Atlantic to the Americas and Europe and who later returned to the African

---

[11] Mark Malisa and Phillippa Nhengeze, "Pan-Africanism: A Quest for Liberation and the Pursuit of a United Africa," *Genealogy* 2, no. 28 (2018): 11. Also, Walter Rodney identified an unequal relationship between underdeveloped countries and the developed world as one of the sources of their exploitation for the benefit of the capitalist world. Walter Rodney, *How Europe Underdeveloped Africa* (London: Bogle-L'Ouverture Publications, 1972), 34.

[12] Sabelo J. Ndlovu-Gatsheni, "Pan-Africanism and the international system." in *Handbook of Africa's International Relations*, ed. Tim Murithi (London: Routledge, 2013), 21–22.

[13] Ikaweba Bunting, "Towards a Pan African Political Culture: Critical Pedagogy, Reparative Justice and the End of Global White Supremacy," *Contemporary Journal of African Studies* 6, no. 1 (2019): 146.

continent, where the movement has continued to evolve over time.[14] It is an old movement, like old wine in new bottles, but its novelty continues to change. Beyond the color of the skin or racial differences, Pan-Africanism has been viewed as a valuable instrument of human dignity as the world aims to promote global justice and human rights protection for all.[15] The hospitable and tolerant/accommodating norms of traditional African society therefore could be translatable to the sustenance of values that promote nationalistic feelings amongst the peoples of the continent.

Edward Wilmot Blyden (1832–1912) was seen as the originator of Pan-African ideas. Blyden was born of "pure Negro descent from the Eboe (Igbo) tribe, in August 1832 on the Danish West Indian Island of West Thomas. His grandfather came to the West Indies from Igboland."[16] As the father of Pan-Africanism, Blyden's studies made him more of an African and, more passionately, the upholder of an African soul, an African culture, an Africa of clearly demarcated and peculiar racial needs.[17] He excelled in his endeavor and succeeded in passing the baton to the younger generation of Africans who took up the task from where he stopped. Just like Blyden, W. E. B. DuBois (1868–1963) also deserves commendation for his relentless efforts in developing leadership in the struggle against imperialism which affected black people and their quest to eradicate exploitation and domination by the imperial powers in Europe, and he was able to devise new tactics against imperialism through his agitations for a common front of all African nations beyond the 1919 Pan-African Congress in Paris.[18] Various circumstances have been responsible for Africa's struggles to take control of her own destiny since the beginning of the last century, which also inspired the first Pan-African Congress that was held in London in 1900.[19] This was highly supported and motivated by Henry Sylvester Williams.[20] All these aspects point to one critical issue, i.e. that Pan-Africanism

---

14 Timothy A. Otunla, "Pan-Africanism with the African Union: Policy Options for Nigeria," in *New Horizons for Nigeria in World Affairs*, ed. Joy U. Ogwu (Lagos: The Nigerian Institute of International Affairs, 2005), 314–315.
15 Kasanda, "Exploring Pan-Africanism's theories," 179.
16 Esedebe, "The Emergence of Pan African Ideas," 81–83.
17 Harry N. K. Odamtten, *Edward W. Blyden's Intellectual Transformations: Afropublicanism, Pan-Africanism, Islam, and the Indigenous West African Church* (Michigan: Michigan State University Press, 2019).
18 Franklin Alexander, "A critique of neo-Pan-Africanism," *The Black Scholar: Journal of Black Studies and Research* 4, no. 10 (1973): 10–13.
19 Benedict Orhioghene Akpomuvie, "Pan-Africanism and the Challenges of Development in the 21st Century," *Africana* 4, no. 2 (2010): 193.
20 Abubakar Momoh, "Does Pan-Africanism Have a Future in Africa? In Search of the Ideational Basis of Afro-Pessimism," *African Journal of Political Science* 8, no. 1 (2003): 43.

remains an African project which unites people desirous of regaining the destiny of the continent with a view to transforming the feelings of dependence and a stranded situation. Despite the significance of color as a symbol of identity in Pan-Africanism, the idea is that this has remained a remarkable building block and source of group definition and mobilization, one that has the capacity to enable Africans to realize their transnational goals hinged on what is described as "anti-colonial nationalism,"[21] which is regarded as a more people-oriented and progressive nationalism.[22] In other words, such nationalism must be anti-imperial, in contrast to many post-nation-state nationalisms that are imperial, as they are directed toward the control of exterior territory.

It is only easy to form a movement and embark on advocacy projects when an idea exists. The people who championed Pan-African ideas were able to ignore whatever differences they had to pursue a common goal of liberation. Various experiences inspired the ideas that led to Pan-Africanism. Such thoughts that later manifested were further strengthened by the perennial neglect of African affairs to the detriment of Africans in other parts of the world. The foregoing made some Africans adopt the Moorish proverb "He who fears something gives it power over him"[23] when confronting their seemingly ugly past. In essence, they chose to shape their destinies for the better. Black people were generally seen as Negroes in most parts of the world. However, the back-to-Africa idea also appealed to African descendants in the West Indies where discrimination and marginalization against Africans manifested in a situation where black people were considered as slaves and people of low status, usually proven by a kind of evidence, as contained in the Antiguan Legislation of 1783.[24]

According to James Africanus Beale Horton (1835–1883), Africa produced many of the famous theologians of the early Christian Church, notably Origen, Tertullian, Augustine, Clement of Alexandria, and Cyril, a reasoned re-assessment of the continent that exposed the ignorance of racists.[25] Pan-Africanists believed in the idea that no condition was permanent, as Horton argued, to develop hope for a grand African future.[26] Through the ideas developed, Africans sought to work on their psyche to eradicate all forms of inferiority in the international community.

---

[21] Brandon Kendhammer, "DuBois the pan-Africanist and the development of African nationalism," *Ethnic and Racial Studies* 30, no. 1 (2007): 54.
[22] Ehimika Adebayo Ifidon, "Did Pan-Africanism beget Nationalism? Race and Territory in the Discourse on Pan-Africanism," *Lagos Historical Review* 8 (2008): 113–131.
[23] Lindsay McKenna, *Commando* (Don Mills, Ont.: Harlequin Enterprises, 2013), 106.
[24] Esedebe, "The Emergence of Pan African Ideas," 81.
[25] Ibid.
[26] Ibid.

Pan-Africanism offered a great opportunity to Africans to enlighten the world that their continent is good and a place of positive realities. Pan-Africanism can be described as an African initiative of mobilization for change to enhance the global understanding of the continent. The development of Pan-African ideas and the movement thereafter led to various congresses in later years.

The significance of these observations is that Pan-Africanism promotes transnational relations in Africa for the entire continent to have a platform for the discussion and management of their affairs in unity.

Theoretical Framework

Several theories have been used to explain issues arising from relationships among groups. Apart from social identity theory, which was developed by Henri Tajfel (1919–1982) in the 1970s and explains how individuals develop their self-conception(s) on the basis of their attachment to a significant group with implications for self-awareness, realistic group theory, formulated by Muzafer Sherif (1906–1988), identifies how the hostility between two groups results from real or perceived conflicting goals.[27] Here, constructivist theory is adopted as the framework for analyzing the new transnational Pan-Africanism in contrast to local nationalisms within states.

The essence of this theoretical consideration is to explore the linkages between nationalism and the new transnational Pan-Africanism, which can be described as dichotomous in Africa, considering the involvement of different groups. There are various groups across the world, and this explains why we have cultural differences within groups and sub-groups with diverse levels of intergroup relations. The characteristics of ethnicity vary with different cultural distinctiveness.[28] The social construction of the identities, interests, and behaviors of people explains the mediative position of constructivists.[29]

According to Andreas Wimmer, Thomas Fredrik Weybye Barth (1928–2016), a renowned Norwegian social anthropologist, pioneered what later became known as "constructivism," which focuses on the claim that ethnicity is the product of a

---

[27] Joaquim Pires Valentim, "Sherif's Theoretical Concepts and Intergroup Relations Studies: Notes for a Positive Interdependence," *Psychologica* 52, no. II (2010): 585–598.
[28] Andreas Wimmer, "The Making and Unmaking of Ethnic Boundaries: A Multilevel Process Theory," *American Journal of Sociology*, 113, no. 4 (2008): 97–99.
[29] Emanuel Alder, "Seizing the Middle Ground: Constructivism in World Politics," *European Journal of International Relations* 3, no. 3 (1997): 321–324.

social process rather than a cultural given, made and remade rather than taken for granted, chosen depending on circumstances rather than ascribed through birth.[30] The works of Fredrik Barth reveal the impact of different peoples with distinct cultures coming together to accommodate themselves in order to develop interest-based understandings, with the stability of ethnic characteristics impacting on inter-ethnic contact, thereby creating the opportunity for group complementarity to determine the positive bond that connects several ethnic groups in an encompassing social system.[31] In other words, inter-ethnic relations sustain interaction for the achievement of various objectives. Also, Emanuel Alder posits that constructivists "believe that 'ideas' have structural characteristics. Ideas – understood more generally as collective knowledge, institutionalized in practices – are the medium and propellant of social action; they define the limits of what is cognitively possible and impossible for individuals."[32] In the same vein, constructivism is the view that the manner in which the material world shapes and is shaped by human action and interaction depends on dynamic normative and epistemic interpretations of the material world.[33] As seen from the foregoing, it can be adduced that the circumstances surrounding the African predicaments necessitated the coming together of concerned people to discuss the issues and identify the ways forward to forge a new identity for black man. With Pan-Africanism, Africa is seen as the 'motherland' and home where people of black origin can identify, irrespective of their cultures within the African family they share, in the form of constructed unity.[34]

Constructivism emphasizes how most enduring institutions are based on collective understandings, while constructivists believe that the human capacity for reflection or learning has its greatest impact on the manner in which individuals and social actors attach meaning to the material world and cognitively frame the world they know, experience, and understand. Thus, collective understandings provide people with reasons why things are as they are and indications as to how they should use their material abilities and power.[35] The nationalist limitations of new Pan-Africanism are obviously situated in this constructivist perspective.

---

[30] Wimmer, "The Making and Unmaking of Ethnic Boundaries," 99–101.
[31] Fredrik Barth, "Introduction," in *Ethnic Groups and Boundaries: The Social Organization of Culture and Difference*, ed. Fredrik Barth (Boston: Little Brown and Company, 1969), 16–22.
[32] Alder, "Seizing the Middle Ground," 325.
[33] Wimmer, "The Making and Unmaking of Ethnic Boundaries," 100–101.
[34] Katharina Schramm, "Pan-Africanism as a Resource: The W. E. B. DuBois Memorial Centre for Pan-African Culture in Ghana," *African Identities* 2, no. 2 (2004): 157.
[35] Alder, "Seizing the Middle Ground," 322.

The Contemporary Significance of Pan-African Congress Resolutions in Paris

In 1919 the Pan-African Congress was held in Paris. Since that time, i.e. in the last 100 years, the position of Africa has remained a source of concern to all who care to think about group survival because it is not disputable that Africans have equal rights like those in other parts of the world. The following resolutions were made during the 1919 Pan African-Congress:
- That the Allied and Associated Powers establish a code of law for the international protection of the natives of Africa, similar to the proposed international code for labor;
- That the League of Nations establish a permanent Bureau charged with the special duty of overseeing the application of these laws to the political, social, and economic welfare of the natives, meaning the people of Africa are in a better position to address their needs;
- The Negroes of the world demand that hereafter the natives of Africa and the peoples of African descent be governed according to the following principles:
  (a) The land: the land and its natural resources shall be held in trust for natives and at all times they shall have effective ownership of as much as they can profitably develop;
  (b) Capital: the investment of capital and granting of concessions shall be so regulated as to prevent the exploitation of the natives and the exhaustion of the natural wealth of the country. Concessions shall always be limited in time and subject to state control. The growing social needs of the natives must be regarded and the profits taxed for the social and material benefit of the natives;
  (c) Labor, slavery, and corporal punishment shall be abolished and forced labor except in punishment of crime, and the general conditions of labor shall be prescribed and regulated by the state;
  (d) Education: it shall be the right of every native child to learn to read and write his own language, and the language of the trustee nation, at public expense and to be given technical instruction in some branch of industry;
  (e) The state: natives of Africa must have the right to participate in the government as fast as their development permits, in conformity with the principle that the government exists for the natives and not the

> natives for the government. They shall at once be allowed to participate in local and tribal government.[36]

This was aimed at promoting the Africans' rights in having an active participation in government.[37] It is believed that the best way to guarantee the interest of people is to offer them the opportunity of participatory development, which gives them a sense of belonging. It is instructive that, at the time of the Pan-African Congress in Paris, most of the black nations were still under the bout of colonialism as they had little or no influence on colonial policies. During this period, they were yet to have the autonomy to have a formidable transnational impact, considering how the demands centered on socio-economic and political rights that gave little priority to decolonization. This notwithstanding, the congress further cemented the foundations for future transnational activities that sought to forge a united Africa.

Nationalism-Oriented Aspects of the Pan-African Idea

Prior to the AAPC, we could see that Pan-African ideas began from identifying the essence of understanding and knowing that the international community has an obligation to listen to the people. The following are nationalism-oriented aspects of Pan-Africanism:

1. The origin is traceable to race consciousness that inspired advocacy programs against domination, discrimination, and anti-African policies.
2. This led to the formation and operation of social movements and sharing of some operational features of social groups.
3. Pan-Africanism offered an opportunity for the people to project the positive past history of Africa.
4. With a transnational outlook, both the movement and its ideology were anchored on popular slogans like "Africa for Africans" and "African personality" (this is based on the goal of projecting Africans as global citizens).

---

[36] Colin Legum, *Pan-Africanism: A Short Political Guide* (New York: Frederick A. Praeger, 1965), 353.
[37] Momoh, "Does Pan-Africanism Have a Future in Africa," 45.

Pan-Africanists adopted the modus operandi of persuading the international community to grant Africa her rights. For instance, the 5th Pan-African Conference was held in Manchester from 15 to 21 October 1945, and this one contributed to the liberation of African countries. They advocated for the freedom of the press in the colonies, among other things. In attendance were Jomo Kenyata (1891–1978), Kwame Nkrumah (1909–1972), Hastings Kamuzu Banda (1898–1997), the South African novelist Peter Henry Abrahams (1919–2017), Jaja Nwachukwu (1918–1996), and Obafemi Awolowo (1909–1987). At the end, they resolved that "We shall complain, appeal and arraign. We will make the world listen to the facts of our condition. We will fight in every way we can for freedom, democracy and social betterment."[38] This period marked the first time that the necessity for well-organized movements as a primary condition for the success of the national liberation struggle in Africa was discussed.[39] The true color of African unity was made manifest through the series of meetings organized in different locations in the name of Africa and for the continent. Apart from the involvement of students in universities and various African educational institutions in promoting black consciousness,[40] the clergy were not left out as the Pan-African conference of clergymen was held in Kampala in 1963.[41] This was the spiritual dimension of the struggle considering the involvement of religious leaders. It developed the perception of African unity, which was backed by the spirit of brotherhood. By implication, it became an active movement that led to decolonization.

The contributions of Pan-Africanists to the actualization of the African dream of liberation and self-determination are noteworthy, from George Padmore, who saw communism as dogmatic and dividing, to W. E. B. DuBois, who had an interest in a Pan-African type of democracy that would strengthen the Pan-African movement.[42] Marcus Garvey's approach to the emancipation of Africans also inspired Kwame Nkrumah. They all motivated themselves in one way or another.

The notable Pan-Africanists like W. E. B. DuBois, George Padmore, Marcus Garvey, Kwame Nkrumah, Jomo Kenyatta, Nnamdi Azikiwe, and Leopold Senghor shared a vision of Africa characterized by freedom and self-determination to position the people to contribute to human culture, science, and civilization

---

38 *Naij, A History of Nigeria*, directed by Jide Olanrewaju (2008). Accessed March 5, 2021. https://www.youtube.com/watch?v=KgrVHrTvxC8.
39 Nkrumah, quoted in Olanrewaju, *Naij, A History of Nigeria*.
40 Malisa and Nhengeze, "Pan-Africanism," 9.
41 Ivan Potekhin, "Pan-Africanism and the Struggle of the Two Ideologies," *South Africa History Online* (October 1964): 41.
42 Momoh, "Does Pan-Africanism Have a Future in Africa," 45.

as a transnational union of states.⁴³ In many ways, Pan-Africanism gave rise to nationalist thought and the emergence of African nationalist movements. Observations have shown that the activities of Pan-Africans also contributed to the socio-economic and political emancipation of the people. By implication, the level of enlightenment has improved to the extent that, beyond education, the people now know their rights and the need to govern themselves without unnecessary external interference.

From various developments and scholarly publications, the new transnational Pan-Africanism is synonymous with the Republic of Ghana, considering how its leaders and institutions hosted people from various parts of the world. Besides, both scholars and the leadership class have identified the transnational efforts of Ghana as a symbolic territory in mobilizing all African states after being the first on the continent to gain independence in 1957.⁴⁴ Likewise, the establishment of the W. E. B. DuBois Memorial Centre for Pan-African Culture in 1985 is proof of Ghana's commitment to the Pan-African cause⁴⁵ by honoring DuBois, who vehemently opposed the colonial occupation and exploitation during his lifetime.⁴⁶ Significantly, the Ghana Studies Association describes the country as at the center of the world both geographically, where the Greenwich Meridian meets the Equator, and also conceptually, where themes that study critical studies on Africa such as Pan-Africanism, the transatlantic slave trade, colonialism, state-building, and development are investigated. From the foregoing, it is not surprising why Ghana hosted the AAPC in 1958 and 2018.⁴⁷ African experiences since the pre-independence era have revolved around the transatlantic slave trade, colonialism, imperialism, state-building, and the need to curb underdevelopment. In fact, after the independence of Ghana, the country became known as "the model of freedom and an inspiration to other African nations."⁴⁸ With the establishment of the Institute of African Studies at the University of Ghana in 1963, Ghana became the center of studies and knowledge development on African history, culture,

---

43 Akpomuvie, "Pan-Africanism," 194.
44 Van den Boogaard, "Modern post-colonial approaches to citizenship," 5.
45 Schramm, "Pan-Africanism as a Resource," 157.
46 Kendhammer, "DuBois the Pan-Africanist," 52.
47 During the 2018 AAPC, participants discussed how the 1958 attendees resolved to use the platform created by Ghana to assist African states to gain their much-desired freedom and self-determination. As Ghana hosted the event, it was another opportunity for the 2018 participants to review achievements, obstacles, and the way forward.
48 Toyin Falola and Chukwuemeka Agbo, "The Prospects and Challenges of Pan-Africanism," *Oxford Research Encyclopedia: Politics*, published online July 29, 2019, https://doi.org/10.1093/acrefore/9780190228637.013.718.

arts, and languages.[49] Earlier, Ghana had hosted Africans living in the diaspora as an icon of Pan-Africanism in theory and practice, to the extent that Eddie Mack Ross sojourned to Ghana on a Pan-African Congress tour where he contracted malaria and died after returning to the United States. This led to his daughter, Shirikiana Aina, producing a film called *Footprints of Panafricanism*, which highlights the diaspora-Ghana connection that demonstrates Kwame Nkrumah's passion and love for blacks.[50] In the early years of independence, Ghana became a safe and peace-oriented home for all Africans desirous of freedom and a safe haven, even when most new states in Africa were crisis-ridden as a result of protracted intra-state conflicts. With Ghana, Africa already had a continent-focused platform for Pan-African nationalism and solidarity for the much-desired transformation through the revolutionary initiative of the AAPC's new Pan-Africanism.

The advent of the AAPC consequently marked a watershed in the history of Pan-Africanism because ordinary people became partners in problem-solving with the leaders of the day. Prior to the AAPC, the Conference of Independent African States was held in Accra in 1958 and hosted eight independent African states (as well as South Africa), comprising five from the Arabic North and three from Sub-Saharan Africa, with the articulation of the idea that Africans needed to project a distinct identity onto the world stage, which Nkrumah termed the "African Personality." The AAPC, which was held in Accra, witnessed the participation of leaders and groups that were still fighting to liberate their territories from European and white settler rule in Africa. It included figures such as Patrice Lumumba (1925–1961) and Holden Roberto (1923–2007). In April 1960, Accra also hosted the Positive Action Conference, which was attended by African nationalists and Pan-Africanists, as well as representatives of leftist organizations largely from the West.[51] Their efforts were focused on advancing the socialist vision in the form of scientific socialism, driven by a united front against imperialism and aimed at embracing a non-capitalist way of development[52] with the hope of actualizing the desired socio-economic justice and black empowerment.[53] As a

---

49 Ghana Studies Association, 2019.
50 Nubia Kai, "Footprints of Pan-Africanism," *Journal of African Literature Association* 12, no. 3 (2018): 362–363.
51 Harcourt Fuller, *Building the Ghanaian Nation State: Kwame Nkrumah's Symbolic Nationalism* (New York: Palgrave Macmillan, 2014), 137.
52 Potekhin, "Pan-Africanism and the Struggle of the Two Ideologies."
53 Said Adejumobi, "Popular Participation and Africa's Development Agenda: Projecting a Citizen-Based United States of Africa," *Politikon: South African Journal of Political Studies* 36, no. 3 (2009): 405.

result, both Pan-Africanism and socialism were linked together, with the latter having the capacity to facilitate "radical social changes" manifested in economic liberation, as identified by Nkrumah,[54] to produce a socialist Pan-African economy, thereby making Pan-Africanism an ideology of development.[55] These meetings, including the first AAPC and the Positive Action Conference, which laid the foundations for the 2018 AAPC, showed the significance of transnational Pan-Africanism in actualizing the objectives of black people in a highly competitive world characterized by global stratification.

Table 1: Levels of Exchanges.

Level	Category
Individual	Paper presentations
Sub-group	Panel discussions/contributions by the audience
Group	Gatherings of all congress participants where all panelists and audience members hold a discussion to draft a communiqué
Publicity	Reaching out to policymakers and the intellectual community

Table 1 shows the levels of exchange from the individual to publicity levels which facilitate the actualization of the new Pan-Africanism through the collaboration of all stakeholders. Transnationalism within this context breaks the colonial boundaries inherited by the independent states of Africa with the aim of forging a new identity through the new Pan-Africanism initiated and sustained by scholars. Such an effort has been a driver of the continental-centered loyalty of the blacks.

Nationalist Limitations of the New Pan-Africanism

Remarkably, the AAPC is a platform for Pan-Africanism because it began as a meeting of African peoples and spread through the conference held at different intervals with the aim of advancing Africans' future in a highly stratified world of white superiority that has scared black people since the pre-colonial era.

---

54 Micah S. Tsomondo, "From Pan-Africanism to Socialism: The Modernization of an African Liberation Ideology," *Issue: A Journal of Opinion* 5, no. 4 (1975): 39.
55 Opeyemi Ola, "Pan-Africanism: An Ideology of Development," *Présence Africaine* 4, no. 112 (1979): 68–77.

The 1958 conference was initiated by the only eight independent African states, namely Ethiopia, Egypt, Ghana, Liberia, Libya, Morocco, Tunisia, and Sudan, and the total liberation of Africa was at the core of their agenda. They resolved to denounce the division of African communities to the extent that brothers became alienated from their relatives and neighbors.

Although this goal was achieved, the liberation of African states through independence has not produced much of an impact in the lives of black people, especially in ending the exploitative and unequal relationship between African states and the developed world where foreign aid flows to Africa with dependency and resource implications. Meanwhile, during the early years of independence, the views of Walter Rodney characterized the relationship between Africa and the great powers. According to Rodney, the control of African societies by the capitalist powers increased the structuring of dependence on developed countries, as well as the exploitation and exportation of surplus natural resources, thereby making the imperialist forces agents of underdevelopment, without any tangible industrialization in the form of factories or a technological approach to food production like mechanized agriculture.[56] The foregoing has been worsened by the poor leadership that makes Africa a mockery of the world, considering the gap between the leaders of the first eight independent African states in 1958 and those in power today.

Although the significance of the new Pan-Africanism initiated in 2018 cannot be downplayed, the fact that the University of Ghana in East Legon played a strategic role in the convening of the AAPC when then-president Kwame Nkrumah organized the program also needs to be seen by other African countries as an acceptance of responsibility rather than as a matter of superiority. This is because Nkrumah refused to have any satisfaction until all African states were liberated in view of his perception and conviction that Africa was not an extension of other continents, and this made him establish contact with other African leaders and their peoples.[57] Also, the landmark 2018 event advanced the ideals of African culture and co-existence, as it created a platform for scholars and civil society to identify and discuss the implications of oppressive tendencies in Africa and outside Africa where blacks suffer different kinds of humiliation because of their roots. It was an opportunity for Africans to reassert their position in the world to discourage the perception of a white-dominated world where every global policy is determined by the West to the detriment of Africa. This

---

56 Rodney, *How Europe Underdeveloped Africa*, 24–34.
57 The discussions during the 2018 AAPC centered on ways of building on the foundation already established by the founding fathers of Pan-Africanism for the actualization of the set objectives.

has the potential to reposition African states in the ever-changing economic world order. The equity promotion themes discussed at the conference will certainly influence the leadership styles of leaders in Africa to run a people-centered governance system rather than excluding minorities from the policy-making and implementation processes.

Although several regimes have been accused of being oppressive and therefore been deposed through external interventions, such external involvement in African affairs must be stopped, but African leaders are expected to learn from the assassinations of Muammar Gaddafi, Thomas Sankara, Amilcar Cabral, and others to prioritize African solutions to African problems.

The 2018 event showed that political will and a combination of ideas can change Africa for good. The program also offered scholars the opportunity to display and share their experiences and publish works on African studies.

Pan-Africanism has become expedient to enable African states and their leaders to overcome the re-colonization trap occasioned by the endless dependency syndrome that is sustained by modernization views and the perceptions of self-centered leaders who think the self-sufficiency of African states is a white elephant project. Overcoming this elite threat demands concerted efforts by all and sundry to confront this limitation through the instrumentality of African solutions to African problems. Such an intervention must be done without any external support to give it the needed socio-economic attributes. One of the lessons from the new Pan-Africanism is that the majority of Africans are desirous of a change that would transform the continent. Through this new Pan-Africanism, scholars and practitioners have made their position known to the ruling class in Africa that what they focus on must not begin and end with winning the next election and initiating oppressive policies to consolidate their grip on power, but rather that the welfare of the people they govern should be prioritized.

Table 2 shows the differences and similarities between the 1958 and 2018 AAPCs. As the leaders in 1958 identified the relevance of the Pan-African conference despite the varying nationality origins, those ruling Africa today do not have excuses. While the Pan-Africanists strategized to counter colonial administrators in the past, the current movement cooperates to project the image and position of Africans to rise above neo-colonialism and recolonization agenda. With the understanding of African leaders that the rule of law and not the rule of men is more development-oriented in every political system that wishes to protect human dignity and create socio-political order, the continent's leadership crisis will become a thing of the past, bearing in mind that the home (Africa) must be stable first before external threats can be overcome by all. Pan-African nationalism can only be result-oriented when leaders use the rule of law to create a platform for

Table 2: Comparison of AAPC 1958 and AAPC 2018.

	AAPC 1958	AAPC 2018
1	Majority were politicians and people from grassroots	Most were scholars and members of civil society
2	Organized by Kwame Nkrumah and held at the Institute of African Studies, University of Ghana	Participants hosted by the Institute of African Studies, University of Ghana
3	Outcome was that leaders resolved to end the oppression and colonization of Africans	Resolved to address bad leadership, dependency, and inequality in international politics
4	Operated like a social movement	Mobilized more scholars than ordinary people
5	Leaders identified the problem of colonialism and the need for liberation	Identified leaders as part of the problem and that they must be part of the solution
6	Identified the need to end neo-colonialism	Identified intractable white superiority as a threat to Africa
7	Showcased Ghana as the center of African affairs	Showed that Ghana is the center of Pan-Africanism
8	Demanded the creation of a common front by all Africans against imperialism	Sent a message to the leadership class and the developed countries
9	Identified the parts of Africa oppressed by Europeans	Identified countries engaging in state-sponsored terror against their own people
10	Nationalistic in nature	Had a transnational outlook

citizens of states to express their patriotism for their countries by only engaging in those acts that edify and contribute to nation-building, which requires the rule of law. With good governance, it would be easier for African states to achieve the unity they desire in promoting equity. Bearing this in mind will give them the opportunity to accommodate people from all walks of life, irrespective of ethnic groups or nationality, for the actualization of Pan-African objectives.

The foregoing has a role to play in addressing the leadership question, which can only become a thing of the past when the leadership class begin to partner with the concerned Africans who have identified the instrumentality of the AAPC as a platform for the revolutionary initiative of the African solution to the current problems affecting the continent's increasing population.

Achieving this would boost the image of Africa and reduce the rate at which the majority of young people are desperate to leave the continent in droves for greener pastures in Europe, Asia, and the Americas. It has the capacity to improve mutually beneficial diplomatic relations between most African states and their counterparts in the core countries of the developed world. The success of the new Pan-Africanism will give Africans their desired voice despite their nationalist differences. Patriotic leaders who wish their people well would promote the effectiveness of the African peer review mechanism by welcoming other stakeholders in supporting them to manage internal problems and cannot allow their people to go through periods of avoidable humanitarian crisis occasioned by their self-centered policies.

One of the notable nationalist limitations has to do with the perception that achieving the unity of all African countries is almost impossible, just like the way it was earlier perceived that Kwame Nkrumah was desperately involved in the Pan-African endeavor in order to be the president in charge of Africa. This mentality of one state or individual trying to dominate others does not promote the needed unity of states despite the efforts of the advocates of Pan-Africanism. Similarly, Pan-Africanism, as it is today, has the limitation of convincing the states that have become the targets of some developed countries to understand the consequences of encouraging them to explore investment opportunities for access to emerging economies and markets in Africa. Moreover, the divisions occasioned by religious and ethnic affiliations are among other threats to Pan-Africanism[58] that continue to hinder the creation of much-desired unity in the continent, which hosts a number of different religious movements.

From the foregoing, unity remains a major requirement in addressing internal and external problems. Ending white superiority for the interests of black people not only demands that the developed world prioritize equality for all but also that Africans begin to look inward and address their problems internally through socio-economic and strategic self-sufficiency rather than searching for development partners in the developed world. This cannot come overnight or by daydreaming by the leadership class, most of whom sometimes indulge in money laundering which remains a major source of capital flight. This negates the ideals of Pan-African progress.

The new Pan-Africanist initiative is an achievement that will sustain African unity through continuous collaboration and strengthening the African Union's Peace and Security Council in initiating peacemaking and peacebuilding activities for the continent's peace culture. African leaders cannot overcome the currency and trade wars fought by the developed countries in Europe and Asia while they are still receiving aid from developed countries. Therefore, advocacy for self-

---

[58] Falola and Agbo, "The Prospects and Challenges of Pan-Africanism," 11.

reliance would boost Africa's position in the current world order, reduce indebtedness, and enable states to address the resource governance crisis.

By implication, the new transnational Pan-Africanism cannot be achieved without the active involvement of scholars and institutions in Africa because they have a role to play in sustaining this desired consciousness in the areas of research and training. A change of perceptions is needed to avoid the probability of some people in Africa perceiving the initiative that has become synonymous with Ghana as a platform of politics for personal gain or benefit for only the advocates of the new transnational Pan-Africanism.

Some of its advocates and contributors cannot be said to be members of any known African country within the context of statehood or based on indigeneship. However, they have been able to identify with the continent in view of the need to create a platform for all to address prevailing continental problems and contribute to the development of Africa.

The new transnational Pan-Africanism as a construct means that different groups in Africa have to come together for specific goals despite their origins and political differences, thereby overcoming the limitations of group-based nationalism at a state level for wider transnational cooperation aimed at fulfilling the interests of black people. It is, however, not a platform for self-determination groups who may wish to use it as an opportunity to push for actualizing their political objectives. This transnational initiative recognizes existing states within the continent rather than the threat of de facto statehood in Africa. As part of the struggle to ensure that blacks overcome nationalist limitations, state-centric nationalism is not to be given the opportunity to overshadow the larger Pan-African need for cooperation and integration that would promote socio-economic justice and equity in the interest of all groups.

The fact that the new Pan-Africanism requires the effort of African leaders is a limitation, considering the differences of perceptions and how such a collaborative endeavor would be realized. Since it has been stated by Johnson and Njoku in their work "Towards a Wholesome Africa" that the leadership question is the greatest problem besetting the African continent, transnational Pan-Africanism is an opportunity for intellectuals and the elite to speak against the sit-tight leadership problem which creates the perception of the continent that harbors a "dictators' club," thereby reflecting the presence of numerous authoritarian heads of state who failed to relinquish power in their individual countries.[59] The goal of this Pan-African initiative is to encourage change for the better for good governance as

---

[59] Paul Reynolds, "African Union Replaces Dictators' Club," *BBC News*, July 8, 2002, http://news.bbc.co.uk/2/hi/africa/2115736.stm.

part of the efforts to reposition Africa for Africans. This would have an appreciable impact on electoral processes and governance, thereby making it difficult for people to manipulate the electoral system to their own advantage, especially by delaying the release of election results, threatening political opponents perceived as stumbling blocks to their success, or rejecting results when defeated. These scenarios were recorded some years ago in the Côte d'Ivoire between Laurent Gbagbo and Alassane Ouattara (the then-leader was captured by soldiers loyal to Ouattara in April 2011), in Zimbabwe between the late Robert Mugabe and Morgan Tsvangirai, as well as in Kenya, Uganda, Equatorial Guinea, etc. With the new transnational Pan-Africanism, the liberation of Africa will be complete when internal oppression by the political elite in various states becomes a thing of the past.

Refocusing the political reality of Africa therefore demands consistent bridging of the institutional gaps in the areas of publication, intellectual exchanges, and elite scholars' collaborations for the development of Africa.

Beyond nationalist limitations, in the context of constructivist theory, transnational Pan-Africanism has several lessons for those engaged in contemporary Pan-Africanism to learn from the founding fathers of Africa who ignored their differences to champion the unity of African peoples. A notable characteristic of the new transnational Pan-Africanism is in its internal motivation rather than previous intervention efforts that were sometimes externally motivated by those in the diaspora. The new transnational Pan-Africanism should serve as leverage in African politics for the desired integration to be sustained by influencing the pattern of leadership, thereby making it more people-centered/participatory.

The coming together of scholars, practitioners, and leaders on the continent in the name of transnational Pan-Africanism will leverage the pattern of leadership among states. As far as the political reality of Africa is concerned, the new transnational Pan-Africanism is instrumental to the much-desired political transformation on the continent where leadership has become part of the continent's many challenges. This is so because getting it right as a people must begin with good governance. The manner in which some African leaders prioritize tenure elongation to the detriment of the populace is something that demands the attention of Pan-Africanists. Tenure elongation has become a continental problem that undermines good governance, which has led to conflicts in various parts of Africa.

Such actions of leaders, if left unchecked, would make it difficult for African states to be united in addressing their internal security challenges, most of which are traceable to the politics of exclusion, greed/grievance, lopsided clamor for presidencies, and resource curse problems. Most African countries are bedeviled by agitations by political leaders to extend their tenure in office by amending the constitution to achieve their goals. What the average present-day African leader wants is the power to establish himself as a dynasty and imperial leader. This is inimical to good governance and transparent democracy. According to John Forje, the origins of indigenous African governments are traced back to Sudan (1956), Ghana (1957), Nigeria (1960), and many other countries that gained their independence in the 1960s.[60] The continent is still far from being liberated from the leadership crises plaguing it, and the only way out is for the people to be united using the platform of transnational Pan-Africanism to leverage the governance processes, thereby making it complex for the ruling powers to become oppressive in office.

The leadership problem in Africa can no longer be allowed to continue without intervention by the people. Unless Africans form a political and economic union to tackle the intractable problems, the revolutions in the north of the continent, religious and ethnic strife, and civil wars in other parts of Africa are inevitable. Kwame Nkrumah already gave this warning in the past, but unfortunately, most leaders do not seem bothered about the consequences of their actions. Instead of political division, unity is the only way Africans can address their problems through effective leadership and all-inclusive and transparent governance.

Conclusion and Recommendations

This contribution has examined the new transnational Pan-Africanism and its nationalist limitations, which are not far from the political reality in Africa. It emphasized how the new transnational Pan-Africanism has sustained the efforts of the people of African descent through the platform of AAPC, which was first held in 1958 and later followed up in 2018. Takeaway lessons from those meetings are numerous. It is apparent that the destinies of African states remain in their hands and that realizing the dreams of the continent must attract African solutions to various challenges. The All-African Peoples' Conference is a contemporary initiative that remains instrumental to the renaissance of African solidarity and the sustainability of African consciousness. The initiative is not only people-oriented but collaborative in nature, requiring more understanding, information, conviction, determination, and cooperation from blacks within and outside Africa.

Despite the nationalist limitations, the new transnational Pan-Africanism has not only revived the Pan-African dream but has also brought awareness of

---

60 John W. Forje, "Self Determination, Nationalism, Development and Pan-Africanism Stuck on the Runway: Are Intellectuals to be Blamed?" *African Journal of International Affairs* 6, no. 1–2 (2003): 66.

it closer to many blacks who may not have understood the origins and essence of such an endeavor, specifically through the platform of the AAPC.

The new Pan-Africanism established by the AAPCs of 1958 and 2018 have shown the readiness of blacks in the diaspora and their counterparts within the continent of Africa to continue from where the pioneers of the initiatives stopped. In keeping the morale as lively as desired, the movement and the ideology of Pan-Africanism emphasize the fact that only Africans, rather than Europeans, Asians, or Americans, are in a position to salvage the people of the continent politically, economically, and socially. It points to the truism that only the people can transform the situation on the continent. If Pan-Africanists in the past could make such remarkable achievements without much technological advancement at that time, contemporary Africans should be held accountable if they fail to galvanize themselves for African unity and development, especially in this 21st-century era of globalization and technological revolution. It is instructive that with social media, Africans can revive Pan-Africanism and create more platforms that would promote intergroup relations for the benefit of the people.

Also, Pan-Africanism is one of the features of intergroup relations in Africa that portrays how Africans and those in the diaspora can discuss and plan for the future of the continent and redeem the battered image of the black race.

The difference between the 1958 and 2018 Pan-African conferences is that the former involved more political thinkers, members of civil society, and those from the grassroots with a focus on issues of decolonization and emancipation, while the latter focused on the need for self-reliance to salvage Africa from the neo-colonial crisis. Given that solidarity is the making of every socio-political movement, like the old Pan-African movement, the new Pan-Africanism remains a remarkable source of social, political, and economic transformations of the African continent. It served as a foundation of post-colonial Africa, creating a platform for peaceful collaboration and unity to achieve a common goal. Pan-Africanism emphasizes the unity of purpose amongst the people of 21st-century Africa, who have realized the urgency and advantages of taking their destinies into their own hands.

The strategic nature of the Pan-African endeavor shows that the post-colonial integration of African peoples is still achievable only if they cooperate beyond what their leaders have been doing through the platform of the African Union. Contemporary Pan-Africanism is a post-colonial endeavor that shifts from decolonization and emancipation to the self-rediscovery of African leaders and the re-evaluation of African culture to the rethinking of the conflict-oriented leadership styles of leaders whose high priority for the self encourages the politics of exclusion.

The study has also shown that the new Pan-Africanism has brought an African renaissance in the form of the reawakening of black consciousness from

Europe and the Americas to Africa, where much-desired transformation has been urgently needed since the neo-colonial era that created a platform for the recolonization of the continent.

This contribution suggests that until African leaders unite, adopt transnational Pan-Africanism, and look inward, it would be difficult to overcome various political, economic, and technological challenges that are linked to neo-colonialism. Options for the eradication of these problems are situated within the framework of new Pan-African nationalism in addressing the leadership question in Africa. Scholars have a role to play in sustaining this desired consciousness in the areas of research and training. The political class and Pan-African scholars have a lot to benefit from the scientific work related to the Kwame Nkrumah Chair in African Studies at the University of Ghana, and this will serve as a knowledge base for countering neo-colonialism as far as overcoming the nationalist limitations of the new transnational Pan-Africanism are concerned.

Works Cited

Adejumobi, Said. "Popular Participation and Africa's Development Agenda: Projecting a Citizen-Based United States of Africa." *Politikon: South African Journal of Political Studies* 36, no. 3 (2009): 403–422.

Akpomuvie, Orhioghene Benedict. "Pan-Africanism and the Challenges of Development in the 21st Century." *Africana* 4, no. 2 (2010): 191–212.

Alder, Emanuel. "Seizing the Middle Ground: Constructivism in World Politics." *European Journal of International Relations* 3, no. 3 (1997): 319–363.

Alexander, Franklin. "A critique of neo-Pan-Africanism." *The Black Scholar: Journal of Black Studies and Research* 4, no. 10 (1973): 9–15.

Aniche, Ernest T. "From Pan-Africanism to African Regionalism: A Chronicle." *African Studies* 79, no. 1 (2020): 70–87.

Asante, Samuel Kwadwo B. *Regionalism and Africa's Development: Expectations, Development, and Challenges*. London: Macmillan, 1997.

Aterianus-Owanga, Alice. "A Pan-African Space in Cape Town? The Chimurenga Archive of Pan-African Festivals." *Journal of African Cultural Studies* (2019): 1–19.

Barth, Fredrik. "Introduction." In *Ethnic Groups and Boundaries: The Social Organization of Culture and Difference*, edited by Fredrik Barth. Boston: Little Brown and Company, 1969.

Boogaard, Vanessa Van den. "Modern post-colonial approaches to citizenship: Kwame Nkrumah's political thought on Pan-Africanism." *Citizenship Studies* 21, no. 1 (2017): 44–67.

Bunting, Ikaweba. "Towards a Pan African Political Culture: Critical Pedagogy, Reparative Justice and the End of Global White Supremacy." *Contemporary Journal of African Studies* 6, no. 1 (2019): 138–157.

Chouin, Gerard and Olanrewaju O. Lasisi. "Crisis and transformation in the Bight of Benin at the Dawn of the Atlantic *Trade*." In *Power, Political Economy and Historical Landscapes of* the Modern World: Interdisciplinary Perspectives, edited by Christopher R. DeCorse, 285–306. Albany, NY: State University of New York Press, 2019.

Davidson, Basil. *The Back Man's Burden: Africa and the Course of the Nation-State*. Ibadan: Spectrum Books Ltd, 1992.

Esedebe, Olisanwuche Peter. "The Emergence of Pan African Ideas." In *Themes in African Social and Political Thought*, edited by Onigu Otite. Enugu: Fourth Dimension Publishing, 1978.

Falola, Toyin and Chukwuemeka Agbo. "The Prospects and Challenges of Pan-Africanism." *Oxford Research Encyclopedia: Politics* (2019): 1–21.

Forje, John W. "Self Determination, Nationalism, Development and Pan-Africanism Stuck on the Runway: Are Intellectuals to be Blamed?" *African Journal of International Affairs* 6, no. 1–2 (2003): 54–86.

Fuller, Harcourt. *Building the Ghanaian Nation State: Kwame Nkrumah's Symbolic Nationalism*. USA: Palgrave Macmillan, 2014.

Ifidon, Ehimika Adebayo. "Did Pan-Africanism beget Nationalism? Race and Territory in the Discourse on Pan-Africanism." *Lagos Historical Review* 8 (2008): 113–131.

Kai, Nubia. "Footprints of Pan-Africanism." *Journal of African Literature Association* 12, no. 3 (2018): 361–363.

Kasanda, Albert. "Exploring Pan-Africanism's Theories: From Race-based Solidarity to Political unity and beyond." *Journal of African Cultural Studies* 28, no. 2 (2016): 179–195.

Kendhammer, Brandon. "DuBois the Pan-Africanist and the Development of African Nationalism." *Ethnic and Racial Studies* 30, no. 1 (2007): 51–71.

Legum, Colin. *Pan-Africanism: A Short Political Guide*. New York: Frederick A. Praeger, 1965.

Malisa, Mark and Phillippa Nhengeze. "Pan-Africanism: A Quest for Liberation and the Pursuit of a United Africa." *Genealogy* 2, no. 28 (2018): 1–15.

McKenna, Lindsay. *Commando*. Don Mills, Ont.: Harlequin Enterprises, 2013.

Middleton, William J. "Pan-Africanism: A historical analysis and critique." *The Black Scholar: Journal of Black Studies and Research* 1, no. 3–4 (1970): 58–64.

Momoh, Abubakar. "Does Pan-Africanism Have a Future in Africa? In Search of the Ideational Basis of Afro-Pessimism." *African Journal of Political Science* 8, no. 1 (2003): 31–57.

Mutiso, Gideon Y. M. and S. W. Rohio, eds. *Readings in African Political Thought*. London: Heinemann Educational Books, 1974.

Ndlovu-Gatsheni, Sabelo J. "Pan-Africanism and the international system." In *Handbook of Africa's International Relations*, edited by Tim Murithi, 21–29. London: Routledge, 2013.

Odamtten, Harry N. K. *Edward W. Blyden's Intellectual Transformations: Afropublicanism, Pan-Africanism, Islam, and the Indigenous West African Church*. Michigan: Michigan State University Press, 2019.

Ola, Opeyemi. "Pan-Africanism: An Ideology of Development." *Présence Africaine* 4, no. 112 (1979): 66–95.

Olanrewaju, Jide. n.d. "The Story of Nigeria. Naij, A History of Nigeria."

Otunla, Timothy A. "Pan-Africanism with the African Union: Policy Options for Nigeria." In *New Horizons for Nigeria in World Affairs*, edited by Joy U. Ogwu, 313–334. Lagos: The Nigerian Institute of International Affairs, 2005.

Potekhin, Ivan. "Pan-Africanism and the Struggle of the Two Ideologies." *South Africa History Online* (October 1964): 36–48.

Reynolds, Paul. "African Union Replaces Dictators' Club." *BBC News*, July 8, 2002. http://news.bbc.co.uk/2/hi/africa/2115736.stm.

Rodney, Walter. *How Europe Underdeveloped Africa*. London: Bogle-L'Ouverture Publications, 1972.
Schramm, Katharina. "Pan-Africanism as a Resource: The W. E. B. DuBois Memorial Centre for Pan-African Culture in Ghana." *African Identities* 2, no. 2 (2004): 151–171.
Smith, Anthony D. S. *Nationalism in the Twentieth Century*. Oxford: Martin Robertson, 1979.
Tsomondo, Micah S. "From Pan-Africanism to Socialism: The Modernization of an African Liberation Ideology." *Issue: A Journal of Opinion* 5, no. 4 (1975): 39–46.
Uzoigwe, Godfrey N. "A Matter of Identity: Africa and Its Diaspora in America Since 1900, Continuity and Change." *African and Asian Studies* 7 (2008): 259–288.
Valentim, Joaquim Pires. "Sherif's Theoretical Concepts and Intergroup Relations Studies: Notes for a Positive Interdependence." *Psychologica* 52, no. II (2010): 585–598.
Wimmer, Andreas. "The Making and Unmaking of Ethnic Boundaries: A Multilevel Process Theory." *American Journal of Sociology* 113, no. 4 (2008): 970–1022.
Yimenu, Shibabaw. "Pan-Africanism and African Economic Development." *The Black Scholar: Journal of Black Studies and Research* 6, no. 8 (1975): 32–40.
Young, Kurt B. "Towards a Holistic Review of Pan-Africanism: Linking the Idea and the Movement." *Nationalism and Ethnic Politics* 16, no. 2 (2010): 141–163.

Section II: **The Fight For and the Creation of Identity: A Cultural Struggle Against the "Other"**

Inessa Kouteinikova

6 Russia's Central Asia: Photographic Symbology of Nationhood

Histories

With the popularization of photography, the medium's role in cultural and natural history followed new directions that reflected the ways in which imperial colonial science was being transformed. Ranging from landscape to portraiture, photography became a focus for various intellectual and cross-cultural encounters and thus not only presented an extraordinary new visual technology but also introduced a new means of discourse between individuals, institutions, and audiences in different parts of the Russian Empire and across the globe. Photography took place under the Western influences in Russia, but swiftly found its own form. Russian peculiarities concerning the principles of empiricism, observation, and analysis, the whole Russian way of thinking about modernization, be it in medicine, mechanics, or education, were not always guided by ideas of efficiency and progress, nor were they always optimistic. Photography set the scene for engagement – at least two-dimensionally – between the different ethnographic groups, disregarding conventional faith-based partitions. This process was carefully calibrated. By alternating between imperial and colonial structures, this research examines the intricacies of these relationships and offers a new perspective on photography's indispensable but complex role in Russian imperial history and the 19th-century colonial exhibitions in which photography was a significant component.

The comparative analysis that frames this study highlights the way nationalism in the Russian colonial era used the merging medium of photography – alongside, but gradually also in place of, other forms of visual culture – to enhance imperial and global networks, support their investigations, advance their careers, and promote exhibitions and their history in novel ways for a new generation of consumers.

Perceiving nationalism through photography asks these various visual arguments about a shared classical "national" past that came to be challenged by or revised in modernist thought. It considers how photography has governed the field of Central Asian media and the media of exhibitions, shaping how these objects and images were collected, displayed, and circulated.

Since Edward Said's (1935–2003) seminal book *Orientalism*,[1] scholars have incorporated the transnational tool in colonial studies, but not to the extent it deserves. At a time when scholars across the humanities are embracing a "global turn," it is important to reassess colonial studies and consider new approaches that allow us to move beyond Euro- and Russo-centrism and simple explanations of "shared" tastes.

The Russian intrusion in Central Asia – unlike the British in India – was an armed invasion by Russia; the British had been in India as inconsequential traders since the beginning of the 17th century.[2] Central Asia remained a relatively unknown area of land and largely unfamiliar politics for the Russians until Emperor Alexander II (1818–1881) ordered it to be explored by force.[3] Within the Turkestan domain (ILL), the more important areas still remained outside Russian control by

---

[1] Edward W. Said, *Orientalism* (New York: Pantheon Books, 1978).
[2] Only in the middle of the 18th century, when conditions in Bengal, the center of the East India Company's trading activities, began to change, was political intervention possible.
[3] The shifting meaning of "law and order" in 19th-century Russian imperial policies can be seen in the history of the Russian colonial conquest of Central Asia through myriad small measures that brought "modern principles" into the Muslim world. Embracing the ideas of the 19th-century Enlightenment all together, themes of Muslim resistance and involvement with Imperial Russian rule have long defined the historiography of Russia and Central Asia. Among the authors whose writings raise many questions about the rich and complex history of the late 19th century Russian colonial relationship – rooted in the classic mistrust of empire – are thinkers as diverse as George Curzon (*Russia in Central Asia in 1889 and the Anglo-Russian Question*, 1889), Petr I. Pashino (*Turkestansky Krai v 1866 godu*, 1860), Eugene Schuyler (*Turkestan: notes of a Journey in Russian Turkestan*, 1877), and Mikhail A. Terentiev (*Istoriia zavoevaniia Srednei Azii*, 1906), none of whom was a xenophobic nationalist. More recent works locate the origins of this anti-imperial tradition in the aftermath of the Great Game and argue for its continued relevance to public life today. See Nathaniel Knight, "Grigor'ev in Orenburg, 1851–1862: Russian Orientalism in the Service of Empire?" *Slavic Review* 59, no. 1 (1998): 74–100; Mark Bassin, "Russia between Europe and Asia: The Ideological Construction of Geographical Space," *Slavic Review* 50, no. 1 (2003): 1–17; Robert P. Geraci, *Window on the East: National and Imperial Identities in Late Tsarist Russia* (Ithaca, NY: Cornell University Press, 2001); Aleksey Miller, *Imperiya Romanovykh i Nazionalism. Esse po metodologii Istoricheskogo Issledovaniya* [The Romanov's Empire and Nationalism. Essay on Historical Research Methodology] (Moscow: NLO, 2010); Jeff Sahadeo, *Russian Colonial Society in Tashkent (1865–1923)* (Bloomington, IN: Indiana University Press, 2007); David Mackenzie, "Expansion in Central Asia: St. Petersburg vs. the Turkestan Generals (1863–1866)," *Canadian-American Slavic Studies* 3, no. 2 (1969): 286–311; Robert D. Crews, *The Prophet and the Tsar: Islam and Empire in Russia and Central Asia* (Cambridge, MA: Harvard University Press, 2009); D. Yu. Arapov, "'Neobkhodimo . . . zanyat'sya obrazovaniem kraya' (Sattar-khan Abdulgafarov o zadachakh russkoi politiki v Srednei Azii" ['It is necessary . . . to improve education in the region' (Sattar-khan Abdulgafarov about the tasks of Russia's policy in Central Asia], *Vestnik Evrazii* [Bulletin of Eurasia] 1: 169–184.

the late 1860s. This was the domain of Zaravshansk and Semirechie, the Khiva, the great plain between the steppes and the deserts, watered by the Aral Sea and its tributaries. The conquest of Khiva in 1873 marked an important stage for Russian rule in Turkestan. Khiva, Bukhara, and Samarkand, the great centers of Asiatic power, retained their political and commercial dominance throughout the 19th century, but a swing in interest and concern took place after 1865. It is not accidental that most of the photographs of Turkestan discussed here are from these parts. The Silk Road's physical landscape, theological impact, and cultural traits were, to a very remarkable degree, synonymous in the Western and Russian imagination with Central Asia. This focus changed after 1865 when Colonel Mikhail Cherniyaev (1828–1898) took Tashkent, and it replaced the Samarkand-Bukhara-Khiva triangle as the primary source of Russian power over Turkestan. The 19th-century colonies were not closed entities but were reliant on the movement of people and geography, their power being dependent on their relationships with other colonies and states. In 19th-century Russia, increased exploration fuelled fierce competition over the control of trade routes and territories and inevitably led to diplomatic entanglements that spanned from the Crimea to Central Asia and Siberia. These entanglements brought about hostile relationships, confusion, and admiration, giving rise to cross-cultural transfer, exchange, and friction as objects, practices, and people moved via trade and diplomacy. This contribution examines colonial encounters during the Russian rule in Central Asia to consider the following questions:

- How were colonial spaces adapted and transformed into national ones through the movement of material things such as photographs?
- Which particular aspects of nationalism and its political, social, and economic infrastructures enabled the exchange of photographic practices?
- To what extent do new nationalist methodologies and approaches need to be developed to consider Russian Central Asia within a global geopolitical network?
- How did such a vast and backward landmass as Central Asia, where the Russians were themselves no more than a large minority, manage to survive for so long under Russian rule? In other words, does national politics present a cogent and persuasive explanation for the Russian Empire's relative stability in its Muslim territories during the 19th century?

The focus of this contribution is fundamentally interdisciplinary: art historical, historiographic, architectural, literary, and religious spaces are the subjects of inquiry, not as discrete or separate entities, but as ones which overlapped, came into contact with one another, and at times into conflict with one another too.

Early Photographic Training, the Distribution of Photographic Prints and the National Media

Considering the drastic changes in the technologies and practices of communication that characterized the 19th century – such as the introduction of electric telegraphy and the development of the railway and the postal system – in relation to and in conjunction with the contemporary emergence of photography, artists and photographers might have had less interest in theoretical explorations and more in practical developments in photography, a business that could serve them well during their travels. Many if not all technical officers of government services in Russian Turkestan were aware of its historical situation. From the beginning of their travels into Russia's Muslim territories,[4] imperial authorities not only made significant efforts to integrate them into the existing routine but often actively employed their curiosity. During the late 19th century, for about sixty years, Central Asian photography was mainly in European and Russian hands. Slowly, members of other ethnic groups and locals moved into the fields, first as translators to the Russians, then as assistants, and a few made it as professional photographers to make money from the business and enjoy the fruits of the industry.

By the 1870s, the St. Petersburg photographic market had developed trans-European relationships, and the photographic catalogs' entries expanded to reflect the training, provenance, and awards garnered by foreign photographers and patent holders, recent photographic processes, and the extended dealers' network. Russian photographic schools lacked the complex system of training of European establishments. Collectors bought primarily through dealers acting as intermediaries who facilitated cultural transfers. Stephen Greenblatt termed these intermediaries "mobilizers."[5] Their photographic perspectives arose from a

---

[4] The khanates of Bukhara, Kokand, and Khiva formed the territory of Central Asia at the time of the Russian conquest that started with conquering Tashkent (1865) and the formation of the Russian Turkestan Government-General (1867) that was officially renamed as the region of Turkestan in 1886. Its borders touched the Ust-Yurt plateau in the west, Jungar Ala-Tau, Pamir, and Tian-Shan in the east, the Khorasan Mountains in the south, and Targobatau and the Aral-Irtysh waterline in the north. These borders are drawn according to V.I. Mushketov's report (1886), confirmed in Vladimir I. Masal'sky, *Polnoe geograficheskoe opisanie nashego otechestva: Nastol'naya i dorozhnaya kniga dlia russkikh liudei* [A Complete Geographical Description of Our Fatherland. Table and Road Book for the Russian People], vol. XIX, *Turkestanskii Krai* (St. Petersburg: A.F. Devriena, 1913), 125.

[5] Stephen Greenblatt, *Cultural Mobility: A Manifesto* (Cambridge: Cambridge University Press, 2010), 251.

vision produced by an archipelago of new schools and national institutions in Tsarist Russia. This cultural and ideological infrastructure reproduced and disseminated new forms of knowledge, new regimes of "seeing," documenting, organizing, measuring, and categorizing the physical and metaphysical world. On the opposite side of the spectrum, the Department of Military Typography, Geodesy, and Cartography at the General Staff in St. Petersburg (founded 1825) immediately grasped the possibilities of the new medium, such as its scientific exactitude, reproducibility, and low cost. As functionaries of the Russian state and products of a new mode of military education – reinforcing the importance of statistics, modern sociology, technological and technical innovations, and political theory –, the officers from the Imperial Technical School succumbed to this very special order and embraced the regime. Russian colonial photography cannot be separated from this perspective. In those years, photographs, in order to be reproduced in maps, books, newspapers, and magazines, still had to be manually prepared. After only a few decades, the advances made in typographical techniques were such as to allow the photomechanical reproduction of the images on the same page as text. The continuous progress made in photographic procedures inside and outside technical institutions contributed to rendering this medium increasingly popular: this permitted obtaining images in a much quicker way and at much lower prices and costs than through other media.

Central Asia obviously immediately attracted a large number of photographers, often from the high military echelon, but not all of them were able to get there easily. Travel remained notoriously difficult, and the construction of the Trans-Caspian Railway, or the Russian Empire's "war railroad"[6] (1880–1888), eased it only partially. The road connected the Caspian Sea to Samarkand but stopped short of the vast steppe up to Tashkent. Only in the 1890s, when the Anglo-Russian diplomatic relationship had rapidly deteriorated and the Andijan uprising took place in May 1898, did the urgent requests of the Minister of War, Aleksey Kuropatkin (1848–1925), reach the court in April 1899. An agreement was drawn up to continue the construction of this strategic railroad.[7] Unlike Europe, whose colonial appetite was rewarded by tourists flowing into the

---

[6] Winfried Baumgart, "Eisenbahn und Kriegsführung in der Geschichte," *Technikgeschichte* 38 (1971): 191–219.

[7] Igor V. Lukoyanov, ed., *Sooruzhenie Zheleznykh dorog v Srednei Azii i Persii* [Construction of the Railroads in Central Asia and Persia] from Sergei Yu. Witte, *Sobranie Sochinenii i dokumentalnykh Materialov* [Collective Works and Documents], vol. I, book 2, part I (Moscow: Nauka, 2004), 413–417.

new countries in Africa and India, Central Asia has never become a tourist destination because of 1) the tremendous difficulties with traveling there; 2) matters of safety (riots and revolts made it unsafe for an adventurous traveler to move through the steppes and desserts), and 3) its languages, which posed natural boundaries, so one had to be equipped with a translator or know local tongues.[8] Expeditions commissioned by national institutions – the Imperial Orthodox Palestine Society, the Imperial Russian Archeological Society, the Russian Geographical Society, the Society of the Amateurs of Anthropology, Ethnology, and Ethnography, and the first museums of national importance – did not always depend on the middlemen – missionaries, traders, and explorers – who had previously made the choices about whom to convert or what to collect, donate, or sell. Photographers observed and documented ethnographic groups, which were merged with expeditions' comprehensive reports on their fieldwork, and carefully documented the data collected and the connections made in the field. Both historical and more recent scholarship has examined the details of the fieldwork and national strategies of these scientific expeditions,

---

[8] The shifting meaning of European supremacy in the Muslim world can be seen in the history of the long 19th century. In arguing their case, European Orientalists take their readers on a fascinating journey over the summits and through the valleys along the Islamic road to the modern world. One of the summits is the study of language, a vitally important subject, often considered in discussions of the modernization imposed on the "Russian" Muslims by reforming the education system. Persuaded or not of the necessity of studying the Russian language – despite formidable religious opposition that was partly the result of the widespread Muslim belief that "who imitates another people becomes one of them" (as a proverb that reflects anxieties about loss of identity) – the Russians were hired by the Mullahs to improve the conversation skills of their subjects, knowing it was a dangerous undertaking. Dangers such as these seemed destructive due to the impact of the real transformations in social attitudes, such as the shift from acceptable to unacceptable, progressive to non-progressive. These ideas and actions were transferable, and they have also entered the Islamic one. They were at work during the Soviet era – even if they were sometimes rebuffed –, as the recent publication edited by Artemy Kalinovsky and Michael Kemper, *Reassessing Orientalism*, demonstrates: "Just as European romantic nationalisms also fed from the knowledge provided by local informants – for instance in the Baltics, where ethnic German folklorists relied on the data provided by Estonian collaborators – so also Soviet and Western Orientlogies incorporated 'Orientals,' first as providers of raw information but increasingly as colleagues; and just as the German folklorists paved the way for Baltic nationalisms, so also Muslim Orientalists from Central Asia used the system of Soviet Oriental studies to develop their own national agendas." Artemy Kalinovsky and Michael Kemper, "Introduction: interlocking Orientologies in the Cold War era," in *Reassessing Orientalism: Interlocking Orientologies during the Cold War*, ed. Artemy Kalinovsky and Michael Kemper (London: Routledge, 2017), 12.

conducted between 1860 and 1914, revealing the complexity of their work.[9] Like the earlier expeditions, they sometimes overlapped with political, imperial, and commercial interests, but Russian colonial photography had always had an ideological edge.[10]

Karl Leberecht Immermann's (1796–1840) ironic comment on "staying home is the exception, now everyone travels at least five hundred miles a year, they travelled for travel's sake, to get away from the daily grind"[11] fell on deaf ears. Turkestan was as distant and foreign to the Russians as it was dangerous. White supremacy movements – which are, ultimately, European supremacy movements – have surged in Russian Turkestan. Yet, Central Asian photography debunks any notion of white supremacy or the inherent grandness of the European genome, or the Russian genome for that matter. Central Asia has always been at the crossroads of the world, a place where immigrant species from the Middle East, Africa, Asia, and Europe have converged, mingled, and hybridized, blending genome with genome to yield a bounty of new species that then colonized new lands. There was no notion of that dangerous concept of racial or genetic purity in Central Asia. This is particularly revealing in photography. Take the *Turkestansky Al'bom* (*Turkestan Album,* 1871–72), for example, the most formidable photographic production to commemorate the mighty Russian presence in Central Asia and produced for the opening of the great Polytechnic Exhibition in Moscow (1872), which featured a Turkestan section. The ethnographic section of the *Turkestan Album* demonstrates the range of people from the regions of Samarkand, Ura-Tyube, Khodzhent, and Tashkent and serves as a storytelling device, in slow motion, allowing Nikolai

---

9 Nikolai P. Ostroumov, *Kolebaniya russkogo pravitelstva vo vzgliadakh na missionerskuy deyatelnost- Pravoslavnoj Ruskoi Cerkvi* [Doubts of the Russian government over the missionary activities of the Russian Orthodox Church] (Kazan: Sotrudnik bratstva Sv. Guriya, 1910), 42; Nikolai P. Ostroumov, "Khrakteristika religiozno-pravoslavnoi zhizni musulman preimuschestvenno Srednei Azii," *Pravoslavnoe Obozrenie* 2 (June-July 1880); Nikolai P. Ostroumov, *K Istorii narodnogo obrazovaniya v Turkestanskom Krae, Lichnye vospominaniya* (Tashkent, 1911); Nikolai P. Ostroumov, *Konstantin von Kaufman, Lichnye Vospominaniya* (1899). Three other accounts – a mix of archival material and anxious revision – may suffice: Paul W. Werth, *At the Margins of Orthodoxy: Mission, Governance, and Confessional Politics* (Ithaca, NY: Cornell University Press, 2002); Geraci, *Window on the East*; Robert P. Geraci and Michael Khodarkovsky, *Of Religion and Empire: Missions, Conversion, and Tolerance in Tsarist Russia* (Ithaca, NY: Cornell University Press, 2001).
10 Inessa Kouteinikova, "Tashkent in St. Petersburg: The Constructed Image of Central Asia in Russia's Nineteenth-Century Ethnographic Exhibitions," in *A l'orientale: Collecting, Displaying and Approving Islamic Art and Architecture in the 19th and Early 20th Centuries* (Leiden/Boston: Brill, 2019), 159.
11 Karl Leberecht Immermann, "The Wonders in the Spessart," in *Tales from the German, Comprising Specimens from the Most Celebrated Authors*, trans. John Oxenford and C. A. Reiling (London: Chapman and Hall, 1844).

Nekhoroshev, the principal photographer for the *Album* whose photographic studio was based in Tashkent, to convey a tremendous amount of ethnographic information while maintaining a plot and point of view. Scenes are vividly, sensorily drawn. We come across over fifty nationalities and ethnic groups and are startled to realize how teeming and diverse Central Asia's "human fauna" used to be. These people are not caught busily going about their routine daily activities; they are carefully staged, posed, and presented as porcelain figures, arranged according to their function and degree of attractiveness. They were a different clientele, representing the new exotic Russia by offering themselves as ethnographic material. The photographs here are anything but neutral documents intended as memoranda.

The *Turkestan Album* probably remains the most fully chronological and veritable description of the colony. Thanks to Nekhoroshev's extraordinary eye, we own portraits of the locals and countless images of the ruins, festivities, and traditional rituals, coproduced by the profession of what can be considered as being the first insightful look into the lives of the colonized. From the 1870s, however, various amateur photographers such as the young explorer and naturalist Aleksey Fedchenko (1844–1873) produced photographs of the principal natural forms of the region. After one examination of his photographic valise, it is impossible to say that the ambiguities of Fedchenko's short life were never apparent in his photographic works and scientific descriptions. His images are examples of faithful documentation, often with clarity and an eager eye. Clearly, he was not trained as a photographer, for the point of view often appears dull, especially when it comes to depicting one unexpected delicate shape after another. They are both stark and lush, bewitching and expressionistic balances of leaves and flowers. His wife, Olga, assorted her own botanical drawings into albums, connecting her scientific work to the decorative art of her own time. Such gentle criticism could be extended to include many images made by Russian and European photographers – the Dane Ole Olufsen (1865–1929), the Swedish explorer Sven Hedin (1865–1952), the Finnish officer at the service of the Russian Empire, or Carl Gustaf Mannerheim (1867–1951), who learned photography at various technical and military schools – and, *in situ*, they could all be described as professionals working in Russian Central Asia, making art in the service of natural and political sciences, quite separate from contemporary aesthetic standards. Yet, they inextricably bound their names to the representation of colonial Turkestan in which the positivist spirit of cataloging often gives way to the taste for the exotic and the picturesque.

With the introduction of photography to Central Asia came the realization that the whole new world was waiting to be photographed. Others modeled their expeditions on the models of the European practices and grand tours, such as

Aleksandr Komarov (1830–1904); Liubov (or Lidia, according to other sources) Poltoratzkaya, the wife of the Governor-General of Semipalatinsk, Aleksandr Poltoratzky; the professor of Persian studies Valentin Zhukovsky[12] (1858–1918); the self-taught photographer, ethnographer and future curator Samuil Dudin (1868–1929); Grigori A. Pankratiev,[13] the army captain serving in Samarkand between 1894 and 1904; Ivan Vvedensky, who was active in Samarkand between 1894–97; Grigori Krivtzov and Nikolai Bogaevsky (1840–1888), who also worked on the *Turkestan Album* hand in hand with Nekhoroshev and the gifted Orientalist Aleksey Kun (1843–1912); or V. F. Kozlovsky, who was active in Central Asia in the 1880s–1890s. Many of them had been trained as mobile photographers and moved from one project to another, gaining tremendous experience.

A great many people made photographs in the later 19th century Central Asia but few as vivid as Nekhoroshev's (ILL). What do we make of certain indigenous photographers who often quietly collaborated with the Russian natural scientists, orientalists and linguists, transforming traditional photographic reproductions of Central Asian objects into original creations.[14] Of course, they all anticipate the Russian Court photographer Sergei Prokudin-Gorsky (1863–1944), the early Soviet scientific and documentary photography, but even more strongly they anticipate what happened when early 20th-century artists like Max Penson, Pavel Kuznetzov, Aleksandr Usto-Mumin (Nikolaev), Aleksandr Volkov, or Georgy Zelma rescued the expeditionary photography from the placid Imperial album. The connection to later experiments is especially suggestive in Nekhoroshev's work.

Where – apart from portraits, which were a given – should they begin? What objects were chosen to be photographed? What were the *criteria* for the colonial albums and the official photographic commissions? How precise did the information have to be? How positive a delivery of the photographic

---

12 Valentin Zhukovsky, *Drevnosti Zakaspiiskogo Kraya Razvaliny Starogo Merva* [Antiquities of the Trans-Caspian Region. Ruins of the Ancient Merv] (St. Petersburg: Tipografiya Glavnogo Upravleniya Udelov, 1894). See also Vasily Bartold, *Pamiati Zhukovskogo, Sochineniya* [In Memory of V.A. Zhukovsky. Selected Works], vol. 9 (Moscow: Izdatel'stvo Vostochnoi Literatury, 1977).

13 Pankratiev enjoyed the patronage of the Great Duke Nikolai Rostovtzev, whose generous stipend enabled Pankratiev to complete the photographic album on Samarkand antiquities with S.A. Lapin's translations from the Arabic inscriptions of the Samarkand mausoleums. All ten copies of the *Album* were published at "a good price". See *Turkestanskie Vedomosti* (Tashkent, 1904), 140.

14 Many Turkestan expeditions and military campaigns have been instructed by leading Orientalists and scientific members of the Archeological Commissions to keep an eye on the antiquities. For example, the eminent Orientalist P.I. Lerkh gave instructions for the Khiva campaign (1873), outlining the priorities for looking for numismatic, archeological, and ethnographic artifacts and keeping them safe.

documentation was expected by the Russian court? Could photographers be critical or neutral of their subjects and sitters? How effective was photography in documenting each object, emphasizing their value as cultural treasures, reflecting aspirations of the time? The possible modifications of contents and format that the colonial album encompassed could make for a complex mobility of meanings, from the publishers' presentation to an individual's collector's personal reconfigurations or additions.

The evocative literary sources (with considerably fewer images) called into question the fixity of the archaeological viewer and the primacy of the three-dimensional object (sculpture and ceramics) over the photograph that could record it. The fact that ancient Central Asian culture made groundbreaking achievements that brought contributions to mathematics, linguistics, astronomy, architecture, politics, military cultures, administration, and medicine was effectively praised by Oriental rationalists and colonialists, but the complexity of the early scientific assignments around the citadel of Afrasiab or other sources of antiquities in Samarkand defeated many great scientists, including Vasily (Wilhelm) Bartold (1869–1930). Neither the one nor the other complexity reduction does justice to Central Asian culture or any other culture, for that matter. This should be remembered not only by those that approach a culture from the outside but also by those who bear that culture within.

Photography as National Media

Several crucial steps took place in the first decade of the Russian campaign in Turkestan – the establishment of the propaganda apparatus, the introduction of the Cyrillic alphabet, the publication of the main titles of Russian literature. The Turkestan government insisted on publishing the educational stories by Aleksandr Pushkin (1799–1837) and Lev Tolstoy (1828–1910), and *Niva* (Field), the populistic Russian publication based in St. Petersburg, flourished by including the lowbrow reports of travels between Moscow and Tashkent and back and missives by Muslim children who described the "Russian customs and culture along the way" (1889). Some steps were done in reverse: the *Tuzemnaya Gazeta* (Local Newspaper), a Russian propaganda tool under Konstantin Petrovich von Kaufmann (1818–1882), the first governor-general of Turkestan, sent an order to bring in the Arabic alphabet and a group of leading specialists in the Arabic language to publish the newspaper in local languages. Based in Samarkand, the newspaper *Okraina* (Outskirts, published between 1890–98) praised the education of Uzbek women. In October 1881, the progressive colonel Nikolai Mayev took the position of editor of the major national forum, the *Turkestanskie Vedomosti* (Turkestan News) and, at around the same time, of the branch of the Russian Telegraph Agency in Tashkent. He inspired the first generations of Russian businessmen to go to Central Asia with his excellent guide written on the occasion of the first Tashkent Industrial Exhibition in 1890. Those novelties changed many things for many people.

In his book *Russian Architecture: Trends in Nationalism and Modernism* (1969), Arthur Voyce sums up the process of Russia's integration with European modernization processes as follows: "With the advance of the modern industrial era and the awakening of the Russian middle classes, an infiltration from Europe of an irrational Classicism and a sugary romanticism could be noted. To combat that sprang up there the Russian National School set itself against the cosmopolitan eclectic aestheticism of the upper classes."[15] While the European influence was significant, nationalism set the scene for a different kind of integration: "The Nationalists were seeking to revive the ancient traditions of Russian art and architecture and to put new life into the old forms by infusing them with the freshness, simplicity and the fantastic picturesqueness of the rustic Russian. It was because of this movement that the direction and the quality of the art of the city began to be seriously influenced by the primitive rural art, an art that had been developing through many centuries in the isolated quietness of the village and in the calm of the limitless steppes and forests."[16] At a time when the Russian architects in Tashkent were persuaded of the necessity to turn the new capital of Russian Turkestan into Moscow,[17] this message could not have been more relevant and urgent.

Russia was part of this new expectation to visualize the world through photography. However, the processes of modernization and globalizing forces unleashed by the Russian Empire led to an awkward juxtaposition. The Russian and Asiatic photographers who were at work in Russian Turkestan were under double pressure from the bullying mentality epitomized in the Russian authorities and the resistance of the local population. This suggests that Russians used the public display of colonial material to define themselves as a nation. They were able to do so because the organizers of such displays constructed them as protean events with numerous possible meanings, even as they used them to disseminate liberal ideas about Russian society, the economy, and Russia's

---

[15] Arthur Voyce, *Russian Architecture: Trends in Nationalism and Modernism* (New York: Greenwood Press, 1969), 121–122.
[16] Ibid., 23.
[17] For a detailed account of Russian colonial life in Central Asia, see Sahadeo, *Russian Colonial Society in Tashkent*.

relationship with Islam and the rest of the world. Russian Turkestan was actively and visibly a colony that was representative of many trends that were occurring throughout the Empire. Scholars such as Mark LeVine, Ali Behdad, and Stephen Sheehi have shown similar transformations in the Middle East.[18] Colonial photographic histories in Russia remain uncharted and deserving of serious scholarly attention.

The aesthetics of photography, no less than those of the other arts, were affected by the general spirit of restlessness and discontent, and the swinging theoretical polemics between the older and younger schools of the profession contributed to rigorous debates between the reactionary and retrospective and the radical and provocative, breaking up the traditional patterns and rhetoric.

A wide range of cultural forms convey the 19th-century Russian fascination with unearthing and exposing – and also reanimating – the unseen and the unknown. It is no mere coincidence that the period in which Turkestan came to public light and attained its greatest prominence comprises those same decades that witnessed the rise of modern museums, in which the emergent historical sciences of geology, palaeontology, and archaeology were coming under the public gaze in an entirely unprecedented way. The representation of extinct species and little-known races held considerable significance for the prospects of colonial and ethnographic museums. Imperial collections, institutions for national interests, relied on a similar set of ideas.

Defending Nationalism, Pursuing Internationalism: The Glory of Colonial Exhibitions

World Fairs and international exhibitions were closely connected to nationalism. They were devised as peaceful contests of nations: from the very start in 1851, the Great Exhibition of spectacular works of industry offered each participating country its own section in London's Crystal Palace to show off its contribution to human progress. The focus on industrial products enabled the host country to emphasize its leading position. Four years later, the Parisian follow-up (the *Exposition Universelle*) added agriculture and fine arts, thus foregrounding

---

18 Mark LeVine, Karin van Nieuwkerk and Martin Stokes, eds., *Islam and Popular Culture* (Austin: University of Texas Press, 2016); Ali Behdad, "Orientalist Desire, Desire of the Orient," *French Forum* 15, no. 1 (1990): 37–51; Stephen Sheehi, *Arab Imago: A Social History of Portrait Photography, 1860–1910* (Princeton, NJ: Princeton University Press: 2016).

fields in which France excelled. Even so, machinery, agriculture, and fine arts offered scant grounds for distinguishing one country from its neighbors. Therefore, at the next Parisian World Fair in 1867, all participating countries were invited to erect a pavilion in a characteristically national style to exhibit their own "authentic" culture. World Fairs accordingly became global platforms where nations learned how to represent their identity in a favorable light. National pavilions in fact were instrumental for a tighter definition of national culture by exhibiting meaningful archaeological finds, important historical artifacts, and traditional costumes and typical artisanal products while also offering characteristic dishes and beverages.

The brand of the colonial and universal exhibitions relied on and drew its value from networks of social, political, and commercial alliances and relationships that were not singularly built but produced through selective energies that drew together individuals, communities, social groups, and institutions through the capital and periphery of each individual nation. Colonial exhibitions were battlegrounds in which different groups within the Russian imperial court, the Directorate of the General Staff, and the Societies for Archaeology, Antiquities, and Sciences fought to present their vision of what sort of nation Russia should be. To analyze the exhibits on display is to argue how inherently antithetical the commercial line was vis-à-vis culture and scientific explorations.

The second argument concerns the forms and directions of industrialization that Russia followed and why, and what would happen if it took a different path and adopted a different model, for example, the British or the French one. Can we insist that the Turkestan exhibition was designed to celebrate Russia's economic successes or to hide its deficiencies? Was it organized to locate the mistakes the colonial policies made alongside the process of conquest or to remedy them through the commercialization of the Fair? Whereas the organizers and many observers portrayed the exhibition as a tribute to a new socio-political order and religious and ethnographic integration, a more careful analysis of attendance patterns might disclose deep, underlying divisions. Did the Turkestan Fair work in reality to segregate the Russian and Asiatic parts of the city of Tashkent, not just by urban zones but on regional, occupational, ethnic,[19] and gender bases as well?[20]

---

19 As Jeffrey Auerbach suggests in his chapter on nationalism and internationalism, "in general, northern Europeans were held in the highest regard, followed by southern Europeans, with Russians, Asians, Africans, and American Indians bringing up the rear. Racial and ethnic groups that were perceived as exotic or different, and nations that were not Westernized or industrialized, were considered lowest in the hierarchy." Jeffrey A. Auerbach, *The Great Exhibition of 1851: A Nation on Display* (New Haven, CT/London: Yale University Press, 1999), 167.
20 Similar questions have been posed by Auerbach but for Victorian society and the British class division that viewed their closest neighbors as the exotic, foreign "other." Ibid., 3.

The 1860s, when Feodor Dostoyevsky wrote *Notes from Underground* (1864) and Nikolai Chernyshevsky published his pamphlet novel *What is to Be Done?* (1863), were a watershed in Russian history, the decade during which Russia began to modernize. It had lost the Crimean War in 1857, which led to a number of reforms, not the least of which was the decision by the Tsar to free the serfs in 1861. The modernization process took longer than anyone expected. Dostoyevsky was both angry and defensive about the achievements of the West: "[I]t was simply inconsistent with the laws of nature."[21] He felt shame at his country's backwardness; the more impressive the achievement, the less Dostoyevsky was able to acknowledge it. What he was really reacting to, in *Notes from Underground*, was not the Western reality of modernization, which was full of conflict and debate, but the Russian fantasy of modernization as a means of silencing that very debate. Nor did all Russians view the Crystal Palace the way Dostoyevsky did. In 1859, Chernyshevsky made a brief visit to London and wrote in his prison work *What Is to Be Done?* about the Crystal Palace, which, for the heroine, appears like a magical vision in a dream, "a symbol of the new modes of freedom and happiness that Russians can enjoy if they make the great historical leap into modernity."[22]

The already famous Silk Road was also high on the agenda of the Imperial Russian Geographic Society and Archaeological Committee in St. Petersburg. The scientific organizations took the lead in setting out to photograph the world of Central Asia systematically. Many expeditions included artists. Vasily Vereshchagin (1842–1904, ILL) set himself an even greater task in covering the colonial campaign in Central Asia, not only because he joined the military campaign of the first governor of Turkestan (1867/68), but also because he took in Samarkand, Tashkent, and Khiva (second Turkestan trip, 1869/70) in addition to other itineraries, which he came back from with something like a thousand drawings and oil sketches. Vereshchagin, who had possibly been instructed in the photographic medium by one of von Kaufmann's officers, was a ruined minor aristocrat who possessed apparently few material possessions but huge personal and artistic ambitions. He always looked for ways to display or publish his art, using some artworks as references for his larger paintings, which he sent out into the world as a complete exhibition, often accompanying the dispatch. He failed to sell many, and most of his art remains in Russia up to this day. His fame is larger than his life, and his life is larger than his travels, which included Central Asia and the Caucasus, the Russian North and the Volga region, Cuba and the Philippines, North America, and India. He died as fearlessly as he lived, during the Russo-Japanese War (1904/05).

---

21 Feodor Dostoevsky, *Notes from Underground* (New York: Dover, 1992), 17, 23–25.
22 Ibid., 26.

He was a great documentary painter and probably a good photographer, a profession he denied, calling it a shameful activity for a good artist: "I'm blamed for using the camera for my paintings, but it's the opposite."[23] As a battle painter, Vereshchagin was an old hand at shocking the public. In 1873, he had provoked St. Petersburg with his Turkestan series, entitled *The Barbarians (ILL)* and completed in Munich (1872/73), the necessary atmosphere being created by the atrocities of war between the Russian army and the locals. Terrifying backdrops with hundreds of scalps suggested the unknown depths of the human tragedy, while Vereshchagin's canvases, cleverly lit and composed, produced still air and cloudless skies: life was turned into death.

Vereshchagin invited the last of the doubters, the journalists and fellow artists, for a private visit to his Munich studio, a rare invitation from an artist whose ferocious temperament kept his friends and enemies at bay. Not unexpectedly, Russia did not take great pride in the native son who had contributed to the glory of the nation. On the contrary, the Russian government and the military authorities saw in his photographic canvases a great threat to their aggressive actions toward Turkistan's rulers. Vereshchagin depicted the chronology of the conquest while the Russian court was more interested in seeing the glorifying aspects of their deeds in the south. No one seemed to notice that Vereshchagin minimized the importance of the role played by his government in the development of the region.

His works encompass structures, ruins, cityscapes, and people – the subjects of his immensely powerful Turkestan series[24] are exactly as imposing, finely wrought, and perhaps even as ancient as his pillars of the minarets of Samarkand. The dimensions of his paintings are enhanced by his frames, which he crafted himself. He was seldom content with a conventionally composed view of a building, or a genre scene, or a portrait. He regarded himself as a "true Russian," a national Russian artist whose duties dictated his righteous deeds. Such morality was seldom taken well even by Vereshchagin's strong supporters. Ivan Kramskoy (1837–1887), another great Russian realist and one of the founders of the *Peredvizhniki* group, attacked Vereshchagin for his bookish documentality instead of being a visionary storyteller, advising him to write down his experiences in a book, not on canvas. This is, perhaps, the highest praise to Vereshchagin as an unknown photographer, something he denied throughout his life. Vereshchagin was an artist rather than a historian, ethnographer, ethnologist, or journalist. His taste for

---

23 Vasily Vereshchagin, *Listki Iz Zapisnoi Knizhki* [Pages from the Artist's Note Book] (St. Petersburg: Tipigrafiya tov. I.K. Kushnerova, 1898), 150.
24 As per Vereshhchagin's intention, they were sold as a series to Pavel Tretiakov, the founder of the Tretiakov Gallery in Moscow, for 92,000 rubles. He later went so far as to build an extra building for Vereshchagin's works.

battles and ruins and his interest in Islamic cultures were all predicated on Orientalist and colonial tendencies in those directions. He deplored the whitewashing peace scenes even though he was aware of their visual necessity because they destroyed the truth and merciless taste of reality. He was in every way a creature of his time, and yet he retained an open eye and an honesty about what he saw. He may have been drenched in preconceived notions of the Russian Academy of Arts, where he studied for a while, but his colonial portfolio does not suggest that it was bent or massaged to accord with an ideology. He preserved the chronicle of the Russian campaign as it stood in the more recent past, and, given how many others of his time have been destroyed or damaged, Vereshchagin's pictures are precious testimony in addition to being vigorous works of Russian national art.

The technique used for the negatives was the dry gelatine process; it would take at least half an hour to shoot the picture and develop each glass negative. Which other techniques were available to photographers? Did he share the process with anyone else? Did he employ an assistant or a team of assistants? Vereshchagin denies it. What was his sole purpose in photography? To officially establish his name as an international photographer, to move elsewhere from the inherited business of his father. Was he interested in witnessing the aftermath of the conquest, in becoming a chronicler and the oracle of the events passing before him? Did he want to live them full-heartedly or as a bystander? By the time he reached Central Asia, Vereshchagin had become quite active working under his own name.

Today, photographic scholars and researchers judge photographs as being artistic using a very different set of standards and which was not applicable in Vereshchagin's time. It was not until the advent of the compact camera and picture negatives that photographic societies, which reflect the Russian interest in the dispersion of the national message around the Empire and beyond, and photographers who had been stationed in or lived in Central Asia were ready to exploit all possible techniques of production. In keeping with the enthusiasm for photography, and later for film and video cameras as media to represent the colonies, the camera ceased to exist as a private tool or one adopted for private use.

Russia was increasingly busy creating the image of Central Asia to suit itself.[25] It was still an image intimately linked to the political and economic

---

[25] A similar spectrum of questions has been posed by Christopher De Bellaigue about "the logic that lies behind such equivalences" in relation to the French idea of liberty and Islamic religious zeal, the tensions between the modern notions of equality and Islamic conceptions of justice, the adaptation of language and dress, etc. Christopher De Bellaigue, *The Islamic Enlightenment: The Struggle Between Faith and Reason, 1798 to Modern Times* (New York: Liveright: 2017).

imperialism that Europe exerted over the rest of the world, one impregnated with exoticism and populated by steppes and deserts, Oriental bazaars, and Asian antiquities. Whether this was the Turkestan wisely governed by the Russian colonists as narrated by numerous Russian and Western European historians and Orientalists is debatable; however, it also should be observed to the detriment of a certain schematism that ends up taking the upper hand in the application of Edward Said's thesis that the very same notion of the Turkestan nation appropriated by the elements that were constructed out of the historical, linguistic and anthropological research carried out in the Russian, Asian, and Orientalist departments of universities, particularly German ones, where the first Russian professors of Orientalist studies worked and the respective languages were taught. Furthermore, from von Kaufmann to Vrevsky, the principal Turkestan governors were formed in the Russian military academies.

Russian colonial photography came into being and spread in less time than any technical process in colonial military history. It was only a few weeks after General Cherniaev's conquest of Tashkent that the first camera arrived in the region. The city did not see its first exhibition until 1887, but the presence of cameras in Tashkent left it dumbfounded. "So far, we have only seen the beginning of it," concluded the *Turkestansky Vestnik*, the leading newspaper of the time in Central Asia.

Conclusion

Colonial photography made for national importance gave feelings of preparation and control, the deliberate transformation of a shadowy circumstance of Russian history into a triumphant act of collecting scientific culture but also transmitting the national interests. Constructing the new image of Central Asia through photography was never so thorough a vice that its energy might not glorify the political deeds, even under the glare of public challenge and rebuke. The Russian conquest of Central Asia shows clearly how rapidly this became evident.

The nationalism of Turkestan had, in fact, little in common with the nationalism of European colonies. Its leaders spoke Russian, and many of them dressed in Russian clothes, but almost all of them came from those classes, especially in Samarkand, Bukhara, and Kokand, who had traditionally been the spokesmen and leaders within the fabric of Turkestan society.

In all the tangled history of the Turkestan subcontinent, nothing is more complex than this interweaving of the political achievement of the Russian and the creation of nation states. The process is almost certainly not yet completed, however, as was demonstrated in 1923 when the Bolsheviks concluded that such remnants of 19th-century liberalism as freedom of the press and unlimited access to the courts were working against the chief ends of the state – the preservation of law and order.

Work Cited

Arapov, D. Yu. "'Neobkhodimo . . . zanyat'sya obrazovaniem kraya' (Sattar-khan Abdulgafarov o zadachakh russkoi politiki v Srednei Azii" ['It is necessary . . . to improve education in the region' (Sattar-khan Abdulgafarov about the tasks of Russia's policy in Central Asia]. *Vestnik Evrazii* [Bulletin of Eurasia] 1: 169–184.

Auerbach, Jeffrey A. *The Great Exhibition of 1851, A Nation on Display*. New Haven, CT/London: Yale University Press, 1999.

Bartold, Vasily. *Pamiati Zhukovskogo, Sochineniya* [In Memory of V.A. Zhukovsky. Selected Works], vol. 9. Moscow: Izdatel'stvo Vostochnoi Literatury, 1977.

Bassin, Mark. "Russia between Europe and Asia: The Ideological Construction of Geographical Space." *Slavic Review* 50, no. 1 (2003): 1–17.

Baumgart, Winfried. "Eisenbahn und Kriegsführung in der Geschichte." *Technikgeschichte* 38 (1971): 191–219.

Behdad, Ali. "Orientalist Desire, Desire of the Orient." *French Forum* 15, no. 1 (1990): 37–51.

Caraffa, Costanza and Tiziana Serena, eds. *Photo Archives and the Idea of Nation*. Berlin/Munich/Boston: De Gruyter, 2015.

Crews, Robert D. *The Prophet and the Tsar: Islam and Empire in Russia and Central Asia*. Cambridge, MA: Harvard University Press, 2009.

De Bellaigue, Christopher. *The Islamic Enlightenment: The Struggle Between Faith and Reason, 1898 to Modern Times*. New York: Liveright: 2017.

Dostoevsky, Feodor. *Notes from Underground*. New York: Dover, 1992.

Fox-Amato, Matthew. *Exposing Slavery, Photography, Human Bondage, and the Birth of Modern Visual Politics in America*. Oxford: Oxford University Press, 2019.

Geraci, Robert P. and Michael Khodarkovsky, *Of Religion and Empire: Missions, Conversion, and Tolerance in Tsarist Russia*. Ithaca, NY: Cornell University Press, 2001.

Geraci, Robert P. *Window on the East: National and imperial Identities in Late Tsarist Russia*. Ithaca, NY/London: Cornell University Press, 2001.

Gies, Jacques, Michel Soymie, Jean-Pierre Drege, Danielle Eliasberg and Richard Scheneider, eds. *Les Arts de l'Asie centrale, la collection Paul Pelliot du musee national des arts asiatiue, Guimet*. 2 vols. Paris: Reunion des Musees Nationaus, 1994.

Greenblatt, Stephen. *Cultural Mobility: A Manifesto*. Cambridge: Cambridge University Press, 2010.

Immermann, Karl Leberecht. "The Wonders in the Spessart." In *Tales from the German, Comprising Specimens from the Most Celebrated Authors*, translated by John Oxenford and C. A. Reiling. London: Chapman and Hall, 1844.

Kalinovsky, Artemy and Michael Kemper. "Introduction: interlocking Orientologies in the Cold War era." In *Reassessing Orientalism: Interlocking Orientologies during the Cold War*, edited by Artemy Kalinovsky and Michael Kemper, 1–15. London: Routledge, 2017.

Knight, Nathaniel. "Grigor'ev in Orenburg, 1851–1862: Russian Orientalism in the Service of Empire?" *Slavic Review* 59, no. 1 (1998): 74–100.

Kouteinikova, Inessa. "Tashkent in St. Petersburg: The Constructed Image of Central Asia in Russia's Nineteenth-Century Ethnographic Exhibitions." In *A l'orientale: Collecting, Displaying and Approving Islamic Art and Architecture in the 19th and Early 20th Centuries*. Leiden/Boston: Brill, 2019.

LeVine, Mark, Karin van Nieuwkerk and Martin Stokes, eds. *Islam and Popular Culture*. Austin: University of Texas Press, 2016.

Lukoyanov, Igor V., ed. *Sooruzhenie Zheleznykh dorog v Srednei Azii i Persii* [Construction of the Railroads in Central Asia and Persia] from Sergei Yu. Witte, *Sobranie Sochinenii i dokumentalnykh Materialov* [Collective Works and Documents], vol. I, book 2, part I. Moscow: Nauka, 2004.

Mackenzie, David. "Expansion in Central Asia: St. Petersburg vs. the Turkestan Generals (1863–1866)." *Canadian-American Slavic Studies* 3, no. 2 (1969): 286–311.

Masal'sky, Vladimir I. *Polnoe Geograficheskoe Opisanie Nashego Otechestva* [The Complete Geographic Description of Our Fatherland], vol. XIX, *Turkestanskii Krai*. St. Petersburg: A.F. Devriena, 1913.

Miller, Aleksey. *Imperiya Romanovykh i Nazionalism. Esse po metodologii Istoricheskogo Issledovaniya* [The Romanov's Empire and Nationalism. Essay on Historical Research Methodology]. Moscow: NLO, 2010.

Ostroumov, Nikolai P. "Khrakteristika religiozno-pravoslavnoi zhizni musulman preimuschestvenno Srednei Azii." *Pravoslavnoe Obozrenie* 2 (June-July 1880).

Ostroumov, Nikolai P. *K Istorii narodnogo obrazovaniya v Turkestanskom Krae, Lichnye vospominaniya*. Tashkent, 1911.

Ostroumov, Nikolai P. *Kolebaniya russkogo pravitelstva vo vzgliadakh na missionerskuy deyatelnost- Pravoslavnoj Ruskoi Cerkvi* [Doubts of the Russian government over the missionary activities of the Russian Orthodox Church]. Kazan: Sotrudnik bratstva Sv. Guriya, 1910.

Ostroumov, Nikolai P. *Konstantin von Kaufman, Lichnye Vospominaniya*. 1899.

Popov, A. *Iz Istorii Zavoevaniya Srednei Azii. Istoricheskie Zapiski* [From the History of Central Asian Conquest. Historical Notes]. Moscow, 1940.

Sahadeo, Jeff. *Russian Colonial Society in Tashkent (1865–1923)*. Bloomington, IN: Indiana University Press, 2007.

Said, Edward W. *Orientalism*. New York: Pantheon Books, 1978.

Sheehi, Stephen. *Arab Imago: A Social History of Portrait Photography, 1860–1910*. Princeton, NJ: Princeton University Press: 2016.

Tashkenbaeva, D. "Formirovanie Osobennostei sredneaziatskikh geopoliicheskikh interesov Rossijskoi Imperiei" [Characteristical Formation of the Central Asian geopolitical interests by the Russian Empire]. *Voprosy Istoricheskoi Nauki, Proceedings from the Third International Conference, Moscow, January 2015*, 130–132. Moscow: Buki-Vedi, 2015.

Vereshchagin, Vasily. *Listki Iz Zapisnoi Knizhki* [Pages from the Artist's Note Book]. St. Petersburg: Tipigrafiya tov. I.K. Kushnerova, 1898.

Vitkind, Nikolai Ya. *Bibliographia Po Sredney Asii*. 1929.
Voyce, Arthur. *Russian Architecture. Trends in Nationalism and Modernism*. New York: Greenwood Press, 1969.
Werth, Paul W. *At the Margins of Orthodoxy: Mission, Governance, and Confessional Politics*. Ithaca, NY: Cornell University Press, 2002.
Zhukovsky, Valentin. *Drevnosti Zakaspiiskogo Kraya Razvaliny Starogo Merva* [Antiquities of the Trans-Caspian Region. Ruins of the Ancient Merv]. St. Petersburg: Tipografiya Glavnogo Upravleniya Udelov, 1894.

Irakli Chkhaidze

7 Georgia's Two Others: Nationalism and the Identity Struggle of a Post-Soviet Nation State

Introduction

Georgia is one of the countries where identity crises and nationalism have led to significant problems and caused political, social, and territorial disintegration during the first years of independence in the 1990s. Later the situation changed: along with Western aspirations, the Georgian national project gradually acquired civil features. The present contribution analyzes the symbolic and real roles of the West in the formation of post-Soviet Georgian public discourse(s) and the importance of attitudes to the West in the development of diverse forms of national identity.

At the end of the 1980s, the country's independence became the foremost goal of the national movement that started in the Soviet Republic of Georgia. After achieving this goal and the establishment of independence, at the beginning of the 1990s, the development of an independent democratic state became the most significant challenge for Georgian society. In the process of deconstructing the Soviet system, Georgians started to construct a new identity and searched for their own place within the international system. Since this period, the idea of the European origin of Georgians and their close links to the West has become widespread in the public and academic circles.[1] The idea of "belonging to Europe" still plays a key role in the process of formation of the Georgian identity. However, the attitude to the West is not positive in all cases. Although Euro-Atlantic integration on the political level is the key message of the Georgian national project, a certain portion of Georgian society is filled with fear and mistrust of the West. Diverse social groups demonize the West, although, unlike in the Soviet era, in this case the "Western Demon" does not threaten the "Soviet motherland." Instead, it threatens a traditional orthodox country with an ancient history. This contribution aims to study two different,

---

[1] Frederik Coene, *Euro-Atlantic Discourse in Georgia: The Making of Georgian Foreign and Domestic Policy After the Rose Revolution* (London/New York: Routledge, 2016), 31.

Note: This work was supported by the Shota Rustaveli National Science Foundation of Georgia under Grant [YS-18-1461].

Open Access. © 2021 Irakli Chkhaidze, published by De Gruyter. This work is licensed under the Creative Commons Attribution-NonCommercial-NoDerivatives 4.0 International License.
https://doi.org/10.1515/9783110729290-007

opposing, yet interlinked tendencies that are widespread in the process of the post-socialist transformation of Georgia.

Identity and nationalism studies is a relatively new research field within the humanities and social sciences in Georgia. In this regard, many problematic issues should be viewed using contemporary theoretical and methodological attitudes. There are only a few works focusing on the given problem from an academically intriguing perspective.[2] Although the empirical material is rich and diverse, its major portion has not been systematized and contextualized based on a certain theoretical framework. This reality proves the significance of the problem under analysis.

From the literature which forms the direct theoretical grounds of the present research, above all, mention should be made of Rogers Brubaker's works. In his work *Ethnicity Without Groups*, the author considers ethnicity, nations, and group identities of various types as construed phenomena. According to Brubaker, when researching nations and ethnic groups, attention should be focused on practical categories, situations, cultural idioms, discourse, political projects, and the changing nature of group membership; phenomena like ethnicity, nation, and race are results of the social and political processes characteristic of the contemporary epoch. A separate chapter of Brubaker's work is dedicated to the dichotomy of ethnic and civil nationalism. The author mentions that similar classifications are often accompanied by analytical and normative ambiguity and geographical determinism, which undoubtedly deserves criticism. Despite this, Brubaker shares the key postulates defining ethnic and civil nationalism.[3]

Other significant works are included in the collection *After Independence: The Making and Protection of the Nation in Postcolonial and Postcommunist States*, edited by Lowell W. Barrington. The book embraces discussions of various post-socialist states, including Georgia.[4] In the introduction of the book, the editor speaks about an important objective of research into nationalism in the post-socialist epoch, namely the study of the role and function of nationalism after it has reached its main goal, i.e. the formation of a sovereign state.

---

[2] Selected works on the issues: Ronald Grigor Suny, *The Making of the Georgian Nation*, 2nd ed. (Bloomington, IN: Indiana University Press, 1994); Jonathan Wheatley, *Georgia from National Awakening to Rose Revolution: Delayed Transition in the Former Soviet Union* (London/New York: Routledge, 2005); Stephen F. Jones, *Socialism in Georgian Colors: The European Road to Social Democracy, 1883–1917* (Cambridge, MA: Harvard University Press, 2005).

[3] Rogers Brubaker, *Ethnicity without Groups* (Cambridge, MA: Harvard University Press, 2006), 27–87.

[4] Stephen F. Jones, "Georgia: Nationalism from under the Rubble," in *After Independence: The Making and Protection of the Nation in Postcolonial and Postcommunist States*, ed. Lowell W. Barrington (Ann Arbor, MI: University of Michigan Press, 2006), 248–276.

The author in addition thoroughly analyzes contemporary debates around the issues of nation and nationalism.[5]

The conceptual frame of the research partly embraces a phenomenon of populism and its theoretical considerations. The study consequently benefits from the famous book *The People* by Margaret Canovan. Discussing difficulties regarding the generalization and contextualization of populist movements, the author claims that ideological movements like socialism, liberalism, or nationalism gained a degree of coherence from a continuous history, willingness on the part of most followers to identify themselves by the name, and distinctive principles and policies. "Populism does not fit this pattern. There is no acknowledged common history, ideology, programme or social base, and the term is usually applied to movements from outside, often as a term of abuse."[6]

This work focuses on the role of a national leader in national populist discourses. In this respect, *The Global Rise of Populism: Performance, Political Style, and Representation* by Benjamin Moffit was found to be very helpful. In the chapter devoted to a leader as a major performer in populist discourses, the author asks important questions regarding populist performers, their audience, and the respective interactions.[7] First of all, populism is a political style aiming to mobilize the people around certain ideas. Post-Soviet Georgia is a field of struggle between pro-Western and anti-Western populist discourses with an explicit role for leaders. Moffit concludes that populist leaders should be seen as key performers of populism: "It is the populist leader who inspires hope in followers, anxiety and panic in detractors, and who attracts the attention of the all-important media through which they broadcast their appeal to 'the people.'"[8] More reflections on the phenomenon of populism will be presented in the section dedicated to the theoretical framework of the research.

There are only a few works in the Georgian language dedicated to the issues of post-Soviet nationalism, populism, and the formation of identity. The field of social sciences is not rich in fundamental research regarding the above-mentioned issues. The reason for this is probably that in the Soviet Union, under the conditions of a strict ideological regime, the study of the given problem was very restricted and only possible when based on a Marxist-Leninist attitude. In the post-Soviet epoch,

---

5 Lowell W. Barrington. "Nationalism & Independence," in *After Independence: The Making and Protection of the Nation in Postcolonial and Postcommunist States*, ed. Lowell W. Barrington (Ann Arbor, MI: University of Michigan Press, 2006), 3–30.
6 Margaret Canovan, *The People* (Cambridge: Polity Press, 2005), 79.
7 Benjamin Moffitt, *The Global Rise of Populism: Performance, Political Style, and Representation* (Stanford: Stanford University Press, 2016), 51–69.
8 Ibid., 68.

despite the absence of ideological pressure, the old attitudes to academic research have been preserved. This proves the necessity of research from a new perspective.

It is necessary to distinguish several works from the literature directly focusing on the issue under analysis. In this regard, mention should be made of Stephen Jones' *Georgia: A Political History since Independence*. A chapter of this book is dedicated to a discussion of Georgian populism.[9] Mention should also be made of Adrian Brisku's article "So Far and Yet So Near, The Image of Europe in Georgia: History of Ideas."[10] In the historical dynamics, this work analyzes the problem of Georgia's attitude to the West. The historical background is also discussed in Ghia Nodia's "The Idea of the West in the Georgian Consciousness"[11] and Tamar Kakitelashvili's "The West in the Georgian Consciousness."[12]

The issue under analysis is part of the recent history of Georgia. The processes that took place in the given period largely defined Georgia's internal and international state and led to the successes and failures in the period of transition after independence. At the current stage of development, it is of crucial importance to implement a critical analysis of Georgia's history since its independence. The study of the processes from the perspective of identity research will help to reevaluate the recent past and define the regional and international contexts of events that have taken place in Georgia.

The empirical grounds for the given research embrace public speeches of representatives of the political and intellectual elite, addresses, interviews, and academic and journalistic works. The post-Soviet Georgian public discourse is a construed phenomenon, developed by the elite and largely transformed in the past decades. The main goal of the project is to observe the stages of the above-mentioned transformation and analyze their dynamics.

The research that the present contribution is based on aims at the study of the formation and development of the Georgian national project from the viewpoint of attitudes to the Western space. The contribution also aims to analyze the factors conditioning the formation of two opposing national narratives. The study is focused on the contradictory nature of the Western orientation of post-

---

9 Stephen F. Jones, *Georgia: A Political History since Independence* (London: I.B. Tauris, 2013), 51–73.
10 Adrian Brisku, "So Far and Yet So Near, The Image of Europe in Georgia: History of Ideas," May 5, 2017, https://ge.boell.org/ka/2017/05/05/ase-shors-da-mainc-ase-axlos-evropis-saxexati-sakartveloshi-ideata-istoria
11 Ghia Nodia, "The Idea of the West in the Georgian Consciousness," *Society and Politics* 2 (1999): 35–74.
12 Tamar Kakitelashvili, "The West in the Georgian Consciousness," *Language and Culture* 1 (2000): 47–54.

Soviet Georgia. The irreversible Western orientation was formed against the background of complicated social processes in the past decades. This can be proved by recent events in Georgia, which reflect the simultaneous processes of the idealization and demonization of the West. This tendency is due to different narratives developed since independence. An analysis of the dynamics of these narratives will explain the controversial attitudes of Georgian society to the West.

Since the end of the 1980s, when the national movement became dominant in the Georgian social space, its key aim was to define the attitude to the West. In the period of Georgia's independence, this issue did not lose its importance; on the contrary, it became more topical and, parallel to political contacts with the West, it turned into a specific problem for Georgian society. The West turned into a source that equally "fed" Georgian orthodox, ultra-nationalist, and liberal-democratic narratives formed in the public discourse. Demonization and idealization of the West have become the most successful means for manipulating public opinion and acquiring political legitimization. The concrete purpose of this paper is to analyze, systematize, and contextualize the empirical material, which clearly reflects the opposing viewpoints in the public space. Based on a preliminary hypothesis, we can assume that, despite radical opposition, the above-mentioned narratives are closely interlinked and make each other topical. Thus, in order to draw a vivid picture, we should analyze them jointly against the background of Georgia's post-Soviet transformation.

Theoretical Basis and Methodology

Contemporary Western scientific circles (e.g. Stephen Jones in his monograph on Georgia) outline the shortage of theoretical attitudes that would enable a thorough analysis of processes occurring in independent Georgia. Academic and political circles share the opinion that the main "culprit" in the destructive processes of post-Soviet Georgia was the intolerant, exclusive Georgian nationalism, which appeared at the dawn of independence. Certainly, Georgian nationalism was an important factor in the period of transition of the 1990s. However, theories of nationalism are insufficient for a thorough study of the issue.[13] An analysis of the transformation of independent Georgia through the prism of nationalism neglects important tendencies of the development of Georgian society. In order to draw a more or less complete picture, it is necessary to dwell on the concept of "populism," which is widely used on the social and political level. In

---

13 Jones, *Georgia*, 217–220.

contemporary humanities and social sciences, there are diverse opinions regarding the concept of populism. Despite being vague from the academic perspective, the concept of populism is quite flexible and often acquires diverse social-economic content. It is revealed in numerous forms within societies in transition, where the degree of awareness of political developments is low and the future is threatening. Populism may be urban, rural, non-liberal, democratic, etc. Different variants of populism may be applied to different social layers. Margaret Canovan offers seven definitions of populism. According to her, populism implies a certain degree of exaltation and appeals to ordinary people; it is always anti-elite and aimed against the dominant ideological narrative.[14] There are several key features that are common to all types of populism, including the search for scapegoats, such as foreign governments, intellectuals, or ethnic and religious minorities. Populism is also characterized by charismatic power, the cult of the chieftain, emphasis on the nation's fate, and so on. Mass demonstrations, plebiscites, the mobilization of people around a concrete idea – these are major tools of populist policies.[15] The above-mentioned elements of populism are important tools for the analysis of processes that took place in Georgia after independence.

Out of the numerous types of populism, within the framework of the given research, I will focus on the concept of national populism. This concept implies a close connection between populism and nationalism. Despite certain criticism, the majority of works dedicated to populism recognize the close connection between the two concepts. Moreover, some famous authors put an equation mark between populism and nationalism. Both nationalism and populism put an emphasis on people's sovereignty. In their article, Benjamin de Cleen and Yannis Stavrakakis attempt to explain a widespread idea regarding the connection between populism and nationalism. In their opinion, although the power of a national state as the key decision-maker has weakened, it still remains the main space in democratic political representations and public debates. That is why the connection between populism and nationalism is quite natural.[16] Ernest Gellner and Ghita Ionescu discuss populism as one of the forms of nationalism.[17] In the ample theoretical literature, nationalism is viewed as an inalienable part of the populist policy.

---

14 Margaret Canovan, *Populism* (New York/London: Harcourt Brace Jovanovich, 1981), 2–13.
15 Jones, *Georgia*, 77.
16 Benjamin De Cleen and Yannis Stavrakakis, "Distinctions and Articulations: A Discourse Theoretical Framework for the Study of Populism and Nationalism," *Javnost – The Public: Journal of the European Institute for Communication and Culture* 24, no. 2 (2017): 301–319.
17 Ernest Gellner and Ghita Lonescu, *Populism: Its Meanings and National Characteristics* (Letchworth: Garden City Press, 1969), 1–5.

The above research is not aimed at a thorough analysis of debates around the concept of populism. We use this concept for the analysis of the context of processes in independent Georgia. Nationalism, appeals to the people, mass mobilization – these are the tools actively used by politicians and leaders of public organizations in the implementation of populist policies, with the aim of developing diverse national projects.

Another methodological basis of this research is the instrumentalist attitude. According to this attitude, national identities are flexible and changeable in time and environment. Instrumentalist theories are based on the idea that nationalism and ethnicity are the results of various political, economic, and social processes. The majority of contemporary researchers agree that such identities represent social constructs.

The main method used in the given research is discourse analysis. Recently, discourse has become one of the most fashionable terms in scholarly literature. It is widely used in political and intellectual debates. Yet the meaning of discourse is not clearly defined. In general, discourse may be defined as a specific language used in the process of perception of the world, or a viewpoint expressed in a certain field of social life, for instance, medical discourse, political discourse, and so on. Discourse analysis is interdisciplinary research; it forms a framework that can be used in diverse academic disciplines.[18]

I use a content analysis method with regard to the empirical material. The researcher who uses this method is interested in a concrete aspect of the analyzed documents – specific relationships reflected in the document, the author's attitude to this or that issue, and so on. In this case, it is interesting to find out the key tendencies represented in the analyzed factual material regarding attitudes to the West, the key peculiarities of the post-Soviet Georgian national discourse regarding Euro-Atlantic integration.

Georgia's Path to Independence

To familiarize readers with the situation in Georgia and provide a context of the processes developed at the dawn of independence, a brief review of the country's path to post-Soviet liberalization is provided here.

A new stage of Georgian nationalism started in the late 1980s, which emerged from the dissident movement of the 1970s. In the initial stage, the movement was

---

[18] Marianne Jørgensen and Louise Phillips, *Discourse Analysis as Theory and Method* (London: Sage, 2002), 12.

of an environmental character. Measures taken for the protection of Georgia's environment and cultural heritage determined the cultural form of Georgian nationalism from the very beginning. At the same time, a "victory syndrome" appeared in Georgian society due to successful street protest marches. The reins of the national movement appeared to be totally in the hands of radically disposed leaders, whose main tools to achieve their political aim were irreconcilability, manifestations, hunger strikes, and other such activities. Toward the end of the 1980s, the Georgian national movement, which was managed from the street, turned into an emotional phenomenon. The rhetoric, approaches, and decisions of radical leaders were mostly driven not by rationalism but by the emotional background in the streets and at rallies.[19]

From the end of the 1980s, against the background of ongoing processes of restructuring and democratization, the strengthening and upsurge of Georgian nationalism significantly determined the fast pace of Georgia's independence. The Communist government was gradually losing real power and made decisions prompted by the Georgian national movement. The sharp rise of nationalism and ruling nationalist rhetoric restricted the area of activities of the governing elite. Despite the dominance of the nationalist discourse, which was also introduced under the Communist government, the latter still managed to control the situation. However, soon the processes turned into a tragic scenario, which forever deprived the Georgian Communist government of legitimacy.

On 9 April 1989, the Soviet authorities violently dispersed a rally demanding Georgia's independence. After that day, radical leaders entirely took hold of ongoing processes, and Georgian nationalism finally took on a radical form, whose main tools were street protests and manifestations.[20] The tragedy of 9 April rallied the Georgian population around the idea of independence, but from then on, the national movement split up forever. Its leaders did not have an established and shared position on how to fight for the independence of Georgia. The emotional background and personal misunderstandings between leaders played a great role in this process; reasons for this can be found in the early stages of the development of the national movement.

After the tragedy of 9 April, Georgia, along with the Baltic countries fighting for independence, happened to be in the leading position among the Soviet Socialist Republics. In May of the same year, the leaders of the radical wing of the national movement, having been released from prison, reached the peak of

---

[19] Irakli Chkhaidze, "From Ethnic to Civic Nationalism: The Dynamics of the National Project in Post-Soviet Georgia" (PhD thesis, Tbilisi State University, 2016), 42–47.
[20] Jones, *Georgia*, 31–38.

their popularity. In order to stabilize the situation, the Soviet leadership made governmental changes: they appointed the head of the Security Committee as the head of the government to replace the previous one, who was discredited. By promoting the person from the security service, the government attempted to restore its control over the situation with its traditional severe methods and a "powerful hand," although the Communist Party had almost lost its legitimacy in the eyes of society. In his turn, the new head of the party had to obey the dominant nationalist moods in the country and take a loyal position toward the national movement. Abuse of the Soviet ideology, Vladimir Lenin, and the central government became common in official and inofficial Georgian discourses.[21] Parallel to open confrontation with the Soviet ideology, which was declared to be immoral, the national movement itself was overwhelmed with romanticism and was wrapped in the mantle of high moral and ethical ideals.

Finally, national forces came to power via elections. The leading figure of the national movement and Georgia's first president, Zviad Gamsakhurdia (1939–1993), confronted other radical leaders. He founded a political organization called "Round Table – United Georgia" and took part in the elections set up by the Communist government on 28 October 1990, in which Gamsakhurdia and his coalition won a resounding victory.

The elections put an end to the 70-year-long period of Communist rule in Georgia. Gamsakhurdia, one of the biggest adversaries of the Soviet ideology for decades and a former dissident, came to power together with his political coalition. Gamsakhurdia was unanimously elected as the chairman of the Supreme Council. The situation was complicated and controversial as the national government started to rule the country while it was still in the composition of the Soviet Union. The fight for the independence of Georgia thus moved to a new stage. The newly elected Supreme Council had to create a constitutional basis for Georgia's secession from the USSR. The government opposing the central power on the one hand and the national movement inside the country on the other was to face a very hard transition period, which required government officials to get themselves out of their role as national movement leaders and become less radical and more rational. However, the processes in Georgia developed even more dramatically and, finally, escalated into a civil war.

The period of rule of the political coalition "Round Table – United Georgia" did not last long but was full of dramatic events: Georgia was declared independent, the country elected its first president, tensions in the breakaway region of Tskhinvali exacerbated, escalating into an armed conflict, and a civil war sparked

---

21 Chkhaidze, "From Ethnic to Civic Nationalism," 48–52.

up in the center of Tbilisi. The so-called "Tbilisi War" resulted in the overthrow of the national government, and the president fled the country.

In Search of the "Lost Glory": The West as "Two-Faced Janus"

At the end of the 1980s, the process of the disintegration of the Soviet system gave rise to radical Georgian nationalism. The nature of the national movement was largely conditioned by its leader, Zviad Gamsakhurdia. Gamsakhurdia's attitude to Georgia's past, present, and future was sacral and emotional rather than rational. According to him, the Georgian people had suffered for centuries. Finally, the time had come when Georgians would occupy their proper place in the contemporary world. Georgia, as a country with a tragic history, had earned this.[22] According to Gamsakhurdia, the mission of Georgia was to restore its historical function as the bridge between the West and the East. He paid special attention to religious issues, saying that Georgians had made a special contribution to the development of Christianity. Due to this emphasis on religion, early Georgian nationalism looked irrational. It was nationalism of an exclusive nature, as it was based on the idea of uniqueness. However, the problems that arose at the dawn of independence were not solely due to Gamsakhurdia. His epoch was characterized by economic collapse and the fragmentation and polarization of society. Gamsakhurdia's policy was a mixture of nationalism, populism, religion, and conservatism. According to Jones, like many other leaders of Third World countries, Gamsakhurdia was a product of the imperial system. Although he radically opposed the Soviet regime, he himself often revealed insularity and intolerance – the characteristic features of the Soviet system.[23]

The Georgian national movement and its leader were initially supported by Western states. Later, under the influence of diverse factors, the relationships with the West changed. In August 1991, US President George Bush accused Georgia of fostering ethnic nationalism. In response to this statement, Gamsakhurdia accused Bush of tyranny and supporting communism. Since this period, a dual attitude to the Western world has become widespread in the Georgian public space: the traditional, ancient, "civilized," moral West was opposed to the contemporary conspiratorial, immoral West. Gamsakhurdia himself thought that Christian

---

22 Zviad Gamsakhurdia, *Spiritual Mission of Georgia* (Tbilisi: Ganatleba, 1990), 8–9.
23 Jones, *Georgia*, 53.

Georgia had formed part of Western civilization since ancient times. In the contemporary epoch, Georgia was to occupy its due place within the European space. At the same time, Gamsakhurdia actively opposed Western governments who, according to him, played a significant role in the dramatic processes taking place in Georgia. In an interview in 1992, Gamsakhurdia declared:

> Western governments aim at the genocide of all other nations, with the exception of one particular group. This group is closely linked to the USA and aspires to domination in the entire world. In fact, I would call it Euro-American Imperialism. Its leading force is the USA. It is obvious that the coup in Georgia was governed by the USA, with the personal support of the Secretary of State J. Baker and with the blessing of President Bush.[24]

In the same interview, Gamsakhurdia added:

> There was one more reason for the Western anger towards us. Being at the head of the Georgian State, we aspired for the restoration of the national culture, unification of people under the national spirit, public awareness of the fact that our history is far more ancient than that of the Europeans . . . . Our policy, which was based on the national orientation, irritated the leaders of the European Commonwealth, because the official West (I mean leaders and not ordinary people) struggles against every national movement. Their aim is to eliminate the nation's will and, in general, create a unified conglomerate with World Government. This World Government will rule the universe and establish the so-called new world order.[25]

In Gamsakhurdia's opinion, it was due to the above-mentioned reasons that the "agent of international imperialism" – Eduard Shevardnadze (1928–2014) – came to power after the coup that removed Gamsakhurdia from power.

Despite his anti-Western national populism, we cannot conclude that Gamsakhurdia was a radical opponent of the West. HHis attitudes were quite prone to changing within short periods of time. Besides, we should take into account the fact that Gamsakhurdia considered Shevardnadze as his main enemy and one of the organizers of the coup. Shevardnadze was supported by Western political circles. This caused Gamsakhurdia's discontent and acute anti-Western attitudes.

The dual attitude to the West became widespread in Georgia in the above-mentioned period, and its pioneer was Gamsakhurdia. In 1992, in his address to Georgian television, Gamsakhurdia denied accusations regarding his anti-Western isolation policy. He condemned the Western orientation, which implied "the cult of pornographic and sadistic films, the 'heroics' of gangsters, the imitation of Western fashion, begging the West for credits, suspicious political deals with some

---

[24] Zviad Gamsakhurdia, "Interview," *Aghdgoma*, December 4, 1992, #20, 1–2.
[25] Ibid.

political adventurists, the invitation of these adventurists to Georgia, selling off Georgia's natural riches, resorts, ports and industries to the West and so on." However, according to Gamsakhurdia, "Western culture, civilization, art, political thinking, philosophy, and social and legislative systems are very close to us. Awareness of all this and the formation of an open democratic society – this is what we should mean by Western orientation."[26]

Such a dualistic attitude to the Western world, which formed a major part of the Georgian public discourse at the beginning of independence, still remains one of the most topical and problematic issues. The idealization of the West on the one hand and, on the other, its demonization are the key characteristic features of Georgia's development since its independence.

Parallel Processes: Official Pro-Western Discourse versus Anti-Western Populism

In March 1992, the former Minister of Foreign Affairs of the Soviet Union, Eduard Shevardnadze, came to power in Georgia. During his presidency, Georgia's foreign policy became obviously pro-Western. Against the background of their complicated relationships with Russia, the Georgian authorities aspired to enhance their relationships with Western states. Alongside practical steps aimed at Euro-Atlantic integration, pro-Western official rhetoric was enhanced. Shevardnadze described the Western course as the only way for the country to develop. In his opinion, close relationships with the West would help the country achieve stability, overcome poverty, and find its way out of the chaos of the civil war. In 1999, after Georgia joined the European Council, the Chairman of the Georgian Parliament declared, "I am a Georgian, therefore, I am a European." These words turned into a slogan of the pro-Western political course.[27]

This political course defined Georgia's civil transformation. With the aim of developing state institutions, on 25 March 1993, Shevardnadze's government adopted a new law on citizenship.[28] When adopting this undoubtedly liberal law, the authorities took into consideration the ethno-political situation in Georgia and granted citizenship to all residents of Georgia. The law did not require any qualifications like the knowledge of the state language or the

---

26 Zviad Gamsakhurdia, "Address to the Georgian People," *Kartuli Azri*, June 1, 1992, #24, 1.
27 Chkhaidze, "From Ethnic to Civic Nationalism," 106–110.
28 "Law on Citizenship" (1993), accessed March 31, 2020, http://mra.gov.ge/res/docs/2013110412031013274.pdf.

history of Georgia. This Law on Citizenship was far more liberal than that of numerous democratic European states.

Another significant act, which finally defined the inclusive civil nature of the Georgian national project, was the Georgian Constitution, adopted on 24 August 1995. The preamble of the Constitution expresses the will of Georgia's citizens to establish democratic order, ensure human rights and freedoms, reinforce state independence, establish peaceful relationships with other nations, and so on.[29]

Since the "Rose Revolution" of 2003, the civil discourse on national identity and Western aspirations have been further enhanced in Georgia. During the presidency of Mikheil Saakashvili, European ideas and the development of a Western state became the main components of the national project. The idea of Georgians being the most ancient Europeans was revived (albeit in a different form from Gamsakhurdia's epoch). Saakashvili's speech from 2013 proves that the authorities considered Western orientation as the key direction of the Georgian national project. According to Saakashvili, a nation is a project which defines its society's present and future. "A project which unites us without regard to our political, social, religious, ethnic or regional differences. A nation is not ethnicity, and it cannot be solely based on common history. Thus, ladies and gentlemen, a nation is a national project," declared Saakashvili in the above-mentioned speech. He also defined the key components of the national project – independence, sovereignty, territorial integrity, democracy, economic development, and European integration. He noted that, in the event that any of the above-mentioned components are damaged, the entire building would be destroyed.[30]

The current government of Georgia also supports the Western orientation. In the past years, the country has achieved significant success on the way to Western integration, such as the EU Association Agreement, signed in June 2014, and the Agreement on Visa Liberalization, signed in 2017, which entails the visa-free entry of Georgian citizens into Schengen countries.

Despite the above-mentioned successes, the "Westernizing" tendency of official policies is developed against the background of the demonization of the West by certain social groups. The steps made on the path to European integration, especially adaptation of the Western legislative basis, have been opposed

---

[29] "Constitution of Georgia" (1995), accessed March 31, 2020, http://www.parliament.ge/ge/kanonmdebloba/constitution-of-georgia-68.
[30] Mikheil Saakashvili, "Address to the People" (2013), accessed March 31, 2020, http://tradebridgeconsultants.com/news/government/president-mikheil-saakashvili-delivers-annual-address-in-national-library/.

by part of Georgian society. For instance, a law adopted in 1999, which implied the extraction of the nationality column from identity cards, was condemned by certain social organizations and politicians. Guram Sharadze, Chairman of the Parliamentary Committee of Immigration, declared: "If we neglect nationality, in several years we will no longer know whether Georgians form a majority among the 80 nationalities and ethnicities residing in Georgia. And if we no longer know whether we represent a majority, we may also question whether our State should still be called Georgia. People will say: if Georgians do not represent a majority of the population, why should this country be called Georgia?" According to Sharadze, Georgia has turned into a polygon of cosmopolitanism. Nations with a much shorter history of existence are teaching Georgians how to be tolerant and respect human rights. According to Sharadze, the USA was such a nation.[31]

In Georgia, contemporary Western values are often criticized by well-known people. One of the representatives of the Georgian business elite, Levan Vasadze, is an active continuer of the vision developed at the beginning of the 1990s. He makes a radical difference between good and bad Europe:

> I am one of the first apologists of Europe and the West. However, I have the impression that historical Europe is one thing and contemporary European culture is another thing. I have nothing to do with the Europe in which homosexual marriage is allowed. I do not want my wife, children and friends to be part of such a Europe. If the Europeans say: "This is our standard and, if you want to join us, become like that," we will answer: "Sorry, we thought Europe was something else."[32]

Two years ago, representatives of the cultural field disseminated a letter in which they addressed the diplomatic corps and the international organizations accredited in Georgia. The authors of the letter accused the Western states of being responsible for Georgia's poverty, territorial disintegration, and demographic problems. According to the authors, all these problems arose as a result of Georgia's pro-Western course and aspiration to NATO. The letter says: "Pro-Western policy and Georgia's aspiration to NATO have complicated Georgia's relationships with its neighbor Russia. This has led to Georgia's territorial disintegration and social-economic problems, hampered the country's development, caused poverty and reduced the population to less than 4 million." According

---

31 Guram Sharadze, "Interview" (1999), accessed March 31, 2020, https://guramsharadze.wordpress.com/devnili/erovnebis-rekviziti/.
32 Levan Vasadze, "Interview" (2013), accessed March 31, 2020, https://www.kvirispalitra.ge/politic/17206–levanvasadzeim-?all=1&add_new=0&reply=0.

to the authors, Georgia, which is a country with ancient history and culture, has never betrayed its allies, unlike the North Atlantic Alliance.[33]

Georgian public space, television, and social and printed media form a kind of battlefield for pro-Western and anti-Western counter-narratives. Recently, anti-Western attitudes have become orderly and purposeful, having penetrated into the highest political bodies, namely, the Parliament. In the elections of 2016, the ultra-nationalist, anti-Western political union "Alliance of Patriots" won a number of seats in the Parliament. The coalition's leaders openly expressed their negative attitude toward Georgia's Western orientation.

Anti-Western populism in Georgia is largely based on negative stereotypes. It appeals to such sensitive and vulnerable topics as territorial disintegration, Orthodox Christian religion, socio-economic issues and poverty, traditional values, family, relationships between sexes, etc.

According to Jondi Baghaturia, one of the leaders of the anti-Western political wing, Georgians have not obtained any benefits as a result of nearly 30 years of pro-Western orientation. Only the political establishment has become richer, while a major portion of the population is suffering. The country has lost territories, and the prospects of their reintegration are becoming vaguer and vaguer. According to Baghaturia, the Russian aggression against Georgia is just an answer to the latter's pro-Western policy, and Georgia would not have fallen victim to this aggression if not for this policy. Baghaturia accuses Western states of being responsible for the hardships affecting Georgia since its independence and also notes that the West has been indifferent to Georgia's problems all this time.[34]

"Where do we want to penetrate? Into NATO or into Sokhumi?"[35] asked opposition MP Ada Marshania while referring to prospects of the territorial reintegration of Georgia. She noted that Georgians must make a choice between the restoration of territorial integrity and Euro-Atlantic integration. The decision to join a Western organization a priori means the rejection of lost territories.[36] The former Chair of the Georgian Parliament, Nino Burjanadze, has also made similar

---

[33] "Letter of Cultural Workers" (2018), accessed March 31, 2020, https://for.ge/index.php/view/50907/kulturis-muSakebis-werili-romelmac-sazogadoebaSi-didi-aJiotaJi-gamoiwvia.html.
[34] Jondi Baghaturia, "Interview" (2017), accessed March 31, 2020, https://www.myvideo.ge/v/3237062.
[35] The capital of Abkhazia, a breakaway region of Georgia occupied by the Russian Federation.
[36] Ada Marshania, "What do we want from NATO and the EU," December 31, 2016, Video, 1:37, https://www.youtube.com/watch?v=aBOqnC1QZMY.

declarations. According to her, the lost territories should be viewed as a price paid by Georgia in return for its membership of Western organizations. It should be noted that Burjanadze was one of the leaders of the "Rose Revolution." While Chair of the Georgian Parliament, she actively made pro-Western statements. After the conflict with President Saakashvili, she moved to the opposition. Since then, she has been trying to take advantage of anti-Western public attitudes and the disappointment of some Georgians in the Western states.[37]

Conclusion

Since Georgia's independence, the issue of her relationships with the West has turned into a key problem for Georgian society. An analysis of the empirical material has enabled us to distinguish two radically opposed and, at the same time, interrelated tendencies, widespread in the past decades. The relationship of Georgia with the West is characterized by official closeness, a pro-Western political course, attempts at an adaptation with the Western space, and certain achievements in this regard. On the other hand, the closer the country becomes to the West, the more enhanced and organized anti-Western populism is. Demonization of the West takes place parallel to its political idealization and gradually influences the part of the population that is dissatisfied and disappointed with Georgia's Western-oriented policy.

Speaking of anti-Western populism and its influence, we should take into consideration the following factors:

1. Georgians have often been disappointed with Georgian-Western relationships. This disappointment has frequently been caused by exaggerated expectations on the part of Georgians regarding their integration with Western organizations and the interference of the West in the processes taking place in Georgia. This disappointment has created a certain space, which is filled with anti-Western populism. Ideologists of this populism manipulate the above-mentioned problem and try to take advantage of the anti-Western attitudes that are widespread in society.
2. Georgia's post-Soviet transformation was characterized by dramatic events. In processes of transition, when state institutions are weak, there are frequent cases of identity crisis, despair, nostalgia for a glorious past, and ultra-

---

37 Nino Burjanadze, "People must decide – Abkhazia and Samachablo or NATO," November 18, 2014, Video, 9:18, https://www.youtube.com/watch?v=mQaOkms6A3s.

nationalist attitudes. The environment is favorable for populist politicians and public figures, hence they manipulate public opinion.
3. Georgia's Soviet experience plays an important role because a major portion of society has long lived in conditions of anti-Western propaganda. These people, including representatives of the former Soviet intelligentsia, are emotionally close to the Russian space and feel nostalgic about the Soviet past. Thus, this group assesses Georgia's Western orientation negatively.
4. Another important factor is Georgia's longstanding isolation from the West. In fact, Georgians discovered the Western world only in the past decades. In Georgian society, there are numerous negative stereotypes and prejudices regarding the West. These prejudices are chiefly connected with the Western lifestyle and vision. Along with other factors, this fact is due to the lack of information about the West. Anti-Western organizations actively manipulate these factors; moreover, they themselves create numerous negative stereotypes.
5. Lastly, we should emphasize the factor of Russia, which views the Euro-Atlantic organizations in the Caucasus as the main threat to its interests. Anti-Western populism is actively supported by pro-Russian political and public organizations in Georgia. These organizations appeal to the idea of common religion and longstanding close relationships between Georgia and Russia. The role of Russia in the above-mentioned processes is far greater than we have discussed in the given paper. This is an issue that deserves a separate discussion, and, at this stage, it is not part of this article's aims.

The present contribution has analyzed the key factors and tendencies of Georgia's attitudes toward the West since the country's independence. Numerous important issues have been left out at this stage, but these issues are planned to be analyzed during further research.

Works Cited

Baghaturia, Jondi. "Interview." Filmed April 2017. Video, 2: 43. https://www.myvideo.ge/v/3237062.

Barrington, Lowell W. "Nationalism & Independence." In *After Independence: The Making and Protection of the Nation in Postcolonial and Postcommunist States*, edited by Lowell W. Barrington, 3–30. Michigan: University of Michigan Press, 2006.

Brisku, Adrian. "So Far and Yet So Near. The Image of Europe in Georgia: A History of Ideas." May 5, 2017. https://ge.boell.org/ka/2017/05/05/ase-shors-da-mainc-ase-axlos-evropis-saxe-xati-sakartveloshi-ideata-istoria.

Brubaker, Rogers. *Ethnicity without Groups*. Cambridge, MA: Harvard University Press, 2006.

Burjanadze, Nino. "People must decide – Abkhazia and Samachablo or NATO!" November 18, 2014. Video, 9:18. https://www.youtube.com/watch?v=mQaOkms6A3s.
Canovan, Margaret. *Populism*. New York/London: Harcourt Brace Jovanovich, 1981.
Canovan, Margaret. *The People*. Cambridge: Polity Press, 2005.
Chkhaidze, Irakli. "From Ethnic to Civic Nationalism: The Dynamics of the National Project in Post-Soviet Georgia." PhD Thesis, Tbilisi State University, 2016.
Coene, Frederik. *Euro-Atlantic Discourse in Georgia: The Making of Georgian Foreign and Domestic Policy After the Rose Revolution*. London/New York: Routledge, 2016.
Constitution of Georgia. 1995. Retrieved from http://www.parliament.ge/ge/kanonmdebloba/constitution-of-georgia-68.
De Cleen, Benjamin and Yannis Stavrakakis. "Distinctions and Articulations: A Discourse Theoretical Framework for the Study of Populism and Nationalism." *Javnost – The Public: Journal of the European Institute for Communication and Culture* 24 (2017): 301–319.
Gamsakhurdia, Zviad. "Address to the Georgian people." *Kartuli Azri* 24, 1992.
Gamsakhurdia, Zviad. "Interview." *Aghdgoma* 20, 1992.
Gamsakhurdia, Zviad. *Spiritual Mission of Georgia*. Tbilisi: Ganatleba, 1990.
Gellner, Ernest and Ghita Lonescu. *Populism: Its Meanings and National Characteristics*. Garden City Press, 1969.
Jones, Stephen F. "Georgia: Nationalism from under the Rubble." In *After Independence: The Making and Protection of the Nation in Postcolonial and Postcommunist States*, edited by Lowell W. Barrington, 248–276. Ann Arbor, MI: University of Michigan Press, 2006.
Jones, Stephen F. *Georgia: A Political History since Independence*. London: I.B. Tauris, 2013.
Jones, Stephen F. *Socialism in Georgian Colors: The European Road to Social Democracy, 1883–1917*. Cambridge, MA: Harvard University Press, 2005.
Jørgensen, Marianne and Louise Phillips. *Discourse Analysis as Theory and Method*. London: Sage Publications, 2002.
Kakitelashvili, Tamar. "The West in the Georgian Consciousness." *Language and Culture* 1 (2000): 47–54.
Law on Citizenship. 1993. Retrieved from http://mra.gov.ge/res/docs/2013110412031013274.pdf.
Letter of Cultural Workers. 2018. Retrieved from https://for.ge/index.php/view/50907/kulturis-muSakebis-werili-romelmac-sazogadoebaSi-didi-aJiotaJi-gamoiwvia.html.
Marshania, Ada. "What do we want from NATO and the EU." December 31, 2016. Video, 1: 37. https://www.youtube.com/watch?v=aBOqnC1QZMY.
Moffitt, Benjamin. *The Global Rise of Populism: Performance, Political Style, and Representation*. Stanford: Stanford University Press, 2016.
Nodia, Ghia. "The Idea of the West in the Georgian Consciousness." In *Society and Politics* 2 (1999): 35–74.
Saakashvili, Mikheil. "Address to the People." 2013. http://tradebridgeconsultants.com/news/government/president-mikheil-saakashvili-delivers-annual-address-in-national-library/.
Sharadze, Guram. "Interview." 1999. https://guramsharadze.wordpress.com/devnili/erovnebis-rekviziti/.
Suny, Ronald Grigor. *The Making of the Georgian Nation*. 2nd ed. Bloomington, IN: Indiana University Press, 1994.
Vasadze, Levan. "Interview." 2013. https://www.kvirispalitra.ge/politic/17206–levanvasadzeim-?all=1&add_new=0&reply=0.
Wheatley, Jonathan. *Georgia from National Awakening to Rose Revolution: Delayed Transition in the Former Soviet Union*. London/New York: Routledge, 2005.

Muhammad A. Z. Mughal
8 New Media and the Narratives of National Identity and Nationalism: A Pakistani Case Study

Introduction

Pakistani national identity has always been associated with Islam since the country was created in 1947. Therefore, Pakistani identity and nationalism are represented through symbols and narratives of Muslim identity in specific religious, historical, and political contexts. The production and dissemination of these symbols and narratives have been limited to traditional media for local consumption until recently. However, an overwhelming use of digital technologies, particularly social media, has given rise to new trends in expressing Pakistani identity, which involve religious symbolism, narratives of modernity, regional cultures, and digital art forms. These expressions in new media, particularly social media, have reasserted the central ideas associated with Pakistani identity while shaping up the ways of representing national symbolism differently in a globalized world. This contribution explores the expressions of Pakistani national identity and nationalism in new media as a transnational space.

The ideologies of integration vs. fragmentation, "us" vs. "them," and borders vs. borderlines are being reshaped in a rapidly changing globalized world.[1] These changing circumstances raise many questions regarding how we describe and analyze identity and nationalism in global and transnational contexts. There is a great deal of literature available to highlight the relationship between mass media and diaspora communities in transnational frameworks.[2] The use of social media has increased in the last few years in education, entertainment, politics, and social movements.[3] Social media is a transnational space, which creates, reacts to, and inspires not only local or national issues but also international situations. Through the interactive nature of social media, different communities and

---

[1] Sheila Croucher, *Globalization and Belonging: The Politics of Identity in a Changing World* (Lanham, MD: Rowman & Littlefield, 2018).
[2] Wanning Sun and John Sinclair, eds., *Media and Communication in the Chinese Diaspora: Rethinking Transnationalism* (London: Routledge, 2015); Kyong Yoon, *Digital Mediascapes of Transnational Korean Youth Culture* (London: Routledge, 2019).
[3] Ramsha Jahangir, "How Social Media has Become a War Zone for Competing Narratives," *Dawn*, January 2, 2019, https://herald.dawn.com/news/1398759.

Open Access. © 2021 Muhammad A. Z. Mughal, published by De Gruyter. This work is licensed under the Creative Commons Attribution-NonCommercial-NoDerivatives 4.0 International License.
https://doi.org/10.1515/9783110729290-008

cultures come in contact with each other and can support or challenge different ideas. Therefore, there is an emerging interest related to social media research on identity and nationalism.[4] Although TV programs and newspapers discuss the trends in social media, very little research is available about social media's use and its impact on society in Pakistan.

This study will explore some new ways of studying the dynamics of Pakistani identity. Pakistani traditional media has been state-owned or has been facing difficult times under different military as well as civil regimes. Several private TV channels started operating in Pakistan from 2000 onward, and their number is ever-growing. However, international organizations have always questioned the governmental control and regulation on print and electronic media regarding the freedom of the press. Due to the uncontrolled nature of new media, several controversial issues are highlighted in social media, which may otherwise be impossible to discuss. This chapter draws on nationalistic symbolism in the digital space, mainly YouTube, Twitter, and Facebook, and the related narratives of nationalism and identity in these platforms contributed by online communities. As identity is ever-changing and evolving, this contribution argues social media in contemporary times provides ways for marginal voices to contribute meaningfully in shaping or reshaping nationalism through alternative expressions and symbolism.

Identity, Nationalism, and New Media

There are various perspectives on identity in different scholarly traditions. However, according to a broader understanding, identity is regarded as socially constructed, fragmented, fluid, and fractured.[5] It is "constructed across different, often intersecting and antagonistic, discourses, practices and positions."[6] Some theorists describe national identity as a postcolonial product. For instance, according to Homi Bhabha, identity has several interconnected and multi-layered

---

[4] Abida Eijaz, "Impact of New Media on Dynamics of Pakistan Politics," *Journal of Political Studies* 20, no. 1 (2013): 113–130; Maqsood Ahmad Shaheen, "Use of Social Networks and Information Seeking Behavior of Students during Political Crises in Pakistan: A Case Study," *The International Information & Library Review* 40, no. 3 (2008): 142–147.

[5] Fredrik Barth, *Ethnic Groups and Boundaries: The Social Organization of Culture Difference* (Oslo: Universitetsforlaget, 1969); Peter J. Burke and Jan E. Stets, *Identity Theory* (Oxford: Oxford University Press, 2009).

[6] Stuart Hall, "Who Needs 'Identity'?," in *Identity: A Reader*, ed. Paul du Gay, Jessica Evans and Peter Redman (London: Sage Publications, 2000), 15–30.

forms that negotiate multiple sources of identification such as language, religion, race, and migration in postcolonial perspectives.[7] The discussions and debates about national identity and nationalism are not completed without the idea of state-formation. Nationalism and the state weave a complicated and, at times, elusive relationship. According to Ernest Gellner (1925–1995):

> In fact, nations, like states, are a contingency, and not a universal necessity. Neither nations nor states exist at all times and in all circumstances. Moreover, nations and states are not the same contingency. Nationalism holds that they were destined for each other; that either without the other is incomplete, and constitutes a tragedy. But before they could become intended for each other, each of them had to emerge, and their emergence was independent and contingent. The state has certainly emerged without the help of the nation. Some nations have certainly emerged without the blessings of their own state. It is more debatable whether the normative idea of the nation, in its modern sense, did not presuppose the prior existence of the state.[8]

Benedict Anderson (1936–2015) describes the imagined aspect of the nation, in which individuals build on mass media to imagine their own and others' membership in a nation state.[9] Nations can be differentiated from other forms of "imagined community" by their size, borders, and sovereignty. Anderson argues every nation is an "imagined community," "because the members of even the smallest nation will never know most of their fellow-members, meet them, or even hear of them, yet in the minds of each lives the image of their communion."[10] These communities are differentiated by various forms of narratives, myths, and stories, which are important with their power to explain the relationship between the "imagined community" and the personal sense of belonging. Nations use mass media to promote national identity by constructing a sense of belonging through emotions and cultural symbols that eventually become integral to national symbolism.

Mass media have been classified variously based on their technologies, mainly print and electronic forms. Mass media are used for mass communication – a two-way process in which the message or information is sent from the sender to the receiver through the medium/channel and the latter sends feedback to the former. However, the interaction between the sender and the receiver has been limited by the technologies used in the mass media, even in radio and television. Therefore, the audience has mostly been passively receiving and or even accepting the media

---

7 Homi K. Bhabha, *The Location of Culture* (London: Routledge, 1994).
8 Ernest Gellner, *Nations and Nationalism* (Ithaca, NY: Cornell University Press, 1983), 6–7.
9 Benedict Anderson, *Imagined Communities: Reflections on the Origin and Spread of Nationalism* (London: Verso, 1983).
10 Ibid., 6.

realities through these channels. This view has mostly been supported by the agenda-setting theory. However, the Internet has changed this scenario. The audience is now alternatively playing the role of receiver as well as sender by using different social media platforms such as Facebook, Twitter, Instagram, and TikTok.[11] New media has thus become a sphere of communication in which new online activists have become influential in competition with traditional political elite actors.[12]

In the 1960s, when Marshall McLuhan (1911–1980) presented his ideas regarding the Internet and the global village, these remained unpopular in the beginning. However, he termed the next form of media as an "extension of consciousness" in which humans would have the ability to interact with the rest of the world in a completely different "communicative act."[13] This had never been so obvious before the advent of the Internet and social media communication. In other words, individuals can now cross national boundaries digitally to interact with "others" in a transnational context.

The uses and gratifications theory, as proposed by Jay Blumler and Elihu Katz, describes how a medium will be used more when the existing motives to use the medium lead to more satisfaction.[14] People use different media for different purposes, such as entertainment, news, and education. A growing number of social media users (e.g. Facebook currently claims to have more than 1.7 billion active users) indicate people's interest in not just receiving information and ideas but also in sharing and spreading their views. It is beyond any doubt that social media has proven to be an effective instrument in enhancing "social capital," as developed by Pierre Bourdieu (1930–2002).[15] Therefore, social media has emerged as an unparalleled platform for public mobilization in social and political movements. For example, social media has been accused of shaping or rather directing voting trends in the USA in recent presidential

---

[11] Henry Jenkins, Sam Ford and Joshua Green, *Spreadable Media: Creating Value and Meaning in a Networked Culture* (New York: New York University Press, 2013).

[12] Ivan B. Dylko, Michael A. Beam, Kristen D. Landreville and Nick Geidner, "Filtering 2008 U.S. Presidential Election News on YouTube by Elites and Nonelites: An Examination of the Democratizing Potential of the Internet," *New Media & Society* 14, no. 5 (2012): 832–849; Julian Ausserhofer and Axel Maireder, "National Politics on Twitter: Structures and Topics of a Networked Public Sphere. Information," *Communication & Society* 16, no. 3 (2013): 291–314;

[13] Marshall McLuhan, *Understanding Media: The Extensions of Man* (New York: McGraw Hill, 1964).

[14] Jay Blumler and Elihu Katz, *The Uses of Mass Communication: Current Perspectives on Gratification Research* (Beverly Hills: Sage Publications, 1974).

[15] Pierre Bourdieu, "The Forms of Capital," in *Handbook of Theory and Research for Sociology of Education*, ed. Dalam J. Richardson (Westport, CT: Greenwood Press, 1986), 241–258.

elections, which led to a legal and political crisis in the country. Similarly, during the "Arab Spring"[16] and the "Russian Spring,"[17] social media provided protestors and activists with an important, and perhaps the only, platform for organizing protests, awareness-raising, lobbying, and networking. In India, social media has been blamed for fueling the rise of extremism, indicating the power of online communities.[18] It is thus not surprising that governments are increasingly concerned with the use of social media, which poses challenges for, but which are not limited to, privacy rights, freedom of rights, and data protection.[19]

Anthony D. Smith (1939–2016) regarded "narrators" (politicians and intellectuals) as important in nation-building processes because the primary roles in the "invention" of a nation are played by "invented traditions."[20] These traditions are communitarian and serve as symbolic markers of the social cohesion of a nation. The "narration" of a nation involves the construction of associated phenomena such as national symbols, myths, and histories. Therefore, the nation provides and serves the interests of a given polity and constitutes the sense of belonging and attachment to the community through shared consciousness. Further, the sense of national community draws heavily on national symbols and myths as parts of its "narration," where the central role in the creation of a sense of community is played by power elites and intellectuals.[21] The myths, symbols, and narratives that shape an "imagined community" today can be traced online in new media where an ordinary member contributes to these

---

[16] Kawa Hassan, "Making Sense of the Arab Spring: Listening to the Voices of Middle Eastern Activists," *Development* 55, no. 2 (2012): 232–238.

[17] Ivan Kozachenko, "Retelling Old Stories with New Media: National Identity and Transnationalism in the "Russian Spring" Popular Uprisings," *East/West: Journal of Ukrainian Studies* 4, no. 1 (2017): 137–158.

[18] Humera Lodhi, Yehyun Kim and Sudipto Maity, "How Social Media is Fueling the Rise of Nationalism and Extremism," *St. Louis Post-Dispatch*, last modified May 12, 2018, https://www.stltoday.com/news/national/govt-and-politics/how-social-media-is-fueling-the-rise-of-nationalism-and/article_71b64021-c958-5fc7-9da4-19414e69d1fe.html.

[19] Ashfaq Ahmed, "Crackdown Starts on 'Misuse' of Social Media in Pakistan," *Gulf News*, February 25, 2019, https://gulfnews.com/world/asia/pakistan/crackdown-starts-on-misuse-of-social-media-in-pakistan-1.62303683; Yasir Hussain, "Social Media as a Tool for Transparency and Good Governance in the Government of Gilgit-Baltistan, Pakistan," *Crossroads Asia Working Paper Series* 22 (University of Bonn, 2014).

[20] Anthony D. Smith, "The Nation: Invented, Imagined, Reconstructed?" *Millennium: Journal of International Studies* 20, no. 3 (1991): 353–368.

[21] Philip Schlesinger, "Media, the Political Order and National Identity," *Media, Culture & Society* 13, no. 3 (1991): 297–308; Aline Sierp, "National Days: Constructing and Mobilizing National Identity," *National Identities* 16, no. 2 (2014): 182–184.

processes. The online representation of national identity is "crystallized" based on a limited set of symbols and narratives on the Internet. Brenda Chan argues that due to these limitations, the online representation of national identity provides distinct options for national belonging (e.g. "patriotic" vs. "critical").[22]

The colonial cultural categories identified the Occident/West as privileged and superior while positioning the Orient/non-West as inferior.[23] The postcolonial approach seeks to analyze and deconstruct practices of neo-colonialism both in Western and non-Western societies. It introduced the notions of multiple, overlapping, and intersecting identity markers or, in other words, hybrid identities. According to Homi K. Bhabha and Jonathan Rutherford, identity is constructed between ever-changing binaries, forces, and cultural influences in the form of global and local, East and West, and national and foreign.[24] Similarly, modern social, cultural, and economic narratives lead to a postmodern perception of self, nations, and cultures. They explain the notion of hybrid identities between various sources of affinity including locality, nationality, religion, race, and ethnicity through the "third space." The third space is a notional realm in which social structures are rearticulated, which underpins the agency of creating the changing expressions of hybrid identities in the postcolonial age. As James Carey noted, mass media work as "national equipment" to construct a shared reality and identity.[25] Consequently, individuals formulate hybrid notions of self by constructing multiple and hybrid media texts.[26]

In light of the above discussions, the following pages present how Pakistani national identity narratives play out in social media. These narratives must be seen through identity discourses theoretically and within the context of Pakistani nationalism and identity.

---

[22] Brenda Chan, "Virtual Communities and Chinese National Identity," *Journal of Chinese Overseas* 2, no. 1 (2006): 1–32.
[23] Edward Said, *Orientalism* (New York: Vintage Books, 1978).
[24] Homi K. Bhabha and Jonathan Rutherford, "Third Space," *Multitudes* 3 (2006): 95–107.
[25] James W. Carey, *Communication as Culture: Essays on Media and Society* (New York: Routledge, 1989).
[26] Marwan M. Kraidy, *Hybridity, or the Cultural Logic of Globalization* (Philadelphia, PA: Temple University Press, 2005).

Pakistani National Identity, Nationalism, and Social Media

Pakistan is located at the crossroads of the Persian Gulf, South Asia, and Central Asia. This location gives geographic, cultural, and ethnic diversity to Pakistan. The country is also home to many ancient civilizations such as the Indus Valley and Gandhara. Many nations and cultures such as the Greeks, Persians, Turks, Arabs, Mughals, and British invaded the area at different times.[27] Therefore, Pakistan has diverse cultures due to a complex history, migrations, wars, calamities, and diverse geographic features, among other factors. The existence of more than 73 living languages and dialects in Pakistan today explains these historical contacts with different cultures.[28] Despite all the cultural diversity, as anthropologist Stephen Lyon notes, "there are patterns of roles, values and world-views which run across the nation."[29] However, since the country's inception, the Pakistani state and societies have always been dealing with the challenging aspects of statecraft and nationalism that gave rise to several political and ethnic tensions.

During the British Raj, Muslim leaders realized that their religious and political rights would not be saved if the British left India because Hindus were in the majority and had a hostile attitude toward Muslims. The Pakistan Movement started as a result of the Two-nation Theory which states that Muslims and Hindus are two separate nations by definition.[30] According to this ideology, Muslims are different from Hindus based on religion, customs, and traditions; therefore, they should have the right to have their own separate country. Consequently, Pakistan came into being in 1947 as a result of the Partition of British India. Given the historical context of the Pakistan Movement, the country's identity has always been defined through Islam, with its Muslim character being its vital and central dimension.[31] There have always been tensions between modernist and

---

[27] Burjor Avari, *Islamic Civilization in South Asia: A History of Muslim Power and Presence in the Indian Subcontinent* (London: Routledge, 2013); Iftikhar Haider Malik, *The History of Pakistan* (New York: Greenwood Publishing Group, 2008).
[28] Gary F. Simons and Charles D. Fenning, "Pakistan," in *Ethnologue: Languages of the World*, 21st ed. (SIL International), accessed May 2, 2020, https://www.ethnologue.com/country/pk.
[29] Stephen M. Lyon, *An Anthropological Analysis of Local Politics and Patronage in a Pakistani Village* (Lampeter: Edwin Mellen Press, 2004), 4.
[30] Abdul Majid, Abdul Hamid and Zahida Habib, "Genesis of the Two Nations Theory and the Quaid-e-Azam," *Pakistan Vision* 15, no. 1 (2014): 180–192.
[31] Akbar S. Ahmed, *Jinnah, Pakistan and Islamic Identity Search for Saladin* (London: Routledge, 1997).

conservative voices in the country over Pakistani identity, modernity, and Islamic values. Indeed, Pakistani society has always presented a blend of tradition and modernity. This blend manifests through marriage ceremonies, symbolism, dress patterns, social norms, politics, and the multiple education systems in the country.[32] Pakistanis make their choices between tradition and modernity through a collective awareness of their needs and aspirations for the future.[33]

The nationalism and national identity of Pakistan have been represented through Islamic symbols in textbooks, television, movies, and other forms of mass media since 1947.[34] In traditional Pakistani media, the narratives and symbolism for national identity have been limited to religious symbolism or the ideas inspired by the Pakistan Movement in specific ways. Some of these symbols include Arabic calligraphy, the depiction of the Quran, the crescent, and the color green. Some historical Muslim figures such as Saladin (1137/38–1193) and Tariq ibn Ziyad (d. 720) are depicted as heroes in textbooks due to their services to Islam, though they did not belong to the area now called Pakistan. For a significant part of Pakistan's history, the country has experienced military dictatorships. Even under democratic regimes, the traditional media has mostly been following the conservative ideologies as laid out by the political elites. Similarly, ethnicities and other factors play an important role in the credibility of the traditional media in the country.[35] However, social media has brought about the possibilities of seeing how common Pakistanis see themselves and others. Some recent studies suggest that social media is gaining an increasing acceptance and legitimacy in Pakistan regarding politics and other social affairs.[36]

---

32 Mohammad Qadeer, *Pakistan: Social and Cultural Transformations in a Muslim Nation* (London: Routledge, 2006).
33 Muhammad A. Z. Mughal, "Calendars Tell History: Social Rhythm and Social Change in Rural Pakistan," *History and Anthropology* 25, no. 5 (2014): 592–613; Muhammad A. Z. Mughal, "Time in Flux: Daily and Weekly Rhythms in Rural Pakistan," *Asian Ethnology* 76, no. 2 (2017): 261–287; Muhammad A. Z. Mughal, "Exchange Relations and Social Change in Rural Pakistan: Rituals and Ceremonies of Childbirth, Marriage and Death," *South Asia Research* 38, no. 2 (2018): 177–194.
34 Naureen Durrani and Máiréad Dunne, "Curriculum and National Identity: Exploring the Links between Religion and Nation in Pakistan," *Journal of Curriculum Studies* 42, no. 2 (2010): 215–240.
35 KyuJin Shim, Guy J. Golan, Anita G. Day, and Sung-Un Yang, "Beyond the Western Masses: Demography and Perceptions of the Credibility of Pakistani Media," *International Journal of Communication* 9, no. 1 (2015): 2282–2305.
36 Shaheen, "Social Networks," 146–147; Dhiraj Murthy and Scott A. Longwell, "Twitter and Disasters: The Uses of Twitter During the 2010 Pakistan Floods," *Information, Communication & Society* 16, no. 6 (2013): 837–855.

Internet penetration rate is increasing in Pakistan at a high pace due to smartphone usage, while social media platforms and blogs are among the most popular sites.[37] Despite this high use of new media in Pakistan, there is a gap in understanding how social media use comes into dialogue with some of the fundamentals of Pakistani identity and nationalism, at least those that have emerged over the course of history under different political regimes.

Methodology

This study is mainly qualitative in design and uses the content analysis of Internet sources including blogs and social media. Social media websites and mobile applications such as Facebook, YouTube, and Twitter have high numbers of users. This chapter uses the interpretive thematic analysis of videos, images, and narratives shared on social media to explore the users' opinions. The content analysis was applied in order to understand expressions of national identity, agendas, and types of information distributed on social media. A "layered analysis" between text, images, and videos is used to compare different forms of social media, groups, and themes.[38]

There are several legal and ethical issues regarding the use of social media or general Internet content for research. It has been argued that publically available content that does not require a password and is accessible through search engines can be used for research purposes with proper citations.[39] However, quotes and images are usually subject to copyright; therefore, these cannot be reproduced without formal permission. In this contribution, publically available information is consequently used for analysis purposes.

---

[37] Huma Yusuf, *Mapping Digital Media: Pakistan* (London: Open Society Foundations, 2013); Pakistan Telecommunication Authority, "Telecom Indicators," last modified December 2019, https://www.pta.gov.pk/en/telecom-indicators.
[38] George W. Dowdall and Janet Golden, "Photographs as Data: An Analysis of Images from a Mental Hospital," *Qualitative Sociology* 12, no. 2 (1989): 183–213.
[39] Jennifer Attride-Stirling, "Thematic Networks: An Analytic Tool for Qualitative Research," *Qualitative Research* 1, no. 3 (2001): 385–405; Virginia Braun and Victoria Clarke, "Thematic Analysis," in *APA Handbook of Research Methods in Psychology*, ed. Harris Cooper (Washington, DC: American Psychological Association, 2012), 57–71.

Narratives and Symbolism of Pakistani Identity and Nationalism on Social Media

There are a lot of examples of the narratives and symbolism of Pakistani identity and nationalism on different social media platforms on the Internet. These represent conservative, traditional voices as well as alternative perspectives through different expressions. Here, these alternative voices as expressed in narratives and symbolism on different social media platforms are presented to highlight how they negotiate expressions generated by and used in traditional media.

Everyday Creativities on Social Media

There is an emerging interest in media studies about the use of the everyday creativities of non-professional artists who use simple mobile phone applications or cameras to share pictures, drawings, poetry, or jokes.[40] Several modernist and liberal images of Pakistan are freely shared on social media and are not easily shown on traditional media. TikTok is one such application where Pakistani boys and girls make parodies or perform mimicries of different songs and famous movies or drama dialogues. Some of these videos present users singing Pakistani national songs in such ways that were neither produced nor tolerated, if ever created, in traditional forms of media.

Another interesting fact regarding most of these everyday creativities on social media, whether posts or tweets, is that the founder of Pakistan, Muhammad Ali Jinnah (1876–1948), is shown as a young person in contrast to his conventional portrayal in traditional media as an old person (which in the Pakistani cultural context is a symbol of respect). One such example is Twitter, where the hashtags #jinnah and #quaid-e-azam present various photos of Jinnah. Several of these photos in which Jinnah's image as a young person is that of a Westernized man that sometimes contradicts the literalist, conservative thought in the country are liked or retweeted by users. Jinnah is also seen as a model of being a good Muslim and true Pakistani (from conservative perspectives). Sharing

---

40 Kate Pahl, "Everyday Creativity," in *The SAGE Encyclopedia of Out-of-School Learning*, ed. Kylie Peppler (New York: Sage Publications, 2017), 263–266.

and liking these photos on social media indicates the acceptance of Jinnah with all his different personality traits and the idealism that the country's youth perceive regarding him as a moderate Muslim. Further, Pakistani users also debate with Indian users over Jinnah and Gandhi to justify their opinions about the former. This creates an open space in a transnational context to redefine or negotiate the traditional expression of how nationalism or national identity has been asserted in local textbooks and television.

Presentation of Kalasha and Other Non-Muslim Cultures

Pakistani textbooks and other traditional mass media always discuss Pakistani identity through Islam and Islamic symbols. The main sites of the Indus Valley, Mohenjo-daro and Harappa, are located in Pakistan. The Indus Valley civilization takes its name from the Indus River that runs mainly through Pakistan. India has embraced the Indus Valley civilization as its markers of identity in contrast to Pakistan where no cultural affiliation or continuity is acknowledged with this civilization in formal ways. The history and Pakistan Studies textbooks do mention ancient civilizations and some other cultures; however, as historian Ayesha Jalal notes, Pakistani identity is typically described through the Islamic history of this area.[41]

National identity in the Pakistani context is defined through Islam, and only Islamic markers of national identity have been used in the traditional media for decades. There are several non-Muslim communities living in Pakistan, such as Hindus, Sikhs, Christians, and Kalasha. Kalasha culture has always attracted foreign media, anthropologists, and international researchers due to its uniqueness within the Pakistani or South Asian cultural landscape. However, many Islamist groups have used the word *kafir* (infidel) for them to distinguish or exclude them from the mainstream Pakistani Muslim society. In many folktales of the community living nearby Kalasha, their area was described as Kafiristan (the land of infidels). Kalasha have rarely been represented as an integral part of the expressions of Pakistani identity and national symbols in textbooks, for instance.

This scenario has changed recently due to social media. Kalasha costumes and dances are almost an integral part of many YouTube videos, Twitter hashtags, and Facebook posts that contain Pakistani culture or even the national an-

---

[41] Ayesha Jalal, "Conjuring Pakistan: History as Official Imagining," *International Journal of Middle East Studies* 27, no. 1 (1995): 73–89.

them or patriotic songs.[42] Similarly, many Pakistani Muslim users congratulate their social media friends on the occasion of Hindu and Sikh festivals. Sikh personnel in the Pakistani police and military are shown with pride and regarded as national celebrities. Embracing Kalasha, Hinduism, and Sikhism as Pakistani cultures and religions helps present the cultural diversity of Pakistan and associates national identity beyond the bonds of Islamic identity and affiliation.

DNA Test Results Videos

There is a general perception about and among Pakistanis that the majority of them came from different regions such as Arabia, Persia, and Central Asia. Showing ancestral links to other nations has been considered as a matter of pride. In India, many Hindu activists still consider all Muslims of South Asia as foreign invaders or their offspring. Many Pakistanis believe that the ethnic groups living in the country have nothing in common except Islam. This has also been discussed by several intellectuals as being the reason behind the lack of ownership of the country by its citizens. However, some interesting YouTube videos in which users discuss their DNA test results show very different perceptions. Most of them describe how happy they feel after knowing that their ancestry belongs mostly to Pakistani regions.

These videos do not directly point to any ethnic discussions regarding local vs. muhajir, Sindhi vs. Urdu speaker, Pukhtoon vs. Afghani, or "son of the soil" vs. outsiders.[43] This does not mean that such ethnic divides do not exist anymore. However, such videos propagate a message of one feeling proud of one's ancestral connection to Pakistan. The context of Pakistani identity and nationalism only being defined through Islam or through an ethnic group in Pakistan is not new. However, taking pride in Pakistani ancestry regardless of religion and ethnicity is something that has been more recently expressed in the media. A significant majority of these videos are made by users of Pakistani origin belonging to the Pakistani diaspora and holding citizenship of the USA or other Western countries as per their introduction in these videos. These videos are

---

42 See, for example, Facebook, "Kalasha People," last modified May 25, 2020, https://www.facebook.com/watch/KalashaPeople/.

43 There is a great deal of literature available about ethnic fissures in Pakistan. See Farhan H. Siddiqi, "Intra-ethnic Fissures in Ethnic Movements: The Rise of Mohajir Identity Politics in Post-1971 Pakistan," *Asian Ethnicity* 11, no. 1 (2010): 25–41; Maryam S. Khan, "Ethnic Federalism in Pakistan: Federal Design, Construction of Ethno-Linguistic Identity & Group Conflict," *Harvard Journal on Racial and Ethnic Justice* 30 (2014): 77–129.

also made in English, which helps them express their identity not only to their Pakistani audience but also to the global community.

YouTube Videos Showing Reactions to Other Videos

Pakistan and India have been hostile toward each other and have fought over different issues, such as Kashmir, since the Partition of British India. Most Indian movies portray Pakistanis as enemies and Indian textbooks regard Muslim historical figures as invaders and particularly cruel.[44] The situation from Pakistani perspectives is no different. This rivalry continues even in debates on social media. Interestingly, Indian movies are very popular in Pakistan, and Pakistani music and dramas are also popular in India. Both countries also share a few similar languages such as Urdu and Punjabi, which become important means of communication on the Internet outside of English.

Social media has provided ways for Indian and Pakistani users to have friendly relations and accept each other by showing mutual feelings of respect. For example, some YouTube channels make what is categorized as reaction videos. Many of these channels by Indian users exclusively make videos on Pakistani digital content and vice versa. There is a great monetary motive behind most of these YouTube channels as well. Therefore, users tend to be generally positive about the content from the other country to gain more "likes" for their videos or "subscriptions" to their channels. However, this has also created a space for people to see the other side of the coin. In many such videos, they even offer their views on or reactions to those media items which are against their own country. In most cases, these reaction videos are made upon the request of other users.

In such Pakistani videos, even if the users make comparisons between India and Pakistan, their main focus remains friendship between the people of these two countries. They show their curiosity to know more about India and appreciate many good things about Indian culture. In almost all such videos, users from both sides show respect to each other and emphasize developing peace between the two countries.

---

44 Sylvie Guichard, *The Construction of History and Nationalism in India: Textbooks, Controversies and Politics* (London: Routledge, 2010).

Ancestral Village Visits and Partition Memories Videos

During the Partition of British India, millions of people were displaced, injured, and killed in riots.[45] Indian and Pakistani narratives about the Partition favor their own side and blame the other side for all the problems. Sikhs from the Pakistani side migrated to India as a result of the Partition, though they have several religious places in Pakistan. There are YouTube channels that discuss the Partition by talking to people who were alive in 1947.

There are multiple YouTube channels in which Punjabis from India and Pakistan share stories of their ancestral villages or cities on the other side. Some of these videos use both Shahmukhi and Gurumukhi scripts.[46] The channel conducts interviews with the people from several villages of Pakistani Punjab who migrated from the Indian side during the Partition. They discuss details of their ancestral villages. The current residents of those villages often comment on these videos to show their respect for the migrants. Some users also post videos of their ancestral villages or cities. In these videos, while people talk about the havoc of the Partition, they respect the national stances of the other side.

Discussion and Conclusion

Social media platforms help users show positive self-representations to "others" while acknowledging the existing tensions and contradictions between ideologies. Social media has provided the Pakistani youth with opportunities to express and hear marginal and under-represented voices. It will remain a question for times to come whether social media can overcome the traditional power spectrum that is shaped by specific ideological and political attitudes toward identity and nationalism.

As Anderson notes, mass media promote national identity by creating a sense of belonging through emotions and symbols.[47] As mass media are owned and regulated by governments, national identity and nationalism are very much shaped by powerful political elites. However, in today's world, social media stimulates new

---

45 Yasmin Khan, *The Great Partition: The Making of India and Pakistan* (New Haven, CT: Yale University Press, 2017).
46 Sikhs use Gurumukhi while Muslims use the Shahmukhi script of Punjabi.
47 Anderson, *Imagined Communities*.

thoughts and emotions by providing alternative narratives. These alternative narratives may range from moderate to radical voices. In Pakistan, radical voices do exist which at times challenge the very fundamentals of nationalism and national identity. However, this chapter focused only on the narratives that reshape the expressions of identity and nationalism in social media. It has tried to explore how these narratives include marginal voices to be heard not through the perspectives of separation but through integration and inclusiveness. Social media has created a new category of intellectuals who contribute to "invented traditions" in the process of nation building and identity formation.[48] In this process, they do not challenge the basic fundamentals of nationalism or the national identity of Pakistan but in fact reiterate these in different ways, aiming to address the existing national problems.

It is critical to understand whether individualized collective actions have the power to change or reshape national identity without state intervention.[49] Social media is used by governments for various purposes, from services to surveillance.[50] Governments can crack down on alternative radical voices, and they certainly do.[51] However, the Internet and social media cannot be regulated by any government in absolute terms.[52] This relatively unregulated dimension of the Internet has given powers to individuals that can be used for different goals. It is obvious from the examples of social media trends among Pakistani users discussed here that they are contributing to reshaping expressions of Pakistani identity and nationalism. Many of these social media narratives make it into the traditional media in Pakistan, just like elsewhere in the world. Consequently, social media narratives influence state decisions as well. Through this process, it appears that, as state and nation are "independent and contingent,"[53] Pakistani social media users are redefining expressions of national identity and nationalism. Whether this will be influenced by the state is yet to be seen.

---

48 Smith, "The Nation," 353–368.
49 W. Lance Bennett, "The Personalization of Politics: Political Identity, Social Media, and Changing Patterns of Participation," *The ANNALS of the American Academy of Political and Social Science* 644, no. 1 (2012): 20–39; Aya Yaldin-Segal, "Constructing National Identity Online: The Case Study of #IranJeans on Twitter," *International Journal of Communication* 11 (2017): 2760–2783.
50 John Carlo Bertot, Paul T. Jaeger and Derek Hansen, "The Impact of Policies on Government Social Media Usage: Issues, Challenges, and Recommendations," *Government Information Quarterly* 29, no. 1 (2012): 30–40.
51 Ahmed, "Crackdown."
52 Caroline Tynan, "Nationalism in the Age of Social Media," *Temple Libraries' Scholars Studio*, last modified December 13, 2017, https://sites.temple.edu/tudsc/2017/12/13/twitter-bots/.
53 Gellner, *Nations*, 6–7.

Works Cited

Ahmed, Akbar S. *Jinnah, Pakistan and Islamic Identity Search for Saladin*. London: Routledge, 1997.

Ahmed, Ashfaq. "Crackdown Starts on 'Misuse' of Social Media in Pakistan." *Gulf News*, February 25, 2019. https://gulfnews.com/world/asia/pakistan/crackdown-starts-on-misuse-of-social-media-in-pakistan-1.62303683.

Anderson, Benedict. *Imagined Communities: Reflections on the Origin and Spread of Nationalism*. London: Verso, 1983.

Attride-Stirling, Jennifer. "Thematic Networks: An Analytic Tool for Qualitative Research." *Qualitative Research* 1, no. 3 (2001): 385–405.

Ausserhofer, Julian and Axel Maireder. "National Politics on Twitter: Structures and Topics of a Networked Public Sphere. Information." *Communication & Society* 16, no. 3 (2013): 291–314.

Avari, Burjor. *Islamic Civilization in South Asia: A History of Muslim Power and Presence in the Indian Subcontinent*. London: Routledge, 2013.

Barth, Fredrik. *Ethnic Groups and Boundaries: The Social Organization of Culture Difference*. Oslo: Universitetsforlaget, 1969.

Bennett, W. Lance "The Personalization of Politics: Political Identity, Social Media, and Changing Patterns of Participation." *The ANNALS of the American Academy of Political and Social Science* 644, no. 1 (2012): 20–39.

Bertot, John Carlo, Paul T. Jaeger and Derek Hansen. "The Impact of Policies on Government Social Media Usage: Issues, Challenges, and Recommendations." *Government Information Quarterly* 29, no. 1 (2012): 30–40.

Bhabha, Homi K. and Jonathan Rutherford. "Third Space." *Multitudes* 3 (2006): 95–107.

Bhabha, Homi K. *The Location of Culture*. London/New York: Routledge, 1994.

Blumler, Jay and Elihu Katz. *The Uses of Mass Communication: Current Perspectives on Gratification Research*. Beverly Hills: Sage Publications, 1974.

Bourdieu, Pierre. "The Forms of Capital." In *Handbook of Theory and Research for Sociology of Education*, edited by Dalam J. Richardson, 241–258. Westport, CT: Greenwood Press, 1986.

Braun, Virginia and Victoria Clarke. "Thematic Analysis." In *APA Handbook of Research Methods in Psychology*, edited by Harris Cooper, 57–71. Washington, DC: American Psychological Association, 2012.

Burke, Peter J. and Jan E. Stets. *Identity Theory*. Oxford: Oxford University Press, 2009.

Carey, James W. *Communication as Culture: Essays on Media and Society*. New York, NY: Routledge, 1989.

Chan, Brenda. "Virtual Communities and Chinese National Identity." *Journal of Chinese Overseas* 2, no. 1 (2006): 1–32.

Croucher, Sheila. *Globalization and Belonging: The Politics of Identity in a Changing World*. Lanham, MD: Rowman & Littlefield, 2018.

Dowdall, George W. and Janet Golden. "Photographs as Data: An Analysis of Images from a Mental Hospital." *Qualitative Sociology* 12, no. 2 (1989): 183–213.

Durrani, Naureen and Máiréad Dunne. "Curriculum and National Identity: Exploring the Links between Religion and Nation in Pakistan." *Journal of Curriculum Studies* 42, no. 2 (2010): 215–240.

Dylko, Ivan B., Michael A. Beam, Kristen D. Landreville and Nick Geidner. "Filtering 2008 U.S. Presidential Election News on YouTube by Elites and Nonelites: An Examination of the Democratizing Potential of the Internet." *New Media & Society* 14, no. 5 (2012): 832–849.

Eijaz, Abida. "Impact of New Media on Dynamics of Pakistan Politics." *Journal of Political Studies* 20, no. 1 (2013): 113–130.

Facebook. "Kalasha People." Last modified May 25, 2020. https://www.facebook.com/watch/KalashaPeople/.

Gellner, Ernest. *Nations and Nationalism*. Ithaca, NY: Cornell University Press, 1983.

Guichard, Sylvie. *The Construction of History and Nationalism in India: Textbooks, Controversies and Politics*. London: Routledge, 2010.

Hall, Stuart. "Who Needs 'Identity'?" In *Identity: A Reader*, edited by Paul du Gay, Jessica Evans and Peter Redman, 15–30. London: Sage Publications, 2000.

Hassan, Kawa. "Making Sense of the Arab Spring: Listening to the Voices of Middle Eastern Activists." *Development* 55, no. 2 (2012): 232–238.

Hussain, Yasir. "Social Media as a Tool for Transparency and Good Governance in the Government of Gilgit-Baltistan, Pakistan." *Crossroads Asia Working Paper Series* 22. University of Bonn, 2014.

Jahangir, Ramsha. "How Social Media has Become a War Zone for Competing Narratives," *Dawn*, January 2, 2019. https://herald.dawn.com/news/1398759.

Jalal, Ayesha. "Conjuring Pakistan: History as Official Imagining." *International Journal of Middle East Studies* 27, no. 1 (1995): 73–89.

Jenkins, Henry, Sam Ford and Joshua Green. *Spreadable Media: Creating Value and Meaning in a Networked Culture*. New York: New York University Press, 2013.

Khan, Maryam S. "Ethnic Federalism in Pakistan: Federal Design, Construction of Ethno-Linguistic Identity & Group Conflict." *Harvard Journal on Racial and Ethnic Justice* 30 (2014): 77–129.

Khan, Yasmin. *The Great Partition: The Making of India and Pakistan*. New Haven, CT: Yale University Press, 2017.

Kozachenko, Ivan. "Retelling Old Stories with New Media: National Identity and Transnationalism in the "Russian Spring" Popular Uprisings." *East/West: Journal of Ukrainian Studies* 4, no. 1 (2017): 137–158.

Kraidy, Marwan M. *Hybridity, or the Cultural Logic of Globalization*. Philadelphia, PA: Temple University Press, 2005.

Lodhi, Humera, Yehyun Kim and Sudipto Maity. "How Social Media is Fueling the Rise of Nationalism and Extremism." *St. Louis Post-Dispatch*, last modified May 12, 2018. https://www.stltoday.com/news/national/govt-and-politics/how-social-media-is-fueling-the-rise-of-nationalism-and/article_71b64021-c958-5fc7-9da4-19414e69d1fe.html.

Lyon, Stephen M. *An Anthropological Analysis of Local Politics and Patronage in a Pakistani Village*. Lampeter: Edwin Mellen Press, 2004.

Majid, Abdul, Abdul Hamid and Zahida Habib. "Genesis of the Two Nations Theory and the Quaid-e-Azam." *Pakistan Vision* 15, no. 1 (2014): 180–192.

Malik, Iftikhar Haider. *The History of Pakistan*. New York: Greenwood Publishing Group, 2008.

McLuhan, Marshall. *Understanding Media: The Extensions of Man*. New York: McGraw Hill, 1964.

Mughal, Muhammad A. Z. "Calendars Tell History: Social Rhythm and Social Change in Rural Pakistan." *History and Anthropology* 25, no. 5 (2014): 592–613.

Mughal, Muhammad A Z.. "Exchange Relations and Social Change in Rural Pakistan: Rituals and Ceremonies of Childbirth, Marriage and Death." *South Asia Research* 38, no. 2 (2018): 177–194.

Mughal, Muhammad A. Z. "Time in Flux: Daily and Weekly Rhythms in Rural Pakistan." *Asian Ethnology* 76, no. 2 (2017): 261–287.

Murthy, Dhiraj and Scott A. Longwell. "Twitter and Disasters: The Uses of Twitter During the 2010 Pakistan Floods." *Information, Communication & Society* 16, no. 6 (2013): 837–855.

Pahl, Kate. "Everyday Creativity." In *The SAGE Encyclopedia of Out-of-School Learning*, edited by Kylie Peppler, 263–266. New York: Sage Publications, 2017.

Pakistan Telecommunication Authority. "Telecom Indicators." Last modified, December 2019. https://www.pta.gov.pk/en/telecom-indicators.

Qadeer, Mohammad. *Pakistan: Social and Cultural Transformations in a Muslim Nation*. London: Routledge, 2006.

Said, Edward. *Orientalism*. New York: Vintage Books, 1978.

Schlesinger, Philip. "Media, the Political Order and National Identity." *Media, Culture & Society* 13, no. 3 (1991): 297–308.

Shaheen, Maqsood Ahmad. "Use of Social Networks and Information Seeking Behavior of Students during Political Crises in Pakistan: A Case Study." *The International Information & Library Review* 40, no. 3 (2008): 142–147.

Shim, KyuJin, Guy J. Golan, Anita G. Day and Sung-Un Yang. "Beyond the Western Masses: Demography and Perceptions of the Credibility of Pakistani Media." *International Journal of Communication* 9, no. 1 (2015): 2282–2305.

Siddiqi, Farhan H. "Intra-ethnic Fissures in Ethnic Movements: The Rise of Mohajir Identity Politics in Post-1971 Pakistan." *Asian Ethnicity* 11, no. 1 (2010): 25–41.

Sierp, Aline. "National Days: Constructing and Mobilizing National Identity." *National Identities* 16, no. 2 (2014): 182–184.

Simons, Gary F. and Charles D. Fenning. "Pakistan." In *Ethnologue: Languages of the World*. 21st ed. SIL International. https://www.ethnologue.com/country/pk.

Smith, Anthony D. "The Nation: Invented, Imagined, Reconstructed?" *Millennium: Journal of International Studies* 20, no. 3 (1991): 353–368.

Sun, Wanning and John Sinclair, eds. *Media and Communication in the Chinese Diaspora: Rethinking Transnationalism*. London: Routledge, 2015.

Tynan, Caroline. "Nationalism in the Age of Social Media." *Temple Libraries' Scholars Studio*, last modified December 13, 2017. https://sites.temple.edu/tudsc/2017/12/13/twitter-bots/.

Yaldin-Segal, Aya. "Constructing National Identity Online: The Case Study of #IranJeans on Twitter." *International Journal of Communication* 11 (2017): 2760–2783.

Yoon, Kyong. *Digital Mediascapes of Transnational Korean Youth Culture*. London: Routledge, 2019.

Yusuf, Huma. *Mapping Digital Media: Pakistan*. London: Open Society Foundations, 2013.

Section III: **Globalized Nationalisms and their National Frontiers**

Tetiana Perga
9 Eco-Nationalism in the Soviet Union in the Late 1980s and Early 1990s: The Ukrainian Case

Discourse on the problems of eco-nationalism has been continuing for several decades. Nowadays, this concept is widely used in national and international debates aimed at justifying the economic, energy, and resource independence of states.

The concept of eco-nationalism was developed by the American researcher Jane Dawson. Analyzing social activism in former Soviet Republics, namely Ukraine, Russia, Armenia, and Lithuania, in the late 1980s, she found convergences of nationalism and environmentalism.[1] However, the concept of eco-nationalism has neither been refuted nor developed. Existing studies therefore focus either on the environmental component of eco-nationalism[2] or on national ones.[3] Meanwhile, the term "eco-nationalism" is rarely used. At the same time, while the failure of the communist ideology and economic failure played important roles in delegitimizing Soviet control, eco-nationalism became an important driving force in the collapse of the Soviet Union. It emerged after the Chernobyl disaster as a result of an understanding of the relationship between the deterioration of the environment in many Soviet Republics and the infringement of the rights of the ethnic groups living in them and contributed to mobilizing the population against the totalitarian Soviet regime. This allows us to view the environmental movement

---
[1] Jane Dawson, *Eco-nationalism: Anti-nuclear activism and national identity in Russia, Lithuania, and Ukraine* (Durham, NC: Duke University Press, 1996).
[2] Murray Feshbach and Alfred Friendly, *Ecocide in the USSR: The Looming Disaster in Soviet Health and Environment* (New York: Basic Books, 1992); Dmitriy Gorenburg, *Minority Ethnic Mobilization in the Russian Federation* (Cambridge: Cambridge University Press, 2003); Anastasia Leukhina, "Ukrainian Environmental NGOs after Chernobyl Catastrophe: Trends and Issues," *International Journal of Politics and Good Governance* 17, no. 1 (2010): 1–12; David Marples, *The Collapse of the Soviet Union, 1985–1991* (London: Routledge, 2016); John Mussey Stewart, ed., *The Soviet Environment: Problems, Policies, and Politics* (Cambridge: Cambridge University Press, 1992); Charles E. Zieger, "Political Participation, Nationalism, and Environmental Politics in the USSR," in *The Soviet Environment: Problems, Policies, and Politics*, ed. John Mussey Stewart (Cambridge: Cambridge University Press, 1992), 24–39.
[3] Taras Kuzio, "Nationalism in Ukraine: Towards a New Theoretical and Comparative Framework," *Journal of Political Ideologies* 7, no. 2 (2002): 133–161; Andrei Shcherbak, "Nationalism in the USSR: A Historical and Comparative Perspective," Basic Research Program Working Papers (WP BRP 27/SOC/2013), https://wp.hse.ru/data/2013/12/12/1339827667/27SOC2013.pdf.

Open Access. © 2021 Tetiana Perga, published by De Gruyter. This work is licensed under the Creative Commons Attribution-NonCommercial-NoDerivatives 4.0 International License.
https://doi.org/10.1515/9783110729290-009

and nationalism as historical forces that can influence the balance of power in a globalized world.

In the context of this research, we consider pre-independent Ukrainian nationalism, which combined features of civil and ethnic nationalism and aimed at obtaining the self-determination of the Ukrainian SSR, which was a part of the USSR.[4] It differs from the Russian "imperial nationalism," which began to form in Russia after the collapse of the USSR and represents a combination of Russian nationalism and imperial consciousness[5] inherited from the Russian and Soviet Empires.

It is apparent that many issues of the eco-nationalism concept remain to be addressed, and the present contribution will consequently analyze peculiarities of the Ukrainian model as well as its transnational perspective in the late 1980s.

Preconditions of Ukrainian Eco-Nationalism

The analyses of the situation in the Ukrainian SSR in the 1960s–1980s allow economic, ecological, political, and cultural preconditions of eco-nationalism's emergence, determined by the totalitarian nature of the Soviet regime, to be found. The Soviet Union sought to demonstrate its superiority over Western countries and the USA, a strategy that was particularly pronounced during the Cold War. Ever since it was a part of the Russian Empire, Ukraine had been considered its industrial nucleus. The USSR continued the tradition, and a disproportionately large number of mining, chemical, and metallurgical enterprises are still located in its territory. During Nikita Khrushchev's (1894–1971) tenure as General Secretary of the Communist Party of the Soviet Union (CPSU) alone, more than 200 chemical enterprises were built in the Ukrainian SSR. It consequently became one of the most economically developed Soviet Republics, ranking just behind Russia. Such industrial areas of Ukraine covered about 3.7% of the territory of the former Soviet Union but produced almost 25% of all its industrial pollution.[6]

---

4 Kuzio, *Nationalism in Ukraine*, 142.
5 Emil Pain, "The imperial syndrome and its influence on Russian nationalism," in *The New Russian Nationalism: Imperialism, Ethnicity and Authoritarianism 2000–2015*, ed. Pal Kolsto and Helge Blakkisrud (Edinburgh: Edinburgh University Press), 46–74.
6 Letter No. 6-1-424 of April 18, 1989 of the First Deputy Chairman of the State Committee of the USSR to the Central Committee, "About the environmental situation in the Ukrainian SSR and measures to improve it," Central State Archives of Supreme Authorities and Governments of Ukraine, F32, D1, File 2611.

Although the Soviet Union declared itself anti-imperialist and a people's democracy, critics argue that it demonstrated tendencies common to historical empires,[7] so the informal term "Soviet Empire" is often used to refer to it.[8] It was not only its foreign policy but also its internal one that was imperial in nature. It has also been argued that the Soviet Union practiced colonialism as other imperial powers did. This applies to the republics that were on the periphery of the Soviet Empire. John A. Hobson states that vast expenditures on armaments, costly wars, and political and social reforms, though fraught with great injuries to the nation, served the business interests of certain groups, industries, and professions of empires well.[9] In the Soviet Empire, everything was subordinated to the interests of the center, the all-Union economy, and the Soviet party elite. Therefore, the Soviet policy on the periphery was a form of predatory exploitation of the Republics' natural resources. A striking example is the Soviet Energy Program, which can be described as ecological imperialism.

The energy strategy of the USSR provided a gradual increase in nuclear energy production that showed its impact after the world energy crisis of the 1970s. These plans of the Soviet leadership directly related to the Ukrainian SSR, as industrial enterprises needed electricity. Ukraine had appropriate natural resources for such facilities; proximity to socialist countries was also important, since the USSR exported electricity to them. According to the Soviet Energy Program, adopted in 1970, in 1977–1986, 16 nuclear reactors (40% of total nuclear power produced in the USSR) were to be built in the territory of the Ukrainian SSR.[10] Environmental issues, as well as the interests of the Ukrainian people and any propositions from or objections by researchers, were not taken into account in the designing of industrial enterprises and nuclear plants.

The political system of the Soviet Union envisaged a strong centralization of power, including in decision-making. Like all Soviet Republics, Ukraine in the USSR did not have any authority in the solving of economic, national, and cultural issues. Important decisions for the Republics were taken by Moscow, and 90% of Ukrainian enterprises were directly subordinated to the Russian capital's control.[11]

---

[7] Michael Dobbs, *Down with Big Brother: The Fall of the Soviet Empire* (London: A. & C. Black, 2013).
[8] George J. Neimanis, *The Collapse of the Soviet Empire: A View from Riga* (Westport: Praeger Publishing, 1997).
[9] John A. Hobson, *Imperialism: A Study* (Nottingham: Spokesman Books, 2012).
[10] Boris Semenov, "Nuclear Power in the Soviet Union," *IAEA Bulletin* 2, no. 25 (1983): 47–59.
[11] Olga Vasiyta, *Ecology and Politics* (Chernivci: Zelena Bukovina, 1998): 172–176.

Although Soviet Republics received certain rights in times of thaw under Khrushchev, they did not deal with economic and ecological decisions; the wave of Ukrainization was very short. The 18-year term of Leonid Brezhnev (1906–1982, in power 1964–1982), who became General Secretary of the CPSU after Khrushchev, was characterized by conservatism, authoritarianism, and Russification. Developing a thesis about the Soviet people as a new national community automatically diminished the significance of nations and nationalities that were classified as "small." This ruled out any equality, humiliated "small" nationalities, and glorified the Russian nation. Based on these theoretical "discoveries," a new wave of Russification started in the second half of the 1970s. The Russian language, which had been promoted as an inter-communication language, replaced the Ukrainian language in education, science, and culture. The Ukrainian language began to disappear from official use. For example, in the 1980s, nearly 90% of theaters and cinemas in Ukraine were performing or showing films in Russian. In 1970, 38.2% of books were published in Ukrainian, but this had decreased to only 21.4% by 1988. Scientific, technical, and educational literature was also published in Russian. The number of Ukrainian-language newspapers also decreased from 80.9% to 70.3% during this period.[12] While in 1950–1951, 80.4% of pupils in general education schools were taught in Ukrainian,[13] this had dropped to only 47.8% by 1988/89.[14] These facts demonstrate the gradual restrictions of the national rights of Ukrainians in the USSR, a development that was similar to the situation in the other Soviet Republics. This trend eventually led to the imminent maturation of the conflict between the center and the periphery in the USSR.

The Disaster at the Chernobyl Nuclear Power Plant

The Chernobyl accident on 26 April 1986 was the result of a flawed design of a reactor that was operated by inadequately trained personnel. It was a direct consequence of Cold War isolation and the resulting lack of any atomic safety culture. As Soviet citizens were not able to get enough information about the 1979 accident at the Three Mile Island nuclear plant in Pennsylvania (USA) or

---

12 Vasyl Bilotserkovsky, *History of Ukraine* (Kyiv: Center for Educational Literature, 2007), 1–536.
13 Ivan Kolyaska, *Education in Soviet Ukraine* (Toronto: St. Martin, 1970), 1–246.
14 *Public Education and Culture in the USSR: Statistical Collection* (Moscow: Finances and Statistics, 1989), 88–89.

the environmental or anti-nuclear activism in Western countries due to the Iron Curtain, they could not officially and publicly assess the risk of radioactive contamination to their health and life. Moreover, due to propaganda about the "peaceful" atom and its benefits to the prosperity of Soviet citizens, they trusted the information produced by the official press. As for the authorities of the Soviet Union and the Ukrainian SSR, due to the high level of politicization of the nuclear industry, it was believed that such accidents could not happen at a Soviet nuclear power plant. This faith resulted in minimal accident preparation, as evidenced by the lack of protective clothing and Geiger counters to monitor radiation at Chernobyl, as well as by inadequate emergency protocols for workers.

The response of the Soviet authorities to the Chernobyl accident that developed into a disaster demonstrated indifference to the fate of citizens of the affected territories and the hundreds of thousands of people who were called upon to deal with the consequences of the disaster (liquidators). The Soviet Union used several strategies aimed at hiding truthful information about the accident. When the cover-up failed and many Western countries demanded clear answers about what had happened in Chernobyl, Soviet authorities decided to conceal the extent of the accident, to falsify information, and to turn attention to nuclear disarmament issues. There is much evidence to support this assertion.

Thus, the first minimal information on the accident was published only three days later – on 29 April.[15] The main message broadcast in the Soviet media space immediately after the accident was the stabilization of the situation. At the same time, the scale of the accident was significantly minimized; it was described as a serious but local accident, an event that some were trying to turn into a global nuclear disaster.[16] Although the governments of the United States, the Federal Republic of Germany, Great Britain, France, Sweden, and other countries requested the USSR to provide clear information on the scale of the accident and radiation levels, the first press conference for journalists was held only on 7 May. Yuri Izrael, the Chair of the State Committee of the USSR on Hydrometeorology and Natural Environment Control and a member of the Soviet Academy of Sciences, wanted to reassure the world community; therefore, he stated at the press conference that the radiation level "has decreased ... which will allow us in the very near future to consider the city of Pripyat safe for living."[17] On 15 May, Mikhail Gorbachev repeated that the situation had

---

15 "From the Council of Ministers of the USSR," *Pravda Ukrainu*, April 29, 1986, 2.
16 "From the Council of Ministers of the USSR," *Izvestia*, April 30, 1986, 2; "Situation under control," *Izvestia*, May 6, 1986, 2; Georgij Arbatov, "Boomerang," *Pravda*, May 9, 1986.
17 Volodymir Gubarev and Mikhaik Odinec, "From Chernobyl to Kiev," *Pravda*, May 10, 1986.

been stabilized and called on the international community to deepen cooperation within the framework of the International Atomic Energy Agency.[18] It was also indicated that the total number of victims was only two.[19]

The All-Union and Ukrainian republican press repeatedly stated that the population did not require special iodine prophylaxis. Therefore, urgent advice on reducing the effects of radiation in everyday life was not provided on time. The Minister of Health Care of the Ukrainian Republic, Anatoly Romanenko, gave the first TV interview only on 6 May. He claimed that the level of radiation in Kyiv and the surrounding areas was within the limits recommended by national and international authorities. Therefore, there was no threat to human health and no special precautions needed to be taken. The only recommendation he made was to limit the ventilation of enclosed spaces and to clean one's feet before entering one's apartment.[20] Demonstrating the insignificance of the situation, the Soviet authorities did not prohibit a festive demonstration on the central Khreshchatyk Street in Kyiv, even though, according to KGB data, a radioactive cloud covered the capital of Ukraine that day.

Besides, the accident contrasted the threat of the nuclear weapons and arms race. The Soviet Union put forward an initiative for the establishment of an international regime for the safe development of nuclear energy based on close cooperation among all states.[21] Therefore, the Soviet Union used the Chernobyl disaster for political purposes and an ideological war against its opponents and failed to provide the necessary protection for its citizens. Meanwhile, many of the 600,000 people who had participated in the emergency response had fallen ill because of radiation exposure. In addition, more than 3.5 million hectares of land were degassed, including 1.5 million hectares of arable land. This covered nearly 12% of the Ukrainian territory. More than 1,000 Ukrainian towns and villages were affected by radioactive contamination.[22]

Attempts by the authorities to conceal the truth and people's fear for their lives and those of their children, as well as different rumors, catalyzed the discontent with Moscow's policy among many Ukrainians and contributed to social mobilization in the Ukrainian SSR. It can therefore be noted that the Chernobyl disaster galvanized discontent with the Soviet regime that had accumulated over

---

18 "Speech by Mikhail Gorbachev on Soviet television," *Pravda*, May 15, 1986, 1.
19 TASS News Agency, "On the Events at the Chernobyl Nuclear Power Plant," *Izvestia*, May 8, 1986, 1.
20 Volodymir Golikiv, "Radiation and Safety," *Argumenti i Fakty*, May 16, 1986.
21 "Nuclear Death – Prohibited," *Trud*, May 5, 1986, 2.
22 Vladimir Vrublevsky, *Vladimir Scherbitsky: Truth and Fiction: Memories, Documents, Rumors, Legends, Facts* (Kyiv: Dovira, 1993), 211.

previous decades. An important role for this development was played by the policies of perestroika and glasnost, initiated by Gorbachev, due to the emergence of new opportunities for communication and social mobilization.[23]

Social Mobilization

The Chernobyl disaster contributed to the development of both the environmental and national movements, although the first groups began to appear only in 1988. In 1989, there were about 47,000 informal groups, and around 10% were engaged in environmental protection activities.[24] The environmental and nationalist movements emerged simultaneously since they had common backgrounds.

The initial stage of the environmental movement was characterized by an increasing wave of civic initiatives. In 1987/88, the first green groups emerged: Indifferent, Green Charity (Kyiv), Ecology (Cherkasy), Noosphere (Ternopil), and For Ecological Restructuring (Zaporozhye), which conducted spontaneous but numerous environmental actions in response to the sharp deterioration of the environment in the Ukrainian SSR. For example, Ecological Initiative (Dnipropetrovsk) organized pickets against atmospheric pollution from the city's metallurgical plants. The main activities during this period were picketing and petitioning. For example, Ecology and Peace (Simferopol) gathered 350,000 signatures against the construction of a nuclear power plant in Crimea between 1987 and 1989, and it organized many rallies and pickets both in Crimea and directly on the construction site.[25]

Certainly, the environmental movement in Ukraine started to form within the framework of anti-nuclear activism. It had a pronounced protest nature and was distinct from the conservation activities carried out by the Ukrainian society of nature protection and brigades of nature protection.

This is due to the fact that in the middle of the 1980s, five nuclear power plants were under construction – Chernobyl, South Ukraine, Rivne, Khmelnytskyi, and

---

23 Karl W. Deutsch, *Nationalism and Social Communication* (Cambridge, MA: MIT Press, 1969).
24 Information message of KGB of the USSR to the Central Committee of the Communist Party of Ukraine, June 24, 1989, "On the work of party committees of the republic with amateur public organizations," Central State Archives of Supreme Bodies of Power and Government of Ukraine, F1, D32, File 2658.
25 Announcement of the KGB of USSR to Central Committee, September 25, 1989, "About Meetings, Paces, Prayers on Crimean, lviv, Ivano-Frankivsk Region" and "About the Situation in the Mines," Chervonograd, Electronic Archive of the Ukrainian Liberation Movement, last modified March 13, 2020, http://avr.org.ua/index.php/viewDoc/11248/.

Zaporizhzhia – and two more were being designed – Crimea and Chyhyryn. The most dangerous was the construction of the last two facilities. The Crimean peninsula was a popular Black Sea resort of all-Union significance located in a zone of high seismic activity. The main arguments advanced against the construction of the Chyhyryn station were that it was to use cooling water filtered from the Dnieper River, already harnessed to capacity; that building work had begun without the necessary inspection and approval of the site and without consulting local residents; and that the area for the plant's location was a well-known historical landmark in Ukraine, the headquarters of the former Hetmanate.[26] Protests on the continuing construction of other nuclear power plants were prompted by people's distrust of the reliability of the type of reactors that were similar to Chernobyl's reactor no. 4.

No less important a branch of social activism in Ukraine in the late 1980s was the nationalistic movement. The first informal groups (clubs, political and cultural associations) emerged in Ukraine only in 1987. By 1988, there were already 25, the most popular of which included the Ukrainian Cultural Club, Heritage, Spadschina, Lion Society, and the Ukrainian Helsinki Group.[27] They started a discussion on the development of Ukrainian language, culture, traditions, etc. Since social disciplines in Ukraine were under the tight ideological control of Moscow, Ukrainian writers, particularly the Union of Writers of Ukraine, became pioneers in the elimination of "white spots" of history, criticism of Stalinism, and protecting national culture and the Ukrainian language from relentless Russification. The main problem raised by writers was the narrowing of the use of the Ukrainian language. After a long struggle with the Soviet regime, the law "On languages" was adopted in 1989,[28] which became one of the most important achievements of the nationalistic movement of that period.

The peculiarity of the Ukrainian context of developing eco-nationalism is the leading role in the social activism of the late 1980s of intellectuals, particularly writers who considered the "conscience" of society. Before the Chernobyl accident, many of them supported the Soviet regime and nuclear power, believing in the official propaganda. The terrible consequences of the Chernobyl disaster changed their minds; in most cases, they led not only the nationalist but

---

26 David Marples, "The Chyhyryn Power Plant in Ukraine and the Soviet Nuclear Energy Program," *The Ukrainian Weekly*, July 23, 1989, 3.
27 Reference of the Department 5 of KGB of USSR, November 15, 1988, "About Amateur Groups of Negative Orientation," Electronic Archive of Ukrainian Liberation Movement, last modified March 13, 2020, http://avr.org.ua/viewDoc/11237.
28 Law of the Ukrainian Soviet Socialist Republic on Languages in the Ukrainian SSR, *Information of the Verkhovna Rada of the USSR*, 1989, Supplement No. 45, Art. 631.

also the environmental movement in the post-Chernobyl period. In 1987, they initiated the establishment of the first official non-governmental environmental organization in the Ukrainian USSR, the Green World Association. The first meetings of the group were organized in the framework of the literature workshops carried out by Sergei Plachinda. The Peace Committee of the Ukrainian SSR, which patronized the organization from 1988 and provided it with office space and material and financial resources, was headed by the famous Ukrainian writer Oles Honchar (1918–1995).[29] Writers had involved many scientists and wide circles of population in environmental activism. Ukrainian scientists were not active in the initial stage of the environmental movement since many scientific developments in the USSR were classified. Moreover, Soviet science was to create a positive image of the USSR. This limited their ability to participate in the protest struggle.

The Development of Eco-Nationalism

In her monograph *Eco-nationalism: Anti-nuclear Activism and National Identity in Russia, Lithuania, and Ukraine,* Jane Dawson correctly notes that in Ukraine, ecological and nationalistic movements developed in parallel, converged, but did not replace each other. A number of factors support this thesis. As the Ukrainian nation was oppressed for centuries by the Russian and Austrian Empires as well as the Soviet Union, national identity became the platform for mobilization. In this context, natural resources – land, water, minerals that Ukrainian inhabitants owned but could not exploit of – became, parallel to language, the subject of the struggle between the center and the periphery. Therefore, the eco-nationalist movement reflected the conflict between the titular nation (Russia) and the ethnic minority (Ukrainians), between an imperialist post-nation state nationalism (Russia) and a pre-independence nationalism (Ukraine), and has been manifested in the struggle for the possession of natural resources. Poorly designed nuclear power plants, in particular Chernobyl, have become clear symbols of the oppression and exploitation of the Ukrainian nation. Rather than approaching the population in terms of abstract environmental ideals, activists were able to present the nuclear power issue as a very real and material threat to the survival of a specific territory and group of people.[30] That is why efforts to shut down nuclear power facilities

---

29 Yuriy Samoilenko, *Green Wave of Independence: Ukrainian Environmental Association "Green World"* (Kyiv: Publishing House Green Patriot, 2017), 30–31.
30 Dawson, *Eco-Nationalism*, 162.

were seen not only as attempts to manage national natural resources but also as possibilities to gain wider national rights. In society, the viewpoint appeared that reasons for the aggravation of the environmental situation were connected with the functioning of the totalitarian system and the colonialist policies of the center. Solving the Chernobyl disaster was associated with the democratization of society, the achievement of sovereignty, and obtaining rights to solve the problems of the country.

Eco-nationalism has manifested itself in the inclusion of many environmental and anti-nuclear requirements in the nationalist movement. Many informal groups engaged in cultural activities therefore raised not only issues of the Ukrainian language and national culture but also issues of environmental protection and those related to the demand for closing nuclear power plants. On the other hand, environmental groups quite often discussed the issue of Ukraine's sovereignty and the extension of the Republic's rights, which, in their view, would help to solve environmental problems. Therefore, it was a mutual convergence. There are some examples supporting this thesis.

In November 1988, the Ukrainian Helsinki Union issued an appeal to the citizens. Appended to the appeal was a petition addressed to the governments of the Ukrainian SSR and the Soviet Union regarding the development of nuclear power in Ukraine. Its authors wrote that as a result of the centralized criminal policy of the Stalin-Brezhnev leadership, which disregarded the interests of the Republics, sovereign only on paper, and as a result of the irresponsibility of the local authorities, which sold out Ukraine to the ruling mafia, the country was oversaturated with energy-producing, metallurgical, and chemical industries, which release the greatest amount of harmful refuse. The Ukrainian scholars, writers, and public activists who signed this paper appealed to the relevant authorities and to the 19th conference of the ruling party, demanding a halt to the further expansion of nuclear energy in Ukraine.[31]

This trend is also evident in the organization of various protests and rallies. It should be noted that the first public protest to mark the second anniversary of the Chernobyl nuclear disaster, which took place on Kyiv's central Khreshchatyk Street on 26 April 1988, was organized by the Ukrainian Cultural Club. At this event, 500 people carried protest banners, which read: "Nuclear Power Plants Out of Ukraine" and "Openness and Democracy to the End."[32]

The KGB archives contain many reports from secret agents on similar rallies in many regions of Ukraine. During a meeting in Poltava on 26 June 1988, participants

---

[31] "Ukrainian Helsinki Union's Statement and Petition on Nuclear Plants," *Ukrainian Weekly*, December 18, 1988, 2.

[32] "500 in Kiev protest against nuclear power plants," *Ukrainian Weekly*, May 1, 1988, 1.

discussed the environmental situation in the region, violations of democracy and transparency, and the denial of privileges and benefits to party and Soviet workers.[33] At a rally in Khmelnytskyi on 4 February 1990, attended by 600 persons, demands for environmental impact assessments and the closure of the Khmelnytskyi nuclear power station, as well as the resignation of local communist authorities, were put forward.[34]

The most obvious example is the first ecological rally in Ukraine that was allowed by the Soviet authorities, which took place on 13 November 1988, at the National Stadium of Kyiv. More than 20,000 participants attended (a KGB note suggests about 3,000 participants). The rally was initiated by both ecological and cultural informal groups – the Green World Association, the Ukrainian Helsinki Union, the Ukrainian Democratic Union, and the Ukrainian Cultural Club – whose leaders, according to KGB agents, "advocated with demagogical and nationalist slogans and, in some cases, held extremist positions."

Speakers at the rally demanded the adoption of drastic measures for improving the ecological situation and even called for the elimination of existing nuclear power plants and chemical industries. The main reasons for the aggravation of the environmental situation were named as the ignorance by the all-Union Ministry of the interests of the Ukrainian Republic in the construction and operation of environmentally friendly companies and the inability of ministries, departments, and deputies of the Verkhovna Rada of the Ukrainian SSR to monitor the environmental situation in Ukraine and give objective information to the population. These requirements formed the basis for the final document of the meeting – the "Appeal" to the government of the time. Oles Shevchenko, a member of the Ukrainian Helsinki Union and dissident, called for a referendum "in which the Ukrainian people will declare their will to live." It was at this rally when Ukrainian writers Dmytro Pavlychko, Ivan Drach, and Sergei Plachinda and activists of the Heritage Group

---

33 Information message about of KGB of the USSR to the Central Committee of the Communist Party of Ukraine, June 27, 1988, "On the collapse of the USSR national flag," Electronic Archive of Ukrainian Liberation Movement, last modified March 13, 2020, http://avr.org.ua/viewDoc/11229.

34 Announcement to the KGB of USSR to Communist Party Central Committee, "On the operational situation in the republic on February 5, 1990," Central State Archives of Supreme Authorities and Governments of Ukraine, F1, D32, File 2873.

proposed to create a People's Movement of Ukraine (RUKH), which later became a major political organization and the party that fought for the national liberation of Ukraine.[35] After the rally on 23 November, a meeting of the group of writers took place in the House of Writers, which began preparations for the creation of this organization.[36]

The Transnational Impact of Eco-Nationalism

Ukrainian eco-nationalism was not inspired by external factors; it had purely Ukrainian roots. In 1986–1988, the Iron Curtain was still dense and information from the West barely penetrated it. It also should be noted that in Ukraine, perestroika began later than in Russia since the First Secretary of the Central Committee of the Communist Party of Ukraine, Volodymyr Shcherbytsky (1918–1990), prevented its development.

Meanwhile, the Chernobyl disaster and the development of the nationalistic movement in Ukraine stimulated the diaspora in the West to find possibilities for establishing contacts with activists of social movements. The most active in this context was the North American diaspora. The first key partners whom it attempted to establish links with were Ukrainians associated with the national liberation movement (as mentioned above, most of them called for solving environmental problems). The bet was on the most influential opposition groups – the Ukrainian Helsinki Union, the Ukrainian Cultural Club, RUKH, and the Green World Association. They were supposed to provide humanitarian assistance to the victims of Chernobyl.

Activists of the Ukrainian diaspora abroad also chose the tactic of establishing face-to-face contacts with Ukrainian activists. This was facilitated by the policy of perestroika which expanded opportunities for tourist and private visits, increasing the number of conferences, exhibitions, and forums visited by foreigners. For this purpose, the diaspora sent special "emissaries" to Ukraine. According to the KGB's information, 18 emissaries were sent during 1987–1988, of whom 16 were interested in both environmental problems as well as the

---

35 Announcement to the KGB of USSR Communist Party Central Committee, November 14, 1988, "About the Meeting on Problems of Ecology in Kiev," Electronic Archive of Ukrainian Liberation Movement, last modified March 13, 2020, http://avr.org.ua/index.php/viewDoc/11231/.

36 Information message of the KGB of the USSR to the Central Committee of the Communist Party, November 24, 1988, "On the creation of an initiative group of public movement in support of perestroika in the Union of Writers of Ukraine," Electronic Archive of Ukrainian Liberation Movement, last modified March 13, 2020, http://avr.org.ua/viewDoc/11239.

attitudes of people toward Chernobyl. These emissaries arrived in Ukraine in different ways: as part of tourist groups, on private invitations, as members of different business and cultural delegations, or as participants of peace walks. They provided moral and material assistance to the opponents of the Soviet regime. The KGB archive documents refer to such emissaries as Bozhena Olshanivska, Chair of Americans for Human Rights of Ukraine (AHRU).[37]

Ukrainian eco-nationalism became a platform for establishing the first contacts with the Ukrainian diaspora in the North American context. Since those living in the diaspora there had supported Ukraine's demand for sovereignty for many years, they were attractive to the nationalist component of the environmental movement. Despite the fragmentation of information on this topic, it is possible to reconstruct the main activities of several North American and Canadian groups. After some private visits in Ukraine, Bozhena Olshanivska also took part in the peace walk held in Ukraine in 1988, where she met with the head of the Ukrainian participants, the secretary of the Green World Association, Svyatoslav Dudko. He told Olshanivska about the green activists in Ukraine. As a result of the established relations, cooperation started between the Green World Association and AHRU. In 1989–1990, AHRU invited Ukrainian green activists to visit the United States. For its part, in 1990, the Green World Association proposed that Olshanivska should occupy the position of one of the eight directors of the ECOFOND Management Board. The Green World Association was chosen as one of the partners from the Ukrainian side for transferring financial and material assistance to the people affected by radiation contamination.

In addition to the activities of AHRU, two groups have been set up in Canada to assist Ukraine in addressing environmental issues. The Committee for Environmental Concerns in Ukraine (CECU), which cared for balding children in Chernivtsi due to thallium poisoning, was established in 1988.[38] On the initiative of the Commission of the World Congress of Free Ukrainians, the ESOLOS group emerged in 1989. ESOLOS provided material assistance to the children of Chernivtsi and sent dosimeters to Ukraine.[39] These groups have done a lot to inform Western society about Ukraine's environmental problems, Chernobyl, and the first Ukrainian green activists.

---

[37] Report of KGB of Ukrainian SSR, "On the subversive activities of the OUN," 32 (1990), Sectoral State Archive of the Security Service of Ukraine, F.16, D.4, File 5, 102–105.
[38] "Toronto Group Focuses on Ukraine's Environment," *The Ukrainian Weekly*, March 12, 1989, 2.
[39] "Ukrainian Ecological Association Begins Joint Projects with North Americans," *The Ukrainian Weekly*, November 25, 1990, 3.

The Canadian ECOLOS and the American AHRU contributed to the promoting of the first Ukrainian green activists in the West and presenting them to decision-makers, businesspersons, civil society, and the public. They organized and sponsored a number of tours of Green World Association executives (Svyatoslav Dudko, Yuriy Mishchenko, Anatoliy Panov) to the US and Canada in 1989–1990.[40] During the tour, the idea of the joint "Vitamin" project (providing vitamins to the victims of Chornobyl) was initiated. Its members were the Green World Association from Ukraine, the Greens, the Clamshell Alliance, AHRU, and the Children of Chornobyl Relief Fund (CCRF) from the USA.[41] Through these activities, the Ukrainian diaspora opened a "window of possibilities" to the representatives of Ukrainian civil society.

Assistance to victims of Chernobyl was an important channel of influence on Ukraine and for establishing bilateral communication. In 1988–89, the activities of the Association of Ukrainian Women, the International Charity Foundation "Help for Chernobyl Children," the Children of Chornobyl Relief and Development Fund, the World Congress of Free Ukrainians (Commission on Chornobyl Affairs), AHRU, ECOLOS, the Union of American Brotherhood; the Ukrainian Peace Council (Children's Rescue Fund), the Confederation of Ukrainian Political Parties and Organizations (CUPPO), the Ukrainian Canadian Committee (the "Promote Ukraine" fund), and many others were engaged with this. Thanks to such assistance, residents of Western countries both became increasingly aware of Ukraine and opened up their world and culture to Ukrainians.

The Achievements of Eco-Nationalism

Due to expanding protests by the beginning of the 1990s, the construction of the Crimean and Chyhyryn nuclear power plants and the Odessa nuclear power and heating station was terminated, while the construction of additional units at the South Ukrainian and Khmelnytskyi nuclear power plants was suspended. In 1990, the Verkhovna Rada (Supreme Council of Ukraine) adopted a moratorium on the construction of the new units at the Zaporizja, Rivne, and Khmelnytskyi nuclear

---

[40] "Yavorivsky, Horbal, and Dudko are in US," *Narodna Volia*, November 9, 1989. See also Walter Bodnar, "Green Movement Activist from Ukraine Tours Communities in United States," *The Ukrainian Weekly*, July 21, 1990.

[41] "'Greens' of U.S. and Ukraine Begin Vitamin Project," *The Ukrainian Weekly*, February 5, 1989, 3.

power plants.[42] It should also be noted that protests organized by activists of the ecological and nationalistic movements contributed to shattering the foundations of the Soviet Union, which further led to its disintegration.

When the main enemy – the Soviet totalitarian regime – and the nuclear plants that embodied it were defeated, eco-nationalism lost its power. However, its achievements were used for political purposes. In particular, the politicization of the environmental movement started. Many activists had begun to use ecological slogans to solve their political problems. During the elections to the Supreme Soviet in the fall of 1989, a few people who actively opposed the construction of the Crimean nuclear plant become deputies. In the early 1990s, many nationalistic and environmental activists became the leaders of different political parties, both ultra-left and ultra-right. Boris Olijnik received a top position in the Communist Party, Ivan Drach became a cofounder of RUKH, Sergei Plachinda became a leader of the Green Party, Volodymyr Lypinos became a leader of the Ukrainian National Assembly, and Dmitro Korchinsky became a leader of the Ukrainian National Self-Defense Organization.

In September 1990, the Green Party of Ukraine was established, based on the Green World Association, the first environmental political party in Ukraine. As noted at the founding congress of the Green Party by its leader Yuri Shcherbak, the "party was generated by Chernobyl, that is, a harbinger of global environmental catastrophe, but the party was not born by fear, but by a courageous determination to fight the nuclear death."[43] Between 1991 and 2004, eco-activism and eco-nationalism continued, expressed by four green political parties that were created in Ukraine in this period.

Conclusions

Nationalism played an important role in the initial stage of the environmental movement in the Ukrainian SSR, because the achievement of the sovereignty of the republic was considered as a pledge to solve environmental problems and close the nuclear power plants. Eco-nationalism as a type of nationalism reflected the conflict between the center and the periphery in the USSR for the right to own and dispose of the natural resources of ethnic groups. It also was

---

[42] Resolution of the Verkhovna Rada of the Ukrainian SSR, "On a moratorium on the construction of new nuclear power plants in the territory of the Ukrainian SSR," Information of the Supreme Soviet of the USSR, 1990, no. 34, art. 498.
[43] "Green Party of Ukraine," last modified March 12, 2020, http://greenparty.ua/.

directed against a supposedly transnational political system of the Soviet Union that exploited the Ukrainian SSR, especially its environment, because this policy led it into a deep economic and ecological crisis and threatened the existence of the entire Ukrainian nation. It can therefore be concluded that the main condition for its emergence was the totalitarian nature of the Soviet Union and its imperial policy toward Soviet Republics.

Although the environmental and nationalist movements in the Ukrainian USSR converged in the late 1980s, they did not replace each other, which can be explained by the wide range of environmental and cultural issues that social activism had to solve during this period. However, the convergence that reinforced these movements into eco-nationalism gave it purpose and strength, which contributed to undermining the foundations of the Soviet Empire.

Eco-nationalism also had an international perspective. It became a platform for establishing initial contacts with the Ukrainian diaspora in the West, which subsequently facilitated the integration of Ukrainian green groups into international environmental activities.

Works Cited

"500 in Kiev protest against nuclear power plants." *The Ukrainian Weekly*, May 1, 1988, 1.
Arbatov, Georgij. "Boomerang." *Pravda* 129, May 9, 1986.
Archive of the Ukrainian Liberation Movement. "Announcement of the KGB of USSR to Central Committee from 25. 09.1989.'About meetings, paces, prayers on Crimean, lviv, Ivano-Frankivsk region' and 'About the situation in the mines Chervonograd'." Last modified March 12, 2020. http://avr.org.ua/index.php/viewDoc/11248/
Archive of the Ukrainian Liberation Movement. "Information message of the KGB of the Ukrainian SSR to the Central Committee of the CPSU dated 14. 11.1988.'On the meeting on the problems of ecology which took place in Kiev'." Last modified March 13, 2020. http://avr.org.ua/viewDoc/11231.
Archive of the Ukrainian Liberation Movement. "Information message of the KGB of the USSR to the Central Committee of the Communist Party of Ukraine dated 24. 11.1988.'On creation of initiative group of public movement in support of perestroika in Union of Writers of Ukraine'." Last modified March 12, 2020. http://avr.org.ua/viewDoc/11239.
Archive of the Ukrainian Liberation Movement. "Information message of the KGB of the USSR to the Central Committee of the Communist Party of Ukraine dated 27. 06.1988.'On the collapse of the USSR national flag'." Last modified March 11, 2020. http://avr.org.ua/viewDoc/11229.
Archive of the Ukrainian Liberation Movement. "Reference of the Department 5 of KGB of USSR of 15. 11.1988.'About Amateur Groups of Negative Orientation'." Last modified March 13, 2020. http://avr.org.ua/viewDoc/11237.
Bilotserkovsky, Vasyl. *History of Ukraine*. Kyiv: Center for Educational Literature, 2007.

Bodnar, Walter. "Green movement activist from Ukraine tours communities in United States." *The Ukrainian Weekly*, July 21, 1990.

Dawson, Jane. *Eco-nationalism: Anti-nuclear activism and national identity in Russia, Lithuania, and Ukraine*. Durham, NC: Duke University Press, 1996.

Deutsch, Karl W. *Nationalism and Social Communication*. Cambridge, MA: MIT Press, 1969.

Dobbs, Michael. *Down with Big Brother: The Fall of the Soviet Empire*. London: A&C Black, 2013.

Feshbach, Murray and Alfred Friendly. *Ecocide in the USSR: The Looming Disaster in Soviet Health and Environment*. New York: Basic Books, 1992.

"From the Council of Ministers of the USSR." *Izvestia*, April 30, 1986, 2.

"From the Council of Ministers of the USSR." *Pravda Ukrainu*, April 29, 1986, 2.

Golikiv, Volodymyr. "Radiation and safety." *Argumenti i Fakty* 20, May 16, 1986.

Gorenburg, Dmitry. *Minority Ethnic Mobilization in the Russian Federation*. Cambridge: Cambridge University Press, 2003.

Gubarev, Volodymyr and Mikhaik Odinec. "From Chernobyl to Kiev." *Pravda*, May 10, 1986.

"'Greens' of U.S. and Ukraine begin vitamin project." *The Ukrainian Weekly*, February 5, 1989, 3.

Green Party of Ukraine. Last modified March 12, 2020. http://greenparty.ua/.

Hobson, John A. *Imperialism: A Study*. Nottingham: Spokesman Books, 2012.

Kolyaska, Ivan. *Education in Soviet Ukraine*. Toronto: St. Martin, 1970.

Kuzio, Taras. "Nationalism in Ukraine: Towards a new theoretical and comparative framework." *Journal of Political Ideologies* 7, no. 2 (2002): 133–161.

Law of the Ukrainian Soviet Socialist Republic on Languages in the Ukrainian SSR. *Information of the Verkhovna Rada of the USSR*, Supplement No. 45, Art. 631, 1989.

Leukhina, Anastasia. "Ukrainian environmental NGOs after Chernobyl catastrophe: Trends and issues." *International Journal of Politics and Good Governance* 17, no. 1 (2010): 1–12.

Marples, David. "The Chyhyryn power plant in Ukraine and the Soviet nuclear energy program." *The Ukrainian Weekly*, July 23, 1989, 3.

Marples, David. *The Collapse of the Soviet Union, 1985–1991*. Abingdon: Routledge, 2016.

Neimanis, George J. *The Collapse of the Soviet Empire: A View from Riga*. Westport: Praeger Publishing, 1997.

"Nuclear death – prohibited." *Trud*, May 5, 1986, 2.

Pain, Emil. "The imperial syndrome and its influence on Russian nationalism." In *The New Russian Nationalism: Imperialism, Ethnicity and Authoritarianism 2000–2015*, edited by Pal Kolsto, Helge Blakkisrud, 46–74. Edinburgh: Edinburgh University Press.

Public Education and Culture in the USSR: Statistical Collection. Moscow: Finances and Statistics, 1989.

Resolution of the Verkhovna Rada of the Ukrainian SSR. "On a moratorium on the construction of new nuclear power plants in the territory of the Ukrainian SSR." *Information of the Supreme Soviet of the USSR*, No. 34, Art. 498, 1990.

Samoilenko, Yuriy. *Green wave of independence. Ukrainian Environmental Association "Green World"*. Kyiv: Publishing House Green Patriot, 2017.

Semenov, Boris. "Nuclear power in the Soviet Union." *IAEA Bulletin* 2, no. 25 (1983): 47–59.

Shcherbak, Andrei. "Nationalism in the USSR: A historical and comparative perspective." Basic Research Program Working Papers Series (WP BRP 27/SOC/2013). https://wp.hse.ru/data/2013/12/12/1339827667/27SOC2013.pdf.

"Situation under control." *Izvestia*, May 6, 1986, 2.

"Speech by Mikhail Gorbachev on Soviet television." *Pravda*, May 15, 1986, 1.

Stewart, John Mussey, ed. *The Soviet Environment: Problems, Policies, and Politics*. Cambridge: Cambridge University Press, 1992.

TASS News Agency. "On the events at the Chernobyl nuclear power plant." *Izvestia*, May 8, 1986, 1.

"Toronto group focuses on Ukraine's environment." *The Ukrainian Weekly*, March 12, 1989, 2.

"Ukrainian ecological association begins joint projects with North Americans." *The Ukrainian Weekly*, November 25, 1990, 3.

"Ukrainian Helsinki Union's statement and petition on nuclear plants." *The Ukrainian Weekly*, December 18, 1988, 2.

Vasiyta, Olga. *Ecology and Politics*. Chernivci: Zelena Bukovina, 1998.

Vrublevsky, Vladimir. *Vladimir Scherbitsky: truth and fiction; assistant notes. Memories, documents, rumors, legends, facts*. Kyiv: Dovira, 1993.

"Yavorivsky, Horbal, Dudko are in US." *Narodna Volia*, November 9, 1989.

Zieger, Charles E. "Political participation, nationalism, and environmental politics in the USSR." In *The Soviet Environment: Problems, Policies, and Politics*, edited by John Mussey Stewart, 24–39. Cambridge: Cambridge University Press, 1992.

Anna Zadora
10 Teaching History in Belarus: Between Globalization and Authoritarian Confinement, Between Europe and Russia

The present Belarusian historiography can be divided into two major schools: Soviet and nationalist. Currently, the Soviet view of history dominates with the support of the political authorities. The education system aims to transmit the official Soviet interpretation of the history of Belarus and to legitimate links with Russia and a specific authoritarian political system. Teaching history in post-Soviet Belarus is extremely complex. The "most Soviet of the USSR's Republics,"[1] Belarus has fully adopted the interpretation of both the Soviet and today's political authorities on the fundamental role played by the Soviet period in the construction of the Belarusian historical narrative, memory, national identity, and political system.

Teaching history is a tool for identity building and for geopolitical strategy legitimation. Identity building, referring to history, is built on the frontier between "us" and "the other." For official identity discourse, the Soviet past and the links with Russia are fundamental elements and the educational system aims to transmit the official Soviet interpretation of a sacred role of the Second World War for Belarus. This contribution therefore investigates the discourse of the Second World War in Belarusian society and in school history textbooks, focusing on the following key themes: the Nazi occupation regime, the Holocaust, the collaboration with Nazi Germany, and the partisan movement. The sacralization of the Soviet interpretation of history has an extreme form going even beyond Russia and cements Belarusian nationalism in the 21st century.

The Context of Belarusian History and Historiography

The history of Belarus, situated at the crossroads of countries and cultural blocs (the Eastern or Eurasian bloc represented by Russia and the Western

---

[1] Valeryi Karbalevitch, "Беларускіфеномен трансфармацыйнага грамадства" [Belarusian phenomenon of a society in transition], *Civic Alternative* 12 (1999): 12.

bloc represented by Poland), is a history of wars and invasions. Until the 20th century, the lands of present-day Belarus belonged to several state formations such as the Principality of Polotsk, the Grand Duchy of Lithuania, the Polish-Lithuanian Commonwealth, and the Russian Empire. In March 1918, the first Belarusian state was created. Belarus declared independence as the Belarusian People's Republic, succeeded by the Socialist Soviet Republic of Byelorussia (SSRB) in January 1919. Belarus was devastated in the Second World War, following which the republic was considerably redeveloped in the post-war years. In 1945, Belarus became a founding member of the United Nations. The SSRB declared its sovereignty on 27 July 1990, and during the period of the dissolution of the USSR, Belarus declared independence on 25 August 1991.

In order to clarify the conflicts between major history and identity paradigms in Belarus, the general context of current Belarusian historiography should be analyzed. The present Belarusian historiography can be divided into two major discourses: Soviet and nationalist. In this configuration, the Soviet view of history dominates with the support of the political authorities, which have monopolized the majority of social sources. The nationalist interpretation of the history of Belarus is pushed to the margins of the system, and its social impact is extremely limited. The pre-eminence of Soviet historiography over other discourses in Belarus is an exception in the post-Soviet bloc. According to numerous research projects devoted to historical discourse and the teaching of history in the post-Soviet countries, Belarus is the only country that does not describe its relations with Russia and the Soviet period in negative terms. Belarus is the only former Republic of the USSR that experienced a turning point in its historiography in the mid-1990s. If the historical narrative of Belarus at the time of perestroika was formed in opposition to Soviet and Russian imperial discourse, the mid-1990s marked a return to a Soviet-style, Russian-orientated, and totalitarian interpretation of history.

Interpretations of History

In Belarus, the construction of a national identity runs parallel to historiographical construction. The early history of the Belarusian lands dates back to the late 19th century when centrifugal tendencies began to undermine the Russian Empire, sparking the beginnings of interest in this particular province. The first book on the history of the Belarusian land, *An Overview of the History of Belarus* by Vaclau Laustouski, was published in 1910.[2] The first Belarusian national states – the Belarusian People's Republic and the SSRB – were created in 1918 and 1919, respectively.

In Soviet historiography, the history of Belarus begins only in 1917 and omits the short-lived Belarusian People's Republic, which existed only for some months. The Belarusian people were able to consolidate themselves, and they began their existence as a nation state only through the framework offered by the SSRB. The Belarusian government is a Soviet creation, and the Belarusian people are primarily a Soviet people. The history of Belarus is the history of the SSRB.

In Soviet times, the history of Belarus did not exist, either as an autonomous academic discipline or as a school subject. The first and only school textbook on the history of the SSRB was published in 1960 in Russian and went through 11 editions, remaining the only educational support on the subject until perestroika. The number of books printed was 9,000 copies (for a country with 9,000,000 citizens), which is an indication of the minor place accorded to the history of Belarus as a school discipline during the Soviet period.

Teaching history in the BSSR prescribed the denial of an independent Belarus and an independent Belarusian history. The history of Belarus was merged into Soviet history. Identity politics transmitted through history teaching aimed at the construction of a Soviet identity above all other identities. The following sentences quoted from the only history textbook on Belarus published during the Soviet period are an illustration of the extent to which Belarusian history was viewed as no more than a constituent part of Soviet history, inasmuch as a fundamental tenet of Soviet historiography was its articulation of the Second World War as the central event in the history of the USSR: "From the first days of the occupation, workers in Soviet Belarus began the People's War. Brigades of partisans were created everywhere. Their number increased daily. The organizer and leader of the partisan movement was the Communist Party."[3] The semantic and stylistic construction of the text is revealing. Short sentences and a dogmatic tone meet the objectives of Soviet propaganda: to point out that the information provided by the textbooks is an ultimate and indisputable truth, despite the fact that objective criticisms of these postulates were made by nationalist historians at the time.

---

2 Vaclau Lastouski, *Кароткая гісторыя Беларусі* [An Overview of the History of Belarus] (Minsk: Kukhty, 1992).
3 Laurentsi Abetsadarski, *The History of the Soviet Socialist Republic of Belarus* (Minsk: Public Education, 1968), 121.

History teaching in the USSR became a propaganda tool underlining the superiority of the Soviet communist model over the Western capitalist model. History as an academic discipline was itself used as an important tool in the construction and legitimization of the Soviet totalitarian state, claiming a specific place for it in world politics. The victory in the Second World War was presented as proof of the superiority of Soviet society over Western society.

Perestroika, Independent Search for Democracy, and European Roots in History

In the post-Soviet bloc, the period known as perestroika was a crucial moment for the building of states and their national identities. New political parties appeared to challenge the political monopoly of the Communist Party of the USSR, claiming the right of the Soviet Republics to an independent history and an independent future. Since the break-up of the Soviet Union, the majority of post-Soviet countries have tended to articulate historical consciousness in opposition to Soviet and Russian interpretations of the past, seeking European roots in their histories.

The writing of history during Soviet times changed completely during perestroika, where history was requisitioned as a legitimizing authority for profound social change, the creation of an independent state in 1990, the establishment of a new socio-political system, and the shaping of a new national identity matrix. Under perestroika, numerous publications appeared in the media relating to the link between education, the teaching of history, and a national renaissance: "Education – the Only Way to a National Renaissance," "Give History Back to the People," or "History Education as a Source of a National Identity." The first school programs on the history of Belarus were inspired by the nationalist party, the National Front program, as was the new Constitution of independent Belarus, which claimed that "the Belarusian people have a long history which can be traced back many centuries."[4] The coat of arms and "nationalist" flag dating back to the era of the Grand Duchy of Lithuania, regarded by Belarusian nationalists as the "Golden Age" of the Belarusian nation, were introduced after the proclamation of independence in 1991.

The gradual gaining of autonomy and the institutionalization of the history of Belarus as an academic discipline and school subject is also linked to perestroika. A decision of the Ministry of Education of 15 September 1986 stated that

---

4 First Constitution of Independent Belarus, 1991.

"during the 1986–1987 school year, the history curriculum must be changed, although the creation of new textbooks is not intended for this year."[5] Changes in the history curriculum were reduced to greater attention to the peculiarities of Belarus within the framework of the history of the USSR. The history of Belarus was incorporated into the curriculum of the history of the USSR, and only 27 hours per year were devoted to it. Only in the early 1990s, when the independence of Belarus was proclaimed, did significant qualitative changes take place in the field of writing and teaching history.

The curriculum of the history of Belarus of 1991 emphasizes the fundamental changes in the teaching of history affecting content, methodology, structure, and teaching. For the first time, issues of national consciousness were discussed in the school history curriculum, and new teaching principles such as historical humanism, democracy, and the rejection of dogmatism and stereotypes were introduced. In December 1992, the Minister of Education held a meeting with the most famous historians in the country – Mikhas' Bitch, Ouladzimir Sidartsou, Vital' Famine, and Pavel Loïka – asking them to write school textbooks to be sent to schools in September 1993.

Manuscripts were submitted for printing in March 1993, while the decision to publish the textbooks was taken in December 1992. All the authors wrote books that were more or less acceptable for the school system within three or four months. The lack of a methodological and didactic base for writing history textbooks in Belarus greatly complicated the work of the authors. The historians invited to write the textbooks were academics and researchers rather than secondary school teachers, and they experienced significant difficulties in adapting their styles to the needs of young readers and the requirements of the education system. The historian Henadz Sahanovitch described the restructuring of Belarusian historiography as "a methodological and pedagogical vacuum."[6]

The National Center for Textbooks at the Ministry of Education was the only body responsible for monitoring the manuscripts in 1993. According to the official procedure, the manual first had to be approved by university professors, which would ensure the academic quality of the works. School teachers would then try out and present the results of the use of the new books in the classroom. At the same time as the review process was conducted by professors and teachers, a series of meetings, round tables, lectures, and discussions were organized by the National Center for Textbooks, where different views were exchanged, discussed, and debated.

---

5 *Official Bulletin of the Ministry of Education*, September 1986.
6 Henadz Sahanovitch, "Ten years of Belarusian historiography (1991–2000)," *Critical Review of Belarusian History* 8 (2001): 14.

The teaching of history and textbook writing during perestroika were the first attempts to move away from the dogmatism of the Soviet period. They encouraged reflection on historical events and personalities and did not contain indisputable dogmas. The authors of the first textbooks put a particular accent on the civic function of the textbooks. The books were supposed to educate patriots and awaken critical thinking skills, which was a novelty, pedagogically speaking, compared with Soviet-era thinking.

Democratization of Society and Condemnation of the Soviet Past

During perestroika in all the post-Soviet countries, contact with Russia and Russians began to be described in terms of disaster. The communist period is thus frequently described in terms of invasion, occupation, and colonization. For the histories of the post-Soviet countries, Russia played the role of "the other," the "convenient" enemy to which it is possible to attribute all errors and all failures. Russians were classified as invaders, and all territorial divisions, whether unions or annexations, are described in very negative terms.

Pluralism, as one of the most important requirements of a democratic society, was an important element of perestroika history teaching policy. Textbook authors and experts stressed the need to present multiple perspectives on historical events in the textbooks: "The author must give at least two divergent opinions on the facts presented. . . . There are many debatable issues in the science of history, however, the author presents some events as ultimate truths."[7] Pluralistic tendencies are strongly reflected in the books of this period. The introduction that opens Sidartsou and Famine's textbook, published in 1993, clearly states the authors' pedagogical point of view.[8] Through their manual, the authors aspire "to explain the contradictory process of the development of our society, to help students become aware of the history of Belarus as our history and as part of our everyday lives today." The authors invite young readers to study "the role of historical figures, to reflect on their actions," and "to put themselves in the place of historical characters to understand their motivations." The authors draw attention to the diversity of opinion on the historical facts analyzed in the book: "Different points of view are represented in the textbook. You can

---

7 Uladzimir Sidartsou, *Падручнік Гісторыя Беларусі. 9* [History Textbook Belarus. 9th Grade] (Minsk: Public Education, 1993), 3.
8 Ibid.

accept them or defend your own opinion; however, you should keep a respectful attitude toward those who have a different opinion from yours. . . . We recommend that students take an active part in debates on controversial issues in order to learn how to defend their points of view." The authors encourage reflection on historical events and personalities, and their book does not contain indisputable dogmas.

The experts who gathered at the National Center for Textbooks at the beginning of the 1990s debated the modalities of revisions of the totalitarian Soviet period, which was a major step toward democratization and openness to democratic values. The condemnation of the Soviet heritage and the search for European roots in Belarusian history was a very important trend in the writing of history textbooks.

During perestroika, the fundamental event of Soviet history – the Second World War – was subject to thorough historical reinterpretation. The myth of the crucial role played by the Communist Party in the victory was debunked, as was the myth of the struggle of the whole people against the Nazis: the whole people did not fight on the side of the Red Army and the partisans. Historians revealed instances of collaborationism and crimes committed by partisans. The Soviet-era glorification of the Second World War was significantly toned down. Stories of victims and of whole communities forgotten by Soviet and Belarusian historiography, such as the Jewish community, were told for the first time in the 1990s.

Search for Links with Europe and the "Europeanization" of History Discourse

The particular attention paid to the Great Duchy of Lithuania, to which the Belarusian lands belonged between the 12th and 16th centuries, was the result of a search for a valid historical alternative to the idea of the Belarusian nation as a constituent part of the Soviet totalitarian state advanced by Soviet-era historiography. Finding an authentic alternative to the Soviet version of Belarusian history was, however, not a simple matter.

In textbooks published in 1993, particular emphasis was placed on the Grand Duchy of Lithuania and on the wars between the Grand Duchy of Lithuania and Muscovy as historical proof of resistance to Russian domination and links with Europe. Even the titles of the chapters underlined the link between Belarusian and European and world history: "Belarusian Culture in the Context of World

Civilization," "The Great Patriotic War in the Context of the Second World War," and so on.[9]

It should be noted that the rejection of Soviet totalitarianism and the national revival took extreme forms during this period. "History today still labors under the burden of dogma inherited from previous decades," remarked one expert, although some scholars recognized that the rewriting of history and the rejection of Soviet dogma created a new nationalist dogma and that it was essential to consider the transitional state of historical consciousness in dealing with difficult issues (documents of the National Center for Textbooks). The school textbooks edited in 1993 contained the headings "Historical Fact" and "Historical Document,"[10] which prove the intention of the authors to support their narrative with historical documents in order to make them objective.

The Second World War: A Fundamental Event in Belarusian History

The historical treatment of the Second World War in Belarus, a post-Soviet state with a unique history and a unique treatment of history, is extremely complex. Belarus has fully adopted the interpretation of both the Soviet and today's political authorities on the fundamental role played by this event in the construction of historical narrative, memory, and national identity. The politics of memory, which are the social framework[11] even for personal memories deployed by the Soviet government, placed the Second World War (known in the former USSR as the Great Patriotic War) at the center of the Belarusian national consciousness as the key event in the development of the Belarusian nation.

In the USSR, victory in the Second World War became a unifying myth for the Soviet people. It was presented as a glorious event where all the people of the USSR joined forces in the fight against Nazism. Heroism, patriotism, and devotion to Soviet ideals under the leadership of the Communist Party led the Soviet people to victory. This victory was presented as an affirmation of the superiority of the Soviet political system in relation to the Western model and was widely used by Soviet propaganda. Neither the Soviet government's responsibility for the war nor the numerous crimes perpetrated against the army and the civilian population before, during, and after the war by the Soviets were revealed.

---

9 Pavel Loïka, *History of Belarus: Textbook for the 7th Grade* (Minsk: Public Education, 1993).
10 Ibid.
11 Gérard Namer, *Halbwachs and Social Memory* (Paris: L'Harmattan, 2002).

As mentioned above, in Soviet historiography, the history of Belarus begins only in 1917. The history of Belarus is the story of the SSRB. For this reason, the major event in the history of the USSR, victory in the Second World War, is accepted as a fundamental myth in the memory of the Belarusian people, who have few competing myths. Even if alternative myths exist on the margins of society, they are too weak to challenge the main Soviet myth.

Europeanization of the Holocaust Memory and Changes in the Belarusian Interpretation of the Second World War

Perestroika and the liberalization of the post-Soviet space in the 1980s opened new pages of the history disseminated by the Soviet regime: the Molotov-Ribbentrop Pact, reprisals against Red Army officers, crimes committed by partisans, and the Holocaust. During perestroika, the fundamental Soviet myth of the Second World War was subject to important reinterpretations. The myth of the leading role played by the Communist Party in the victory was debunked, as was the myth of the struggle of the whole people against the Nazis: not everyone fought on the side of the Red Army and the partisans. Historians revealed instances of collaborationism and crimes committed by partisans.

The memory of the Holocaust is a founding historical experience and a unifying memory for Europe. Eastern Europeans had to confront the fact that for Western Europe, the founding historical experience had become the Holocaust, which, for them, was only one part of their history. The newcomers had to tell their own historical experience, unknown to the West, and make it officially part of the European identity. By 1989, the representational modes of the Holocaust memory had become normative in an emerging transnational social space of memory politics, into which Eastern European states entered after the collapse of states' socialist regimes. After 1989, it gradually transformed into a "Europeanized" regime of memory politics in the Western world.[12]

Representation of Holocaust memory in Western Europe served as a model for Eastern European countries, and the canonization of the Holocaust memory became a criterion of Europeanness in order to be considered as a member of the European family by joining the Council of Europe and the European Union. The Holocaust has become a meta-historical, supranationally decontextualized discourse, forming a transnational normative regime of memory.[13] To recognize

---

12 Aline Sierp, *History, Memory, and Trans-European Identity* (London: Routledge, 2014).
13 Michael Rothberg, *Multidirectional Memory. Remembering the Holocaust in an Age of Decolonization* (Stanford: Stanford University Press, 2009).

the Holocaust memory and to learn lessons from history became moral obligations in order to prevent human rights violations in Europe, to prevent the atrocities of the past being repeated. The European Union is founded on the indivisible, universal values of human dignity based on the Holocaust memory deprived of its historical context and turned into an ethical inoculation against totalitarian crimes.

The post-Soviet space faced the issue of the Holocaust memory after perestroika and liberalization when the change of political regimes historically coincided with the memory boom in Europe. The Holocaust became a subject of public discussion after decades of Soviet silence on the issue. Belarus, which had a very important Jewish community before the Second World War, found documents proving that more than 600,000 Jews were murdered by the Nazis. The Maly Trostenets extermination camp near Minsk is one of the biggest concentration camps in Europe.[14]

Belarus discovered institutionalized commemoration of the Holocaust in Europe only after the collapse of the Soviet Union, and this helped in recognizing the Holocaust in Belarus. Perestroika was used to claim "Europeanness," and, like other post-Soviet countries, Belarus opted for the European model of the history of the Holocaust.

Re-Sovietization of History Teaching

The year 1994 witnessed a major shift in the liberalization of Belarusian society. The political forces which came to power in 1994 forged their victory by promising a people in disarray that they would restore the Soviet legacy, fraternal ties with Russia, and the welfare state inherited from the Soviet period. The new government began to use methods inherited from Soviet leaders. A referendum in May 1995 focused on changing state symbols, building a union with Russia, and implementing (?) the Russian language as the state language. The arms and "nationalist" flag dating back to the era of the Grand Duchy of Lithuania, regarded by Belarusian nationalists as the "Golden Age" of the Belarusian nation, were introduced after the proclamation of independence in 1991. After the 1995 referendum, these nationalist symbols were again replaced by those of the Soviet era. The majority of the electorate voted for union with Russia and two state languages: Russian and Belarusian. In 1991, Belarus's Independence Day was established as 27 July in commemoration of the vote for the Declaration of

---

14 Martin Dean, *Collaboration in the Holocaust: Crimes of the Local Police in Belorussia and Ukraine, 1941–44* (London: Palgrave Macmillan, 2000).

Sovereignty by the Supreme Soviet (the legislative body of SSRs). In 1996, however, Independence Day was changed to 3 July, the day of the liberation of Minsk from the Nazis: further evidence of a return to a Soviet model of writing and interpreting modern Belarusian history.

The referendum institutionalized a return to the Soviet era and to Russian-orientated interpretations of history. This legalized Sovietization also affected history writing and teaching and official policies on Belarusian national identity. An edict of the President of Belarus, Alexander Lukashenko, of 16 August 1995 stated: "[G]iven the results of the referendum, it is necessary to replace the books published between 1992 and 1995 with new textbooks." Concerned with defending the Soviet legacy, history textbooks seen by the president as having a nationalistic content were condemned to be replaced by books that better met the aspirations of the new political authorities, who took the Soviet heritage as the basis of their political legitimacy.

The intervention of the political authorities in history teaching and textbook writing provoked heated debates in society. Discussions in the press reflected the negative attitude of teachers and the intelligentsia toward the hardening of control over and manipulation of school history teaching. The round table on history textbooks organized by the *Belarusian Historical Review* was a response to the decision to remove all textbooks published between 1992 and 1995. Authors and teachers strongly criticized state intervention in textbook rewriting. The author Mikhas' Bitch criticized the authoritarian ban on books edited in 1993: "The history curriculum was openly debated and discussed in 1991 and 1992. Where were the people who are now raising their voices to criticize our textbooks in 1992?"[15]

Proof of Authoritarian Confinement: Teaching History under Political Censorship

In the mid-1990s, the creation of the State Commission for the Control of School Literature in the Field of the Humanities and Social Sciences, called into being by a presidential order of 24 August 1995 and answering directly to the presidential administration, marked a new stage in the Belarusian politics of history teaching and textbook writing. This structure responded to the aspiration of the Belarusian political authorities to bring the writing of school history under their

---

15 Quoted in an unpublished document in the archives of the National Center for Textbooks, Ministry of Education.

control. Countless mechanisms introduced in the procedure of textbook publishing stifled any attempt to go against the official government conception of history. The purpose of the Commission is to monitor and directly control textbook writing. Thus, the Commission remains the ultimate judge of textbook manuscripts. Before being monitored by the Commission, however, a manuscript must pass many stages of correction and review.

First, a manuscript is read by two experts at the Institute of Education of the Ministry of Education. The experts appointed by the Institute check the didactical and ideological quality of the work. If the manuscript corresponds to the pedagogical requirements of a textbook and is not openly opposed to official ideology, it obtains approval in the first instance. A manuscript can be subjected to a number of criticisms, and the author is obliged to make corrections in response to the experts' objections. The secretariat of the Ministry can send the manuscript back for "improvement" many times until it is accepted by the Commission. The next step is expert analysis and deliberation within the Section of History Textbooks of the Ministry of Education. The Section verifies whether the work corresponds to the official curriculum, the didactical characteristics of the manuscript, and the ideology expounded by the author in the book. The manuscript is submitted to different experts, and if there are points to rework, it is returned to the author(s) for corrections. The officials of the Ministry of Education know which points to "polish" so that the manuscript can be analyzed first by the Presidium of the Academic Council of the Ministry of Education and then by the Commission. Points relating to political history, the Soviet period, and the Second World War are considered to be difficult. After the approval of the Section, the manuscript is submitted to the examination of the Presidium. Its members are appointed by the Ministry of Education, and it is chaired by the Minister of Education. Before deliberation in the Presidium, the manuscript is submitted to the experts of the Commission, and although this does not form part of the official procedure, their opinion carries much weight during deliberations. It is the Presidium that gives the greatest number of negative verdicts to manuscripts. This makes sense, because the next step is the Commission, which makes the final decision on manuscripts, so they must correspond to official ideology by the time they reach this stage. The Commission controls politically important school subjects such as world history, geography, and the literature and history of Belarus. These are the most controversial and politicized academic disciplines, so the political authorities control how they are taught with particular vigilance. The file concerning each manuscript considered by the Commission includes nearly ten expert conclusions, the authors' responses to the corrections made on the basis of objections, and the reports of all the meetings of all the bodies that have analyzed the manuscript. The Commission issues the final verdict. If the manuscript gets the approval of the

Commission, the Ministry sends the manuscript to the publisher specifying the number of copies to be printed. Such openly authoritarian control over history teaching and textbook writing goes even further than former Soviet methods of control within the educational system.

Forward to the Soviet Past?

The return to the Soviet interpretation of history resulted in the reselection of topics. Some of them were accentuated, others disappeared. Collaboration during the Second World War is a very problematic issue, which "disappeared" from the present Belarusian historiography. During perestroika, this issue started to be analyzed. It was important to study this phenomenon, the motivation of collaborators who very often were the executioners of Jewish, Roma, and other communities, which is why neighbors became executioners, according to Martin Dean's expression.[16] In Belarus textbooks edited after 2005, the term "collaboration" is not even mentioned. It is impossible to conduct research on collaborationism in state institutions or to publish research on collaboration in Belarus.

The present Belarusian administration is also aware of the role of education in weaving social ties and building identity: "[H]istory teaching is also a struggle for the minds and souls not only of individuals but also of nations."[17] On the one hand, it is imperative to overcome the shortcomings of education within the family in the context of a dramatic decline in the general level of the education of children, to the degree that "textbooks are probably the only books which many children lay their hands on." On the other hand, the school system plays an almost exclusive role in the training of young citizens. Textbooks are the preferred and often the sole instrument of the transmission and legitimization of the particular interpretation of history and narrative of national identity that a political administration aspires to convey.

Within this context, history teaching and school textbooks on history are extremely effective instruments of identity construction. Messages on identity, on "us and the other," can be transmitted and perpetuated across generations through history textbooks distributed to citizens in millions of copies. Their texts, illustrations, and typography can become common references all over a country, guaranteeing a broad, thorough, and continuous impact on the entire population of a territory. The adaptation by several generations of the same

---

16 Dean, *Collaboration in the Holocaust*.
17 Alexander Lukashenko, "The Problems of Textbooks," *Teachers' Journal* 55 (April 2000).

message, photographs, and historical images transmitted by textbooks can play an important role in legitimizing an official narrative on history and identity within a school system.[18]

Identity discourse transmitted by educational systems becomes a starting point, a basis on which individuals can construct their identity, worldview, and view of the past and history. They begin to assume their belonging to certain groups and their non-belonging to "others" to the point that this perception guides their behavior and becomes a generator and an organizer of practices and opinions. The narrative of the history of a nation as taught in its school system tends to center around certain key events which become markers used in the construction of links between a nation and its past.[19]

In official historiography, alternative historical interpretations are not completely erased but pushed to the margins of the socio-historical narrative. Among the few alternative institutions that can escape the official historiographical dogmas outside the system, there are some institutions in exile that are now located in Vilnius (see below) and the "History Workshop," a German-Belarusian institution in Minsk. The Workshop, located in the territory where the Minsk ghetto was situated, is trying to reveal the "white spots" of the war and of Nazi occupation, including the destiny of the Jewish community and collaboration.[20] The protection of a diplomatic institution, the German embassy, guarantees it a certain flexibility and freedom of expression.

Soviet historical dogma, and in particular the cornerstone of the Soviet legacy – the glorification of the Second World War –, has marginalized other historical interpretations. The pre-eminence of the Soviet interpretation of the war is reflected in partial and biased discourse, full of lacunas and omissions, in school textbooks. Current definitions of Belarusian past and memory cannot be sustainable and will always be weak and susceptible to political manipulation because they are based on partial and lacunar historical references in which the heroic interpretation of the Second World War is incompatible with the victims' narrative. The Holocaust memory was evicted not only from official discourse but even from personal memories. As such, the pre-eminence of the Soviet and Russia-orientated interpretation of history resulted in animosity in analyses of relations with Europe.

---

18 Hanna Schissler, *The Nation, Europe and the World: Textbooks and Curricula in Transition* (New York: Berghahn Books, 2005).
19 Mark Bassin and Catriona Kelly, *Soviet and Post-Soviet Identities* (Cambridge: Cambridge University Press, 2012).
20 Kouz'ma Kozak, *German and Collaborationist Loss in Belarus during the Second World War (1941–1944): An Analysis of the Results* (Minsk: Logvinov, 2012).

With Russia and Against Europe

Animosity between Poles and Belarusians was methodically cultivated over the centuries by the political authorities. The policy of hostility between Belarusians and Poles has been encouraged for centuries by the ruling elite in Belarus, be they Russian, Soviet, or the present-day Belarusian authorities. The goal of this policy is the establishment of a multidimensional border between these peoples in terms of mentality, territory, religion, and language, obscuring the fact that Poles, like Belarusians, are a Slavic people, who are in fact very close to the Belarusians in all these areas. The Belarusian language, for example, is the most "Westernized" of all the Eastern Slavic languages and thus is close to both the Polish and Russian languages.[21] This artificial and unfounded cultural boundary between Belarus and Poland makes Poles out to be the "worst enemies"[22] of Belarusians in all official discourse and political propaganda, which have declared a "war against Poles,"[23] evidence of which can be found even in the public sphere and in narratives on education.

If identification is defined as a conscious act of choosing to belong to one particular group rather than to "another" one,[24] knowledge of national history, which contains a considerable number of questions and answers to issues relating to identity, to common features of the nation and to differences with "others" is the cornerstone of this identification process.

Alternative Historical Interpretations of the Second World War: Marginalized Discourses

The Soviet view of the history of the Second World War is currently dominant in Belarus; however, it is not the only view. The perestroika period saw a revolution in historiography. In the mid-1980s, history was at the center of social change. The destruction of Soviet dogma led to the search for "new truths," a new concept for the Belarusian nation. The revision of history resulted in a change in social paradigms: what was sacred became profane and vice-versa. Sacred topics in Soviet historiography were reinterpreted and rewritten to match the new nationalist

---

21 Alexander Boulyko, *Typology of Bilinguistic and Multilinguistic Situation in Belarus* (Minsk: Belarusian Science, 1999).
22 Leonid Zaiko, *National Interests of Belarus* (Minsk: Skakoun, 1999).
23 Petar Eberhardt, *Demographic Situation in Belarus 1897–1989* (Minsk: Soros Foundation, 1997).
24 Stephen Recher, *Self and Nation* (London: Sage Publications, 2001).

narrative. Historians revealed instances of collaborationism and crimes committed by partisans. The heroic and glorious interpretation of the Second World War was significantly reduced. The stories of the victims, of whole communities forgotten by Soviet and Belarusian historiography such as the Jewish community, found their place for the first time in the 1990s.

The historiography of the 1990s highlighted features of the Second World War in the USSR ignored by Soviet historiography: the Molotov-Ribbentrop Pact, the purges in the ranks of the officers of the Red Army on the eve of the war, collaborationism, crimes committed by partisans, and so on. Some researchers, such as the Polish historian Yury Touronak[25] and the German historian Bernard Chiari[26] (condemned by the Belarusian authorities), study collaborationism and present it as a mass movement (the only Belarusian Youth Union created by collaborationists on the model of the Hitler Youth counted more than 10,000 members), which goes against official discourse that completely erases this historical fact.

The current socio-political system is making significant efforts to impose the Soviet vision of the Second World War as a holy heroic war of the whole people, the Belarusian nation that defended the home country against Nazi invasion and occupation. Alternative resources are required to defend the alternative version of the war, but these are almost non-existent in Belarus. Only academics who are able to conduct historical research in institutions located outside Belarus, such as the European Humanities University, the Independent Institute of Socio-Economic Research and Political Studies, and the Belarusian Institute for Strategic Studies, all of which are exiled in Vilnius (Lithuania), or those placed under the patronage and protection of foreign bodies (such as the "History Workshop" in Minsk) can afford to challenge the official discourse. In Belarus, in the context of a system that derives its legitimacy from the Soviet legacy, the defense of an alternative interpretation of the war is extremely problematic. Besides costing a great deal, the ability to protest and to defend an alternative interpretation of history is conditioned by how much influence the person protesting is able to exercise.[27] There are very few historians who feel able to influence the writing and teaching of history, which inhibits protests. Among the few alternative institutions which can escape the official historiographical dogmas outside the system is the already cited "History Workshop" in Minsk, whose central area of research is the Second World War.

---

25 Touronak 1993.
26 Chiari 1998.
27 Hirschman 1970

History of the War in the Education System

The school system is a powerful tool for transmitting collective memory, for building a sense of belonging to a nation state and a national community, and for reinforcing the acceptance of an institutional order by creating a sense of belonging, i.e. an "imagined community."[28] Textbooks are an effective way of transmitting historical narratives concerning national identity. History teaching and history textbooks for schools are extremely powerful and effective tools in shaping national identity in education for many reasons. First of all, the compulsory character of primary and secondary education for children and adolescents must be stressed: no one escapes the educational system of the countries in which they grow up. Secondly, in the Belarusian context, the state educational system has few concurrent agents of education: even the family often delegates its educational function entirely to the school system. Textbooks constitute a powerful force of integration since they "are diffused in hundreds of thousands, taken over several generations even in millions of copies: their texts, illustrations, and typography have been common references . . . for a long time."[29] The role played by history textbooks in the construction of national identity is very important. The content of history textbooks relates directly to questions of national identity. It teaches us to be and think nationally through the interpretation of the events of a particular national history and brings information about the distinction between "us" and "the other" to schoolchildren and young adults in the context of the country in which they are educated.

Many political authorities of different countries and different periods have been aware of the power of history in the formation of the consciousness of citizens, a fact proved by the resolution "On the teaching of history in secondary schools of the USSR" adopted by the Central Committee of the Communist Party of the Soviet Union on 16 May 1934, personally approved by Stalin. This resolution stated that "the teaching of history should no longer refer to abstract patterns of the evolution of sociopolitical formations, but the history of the Soviet state must be presented in a lively and interesting way."[30]

After the fall of the Soviet Union, historians were asked to debate and justify a new historical discourse and the political project of an independent Belarus, diametrically opposed to the Soviet project. New history textbooks were written on political control in post-Soviet countries at the beginning of the 1990s. Most Soviet

---

[28] Benedict Anderson, *Imagined Communities: Reflections on the Origin and Spread of Nationalism* (London: Verso, 1983).
[29] Marc Ferro, *Histoire et ses interprétations* (Strasbourg: Conseil de l'Europe, 1997).
[30] Stalin 1934.

Republics conducted a selective inventory of their histories, searching for historical facts and "useful" events which could be mobilized in order to build and legitimate an independent state and national identity.[31] The highlighting of certain events, such as victory in the Second World War, necessarily entails the treatment of other related issues, such as the responsibility of the Soviet government for the war, the purges on the eve of the war, and the occupation of liberated territories by the Red Army, including the Baltic countries. Such a reduction of history, a "happy eclecticism,"[32] is not only problematic from the standpoint of historical research, but also creates significant political and diplomatic tensions visible in the example of the complex relationship between Russia and the Baltic countries.[33]

School history teaching is now subject to tight political control. The establishment by presidential decree on 24 August 1995 of a State Commission responsible for overseeing the publishing of textbooks in the field of social sciences, reporting directly to the presidential administration, was a milestone in Belarusian historiography. This body responds to the aspirations of the current political masters of Belarus to control the teaching of history in schools. The purpose of the Commission is to monitor and directly control the content of school textbooks.

Soviet Interpretation of the War in Schoolbooks

To illustrate how the myth of the Great War was created and perpetuated at an academic and scholarly level, it is advisable to refer to the section devoted to the Great Patriotic War in the only textbook of the history of the SSRB published in Belarus during the Soviet period.[34] The section devoted to the Second World War occupies 6% of the editorial content of the textbook, proof of the difficulties in interpreting the events of the war in the USSR and of the difficulties to attribute a fundamental role to this event. A major event in the history of the USSR and the SSRB should be developed in depth and deserves more editorial space. The interpretation of the war is only partial. The paragraph begins with the following dogmatic assertion: "On 22 June 1941, Nazi Germany attacked the USSR. Upon the call of the Communist Party, the whole people stood up to fight against the Nazi invaders." A subparagraph concerning the partisan movement entitled "The partisan war of the whole people" occupies half of the chapter on

---

31 Bassin 2012.
32 Berger 2007.
33 Lisovskaya Karpov 1999.
34 Abetsadarski, *The History of the Soviet Socialist Republic of Belarus.*

the war, and this movement is described in glowing terms. Three elements are highlighted. Firstly, the partisan war was a war of the whole people of Belarus. Secondly, the direction of the movement was provided by the Communist Party. Thirdly, the success of the partisan struggle is emphasized, and no mention of failures or crimes committed by partisans is made. The following sentences quoted from the only textbook of Soviet Belarus illustrate how the history of the Soviet partisans is written about: "From the first days of occupation, workers in Soviet Belarus started the war of the whole people. Brigades of partisans were created everywhere. Their number increased daily. The organizer and leader of the partisan movement was the Communist Party."[35] The semantic and stylistic construction of the text are revealing. The short sentences and dogmatic tone meet the objectives of Soviet propaganda, pointing out that the information provided by the textbooks is an ultimate and indisputable truth, while objective criticisms were leveled by nationalist historians at these postulates of the Soviet interpretation of the war.

An interesting illustration of the continuity of the Soviet tradition, of the social use of collective memory and the importance of the Second World War, is the textbook summarizing the history of Belarus entitled *A Gift of the President of Belarus*,[36] which since 2004 has been given to all first-year primary school pupils in Belarus. The book particularly emphasizes the history of the Second World War, both through its text and its illustrations. In the same year, when Belarus celebrated the 60th anniversary of the victory in the Second World War, a special course on this event was introduced for students in the final year of high school and the first year of university. Specific textbooks were published as didactical support for these courses. These textbooks present a Soviet version of the war and scarcely evoke the crimes of Soviet leaders and the complex issue of collaborationism, and reduce the role of the Allies in the victory to a minimum. The Molotov-Ribbentrop Pact and its secret protocol are mentioned, but without explanation: "On 23 August 1939, a German-Soviet agreement of non-aggression was signed (the Molotov-Ribbentrop Pact). At the same time, a secret protocol was signed."[37] In the same textbook, a preface written by the Belarusian president (who has a degree in history) reads:

---

35 Ibid., 147.
36 Lukashenko 2004.
37 Alexander Kovalenya, *Великая Отечественная война советского народа (в контексте Второй мировой войны). 11* [The Great Patriotic War of the Soviet People (In the Context of the Second World War). 11th Grade] (Minsk: Belarusian State University, 2004).

> Some pseudo-academics try to rewrite the history of the Great Patriotic War, diminishing the role of our grandfathers and rehabilitating traitors, collaborators, and slaves of the Nazis. Young people are the main target of these lies. I have confidence in your clear minds and the honesty that allow you to distinguish between truth and falsehood. The living memory of the past will help us to build the future. To know the history of our homeland is a sacred duty of every citizen. Patriotism is the foundation of the courage and heroism with which the Belarusian people has survived all its wars and defended its independence.[38]

The Great Patriotic War is a sacred event in the history of Belarus. Political discourse underlines the heroic role of the Belarusian people, which "together with the peoples of the USSR saved Europe from Nazism."[39] This is a winners' version of events; no mention of the victims of the war is possible. In official rhetoric, the Great Patriotic War is thus presented as a sacred event at the base of Belarusian history, and divergent interpretations are erased.

The Holocaust in Belarusian Textbooks

Another important argument of the continuity of the Soviet tradition of the Second World War's interpretation in history textbooks is the representation of the Holocaust. In Soviet historiography and textbooks, "Holocaust" is an absent term. Now, it is not possible to avoid the events related to the Holocaust completely, but their interpretation is partial and distorted.

Four textbooks on the history of Belarus treating the Holocaust are analyzed here: Evguenii Novik's *История Беларуси 1917–1945. 10* [History of Belarus 1917–1945. 10th grade], Ouladzimir Sidartsou's *Падручнік Гісторыя Беларусі. 9* [History of Belarus. 9th grade], Petar Petrykau's *Гісторыя Беларусі. 11* [History of Belarus. 11th grade], and Alexander Kovalenya's *Великая Отечественная война советского народа (в контексте Второй мировой войны)* [The Great Patriotic War of the Soviet People (In the Context of the Second World War). 11th grade].[40]

---

[38] Alexander Lukashanko, "Preface," in Alexander Kovalenya, *Великая Отечественная война советского народа (в контексте Второй мировой войны). 11* [The Great Patriotic War of the Soviet People (In the Context of the Second World War). 11th Grade] (Minsk: Belarusian State University, 2004).

[39] Alexander Lukashenko, *The Historical Choice of Belarus* (Minsk: State University Press, 2003).

[40] Evguenii Novik, *История Беларуси 1917–1945. 10* [History of Belarus 1917–1945. 10th Grade] (Minsk: Public Education); Sidartsou, *History Textbook Belarus*; Petar Petrykau,

The official curriculum mentions: "The 'West' plan the Nazi occupation regime. The genocide." No clarification is given by the curriculum on the teaching of the reasons for the Holocaust, or its consequences, or its remembrance. The program of the special course on the Great Patriotic War does not mention the term "Holocaust." Concerning the time allocated to teaching and learning about the Holocaust in schools, 11 hours are devoted to the topic "The BSSR during WWII and the Great Patriotic War" for the 11th grade, of which two hours are given to the occupation regime and the genocide. (Within the framework of the special course on the Second World War and the Great Patriotic War, two hours are devoted to the occupation regime.)

The Belarusian textbooks present the Holocaust within the context of the Second World War and, more specifically, in the context of occupation during the "Great Patriotic War." Some textbooks present the Holocaust in the framework of chapters entitled "Struggle against Nazi aggression," "The regime of occupation," and "A policy of genocide and violence," offering brief chronologies of the event in some sentences or paragraphs. The average number of pages devoted to the occupation regime varies from one to three in books of approximately 200 pages.

The terms used to describe Holocaust are "genocide," "mass murder," and "planned extermination of the Soviet people." The only Belarusian textbook to use the term "Holocaust" is Kovalenya's for the special course on the Second World War in the following sentence: "The Holocaust is the extermination of the Jewish population of Europe by the Nazis during WWII."[41] Other textbooks offer the following vague explanations: "According to the plan of the 'West,' Jewish people, communists, and representatives of Soviet authority were all condemned to total extermination . . . '[a] racially harmful' part of the population – Jewish people, gypsies, and the physically and mentally ill – were condemned to extermination in a particularly cruel manner." The extermination of Jewish people in Belarus is treated as part of the extermination of Soviet people.

The books do focus on military warfare and political events but without giving space to individual experiences or testimonies. The lives of Jewish people before and after the Second World War in Europe are not depicted. No dates are ascribed to the Holocaust to mark the main occurrences or its beginning and end. This event is not linked to earlier events of the 18th or 19th centuries. The genocide of the Jewish people is treated within the context of the Second World

---

Гісторыя Беларусі. 11 [History of Belarus. 11th Grade] (Minsk: Public Education, 2002); Kovalenya, *The Great Patriotic War*.
41 Kovalenya, *The Great Patriotic War*, 36.

War, but without a relevant explanation and without a clear indication of the relationship between the Holocaust and the Second World War. The explanation of the genocide of the Jewish people is very short and so disconnected from the general context that it is impossible even to begin to understand the Holocaust as a phenomenon based on the text in the textbooks.

The representation of the Holocaust in Belarusian textbooks does not establish the links with the European context. Though Kavalenya's textbook's maps depict the sites of camps on a European scale and show the sites of ghettos and extermination camps in Belarus and the Soviet Union, the textbooks do not establish a spatial link with Europe or the Soviet Union. The textbook for the special course on Second World War history only mentions the Maly Trostenets camp near Minsk, as well as Auschwitz, Majdanek, and Treblinka, without any reference to the Holocaust as a European phenomenon. In this textbook, and in spite of the maps of Europe showing the sites of camps, the text does not explain the geopolitical dimensions of the Holocaust, but rather presents it only insofar as it affected Belarus.

Concerning the names of the protagonists, the emphasis is put on Soviet people in the abstract, while Jewish victims, Gypsies, and "racially harmful" parts of the population, including "the physically and mentally ill," are only mentioned in passing. The main focus of all textbooks is a factual and impersonal account of the extermination, detailing the number of camps, people murdered, villages destroyed, etc. There is no portrayal either of the victims or of the perpetrators. Novik's textbook names the victims as "people," without any reference to the categories defined by the National Socialist regime. There are no distinctions between the treatment of various victim groups, such that the murder of Jews in Belarus in Sidartsou's textbook, for example, is presented within a passage about the murder of Soviet people; likewise, different victim groups are lumped together indiscriminately in Petrykau's textbook, that is, as "people who perished" and as "all who were condemned to total extermination." All books list the numbers of "people" killed in the Maly Trostenets camp, and all books list the numbers of "people" or "Jewish people" killed in the Minsk ghetto. Perpetrators are referred to as "Hitler's soldiers," "Nazis," "collaborators," "occupiers," "Germans," and "aggressors." None of the textbooks contain images of Hitler in connection with the Holocaust, nor do they address the role of the Allies, bystanders, or individual stories. The motivations of the defined individual persecutors (e.g. a desire for revenge, a sense of duty, peer pressure, the wish for power, a sense of justice, fear, etc.) are not provided. No space is devoted to ambivalence and human error, refusal or heroism, beyond the polarized depictions of victims and perpetrators. A characteristic of all the books covered in the survey is a general silence regarding local people who participated in extermination operations or people who risked their lives to save members of the Jewish population during the Second World War in Belarus. There are numerous instances of such acts. As of 2014, Yad Vashem listed 601 names of Belarusians among the Righteous Among the Nations. However, none of the books mention either helpers, rescuers, or local people who participated in or abetted killings or collaborated with perpetrators of the Holocaust in Belarus. The Belarusian national narrative is consequently relatively limited with regard to the historical perspectives that are offered to pupils and thereby the next generation. As highlighted by Peter Carrier et al., in contrast, "partisan resisters feature prominently in all books," and the fate of individual women is indicated visually in Kovalenya's textbook via an image of a child next to his dead mother; although the child is named as Tolia Markovets, no information concerning the place and date of, or the reason for, the killing is provided.[42] The partisan-maquis movement is dealt with in detail, as befits its quasi-'sacred' status within Belarusian historiography and national politics of historical memory. The impersonal style explains the very small number of pronouns used. There are only some rare instances of personal pronouns in all the textbooks. Passive constructions dominate the text, such as: "The territory of Belarus was covered with a network of concentration camps,"[43] "In the occupied territory a 'new order' was established, a regime based on genocide, mass extermination, and the theft of national resources,"[44] and "The extermination was carried out."[45] None of the textbooks use superlative or emotive terms. The sections dealing with the Holocaust do not reflect a general decline (of morality, human rights, or modernity), nor do they include elements of hope or redemption. No comparisons are made between the Holocaust and similar events in other parts of the world (e.g. genocides, the effects of dictatorships).

The extermination of the Jewish people, without the term "Holocaust," is depicted in a factual manner: the numbers of instances of mass extermination and of concentration camps and ghettos are given. The presentations of the Holocaust are not comprehensive or historical but consist of brief statements outlining facts of the event, such as the numbers of camps and ghettos and the identity of selectively chosen perpetrators and victims. These statements are generally short and disconnected from the context of the Second World War and do not constitute explanations of the event. The aims of perpetrators are described in the context of the *Generalplan Ost* (General plan for the East),

---

42 Peter Carrier et al., *The International Status of Education about the Holocaust: A Global Mapping of Textbooks and Curricula* (Braunschweig: UNESCO, 2015), 85.
43 Novik, *History of Belarus*.
44 Sidartsou, *History Textbook Belarus*.
45 Petrykau, *History of Belarus*.

according to Novik, in which 75% of Belarusians were to be killed or displaced and 25% of them used for forced labor, while all Jews and "Gypsies" were to be killed. Sidartou describes the aims of the perpetrators as a "new order . . . based on genocide, mass extermination, and the theft of national resources." The causes of and motives for the Holocaust are not explained, although references to "racially harmful" people in Kovalenya's textbook suggest that causes of the event were rooted in ideological motivations.

The average number of illustrations and documents relating to the Holocaust is three in all analyzed textbooks. Beyond administrative documents, including a letter from the General Commissar of Belarus about the killing of Jews in Novik's textbook and an official order concerning the "Jewish district" of Minsk in Kovalenya's textbook, the textbooks contain few iconic images of the Holocaust, such as the camp badges used to identify people from Eastern Europe or the entrance to Auschwitz (in Sidartsou's textbook). Historiographical or commemorative issues are not addressed.

All authors adopt a neutral voice, providing a single authorial point of view with minimal indications of other points of view. This imbalance is reflected in the fact that 90–100% of sections about the Holocaust are devoted to authors' texts alongside up to 10% of documents or maps, while Kovalenya's textbook devotes 60% of the available space to documents alongside 40% of text. The authors offer no meta-historical reflection about historical methods or commemorative uses of the Holocaust. By confining the scope of the narratives to the period of the war and to Belarusian territory, they likewise provide fatalistic moral accounts with no reference to the long-term causes or consequences of the Holocaust. The references to "occupiers" reveal a narrative bias toward a national Belarusian standpoint. The narrative is also not organized according to specific themes or problems (such as morality, politics, or psychology) but is reduced to a catalog of facts.

Novik's textbook requires pupils to explain the meaning of "genocide" in relation to a document and secondary literature. Sidartsou's and Petrykau's textbooks each contain one question about the Holocaust requesting pupils to define the characteristics of the "occupying regime." In Novik's textbook, there is one question asking pupils to explain the *Generalplan Ost* and one relating to the genocide requiring an explanation of the term together with a description of the phenomenon through an analysis of the document in the textbook and complementary literature. Sidartsou's textbook contains only one question related to the genocide, asking pupils for a characterization of the occupation regime using the map of concentration camps. Petrykau's textbook has one question related to the extermination policy, asking pupils for a characterization of the occupying regime. Kovalenya's textbook requires an explanation for the forced dislocation of Jews from Minsk and a definition of the characteristics of the genocide in occupied Belarus. The authors' general didactic approach to the Holocaust therefore offers pupils the opportunity to learn *of* the Holocaust, but little *about* or *from* it.

The textbooks present the Holocaust strictly in the context of local or national Belarusian history, in line with the stipulation for Belarusian curricula that teaching about the Holocaust should take place within the context of the history of Belarus and, more specifically, of the "Great Patriotic War." Repeated references to the occupation of Belorussia in the context of the Holocaust suggest that the Holocaust primarily involved a violation of Belarusian territory. Sidartsou, for example, refers to "the occupied territory" and Novik to that fact that "[t]he territory of Belarus was covered with a network of concentration camps," while exercises in Petrykau's and Kovalenya's textbooks ask pupils to describe the Holocaust from the point of view of members of an occupied country. This local vision of the event is reinforced by further references to camps, above all to the Maly Trostenets camp and the Minsk ghetto in Belarus; to the equal status accorded to Jews, "Gypsies," and Belarussian nationals as victims of the *Generalplan Ost* in Novik's textbook; and by reproducing images of badges worn by Eastern Europeans and Belarussians in camps in Sidartsou's textbook. There is a tendency to nationalize victimhood. The numbers of Jewish victims listed in all books refer only to those who were killed in either Maly Trostenets or the Minsk ghetto, although Novik does not name the categories of victims and Sidartsou focuses primarily on Soviet victims. By naming the perpetrators as "Hitler's soldiers," "Nazis," "collaborators," "occupiers," "Germans," and "aggressors," the textbooks testify to a further tendency to externalize perpetration, which is not embodied in the person of Hitler but in multiple, largely national, German agents.

Conclusion

The recent Belarusian historiography and identity matrix is divided into two competing interpretations of history and two approaches to producing historical narratives: nationalist and Soviet. Each of these approaches mobilizes and articulates facts and historical events in order to legitimize a political discourse and a narrative of historical identity. In current Belarusian historiography, a clear imbalance exists between the historical narratives in favor of the Soviet doctrinal and dogmatic narrative. The history of the 20th century witnessed the misuse of history in the USSR to justify crimes, exterminations, and reprisals. The use of nationalist history in different contexts also showed the dangers of an aggressive nationalism. A single perfect historical narrative, a unique historical consciousness, a single way of interpreting the past cannot exist, but this narrative must be plural, open, without dogma, and without monopoly, which is not the case in Belarus today.

The nationalist discourse on historical consciousness and national identity is condemned to obscurity due to the lack of opportunity for its transmission and legitimization. The only model for historical consciousness and national identity for Belarusians is the Soviet model defended and promoted by the authorities. The alternative project promoted by nationalist forces is also a negative project, incapable of becoming a reference for national unity. The problem of the lack of a regular and stable point of reference is the absence of a necessary consensus on national identity. Soviet historical dogma, and in particular the cornerstone of the Soviet legacy – the glorification of the Second World War –, has marginalized other historical interpretations. The pre-eminence of the Soviet interpretation of the war is reflected in partial and biased discourse, full of lacunas, on the Second World War in identity discourse and school textbooks. Thus, ideas of Belarusian national identity are once again based exclusively on negative and destructive references to war. Remembrance of the past and historical discourse, where it relates to national identity, should have an open, peaceful, pluralistic, and discursive basis and should transcend controversial issues like wars and conflicts. Current definitions of Belarusian identity cannot be sustainable and will always be weak and susceptible to political manipulation because they are based on destructive historical references.

The acceptance of official discourse on historical memory is due to the marginalization of other discourses. The formative influence of the politics of memory is powerful if society remembers the past in a similar but not identical way, generating an idea of historical truth and reinforcing belief in the version of history commemorated. The current Belarusian political authorities aspire to disseminate a Soviet, Russia-orientated version of Belarusian history and national identity in the interest of justifying their own legitimacy. In order to do so, they need an interpretation that can be accepted without discussion by the population. In this specific context, any interpretation of national identity must be as simplistic and dogmatic as possible. The result of mixing Soviet and nationalist references are weak and contradictory discourses and textbooks, unfit to be consistent and stable referents for the construction of national identity, for fostering a sense of belonging to a national community, or for justifying the place of a nation in the global system. This is extremely important for Belarus, as its Democracy Index is continuously ranked the lowest in Europe. It is the only country on the European continent not to be a part of the Council of Europe and the only one that still implements the death penalty.

Works Cited

Abetsadarski, Laurentsi. *The History of the Soviet Socialist Republic of Belarus*. Minsk: Public Education, 1968.
Anderson, Benedict. *Imagined Communities: Reflections on the Origin and Spread of Nationalism*. London: Verso, 1983.
Bassin, Mark and Catriona Kelly. *Soviet and Post-Soviet Identities*. Cambridge: Cambridge University Press, 2012.
Boulyko, Alexander. *Typology of Bilinguistic and Multilinguistic Situation in Belarus*. Minsk: Belarusian Science, 1999.
Carrier, Peter et al. *The International Status of Education about the Holocaust: A Global Mapping of Textbooks and Curricula*. Braunschweig: UNESCO, 2015.
Dean, Martin. *Collaboration in the Holocaust: Crimes of the Local Police in Belorussia and Ukraine, 1941–44*. London: Palgrave Macmillan, 2000.
Eberhardt, Petar. *Demographic Situation in Belarus 1897–1989*. Minsk: Soros Foundation, 1997.
Ferro, Marc. *Histoire et ses interpretations*. Strasbourg: Conseil de l'Europe, 1997.
Karbalevitch, Valeryi. "Беларускі феномен трансфармацыйнага грамадства" [Belarusian phenomenon of a society in transition]. *Civic Alternative* 12 (1999).
Kovalenya, Alexander. *Великая Отечественная война советского народа (в контексте Второй мировой войны). 11* [The Great Patriotic War of the Soviet People (in the context of the Second World War). 11th Grade]. Minsk: Belarusian State University, 2004.
Kozak, Kouz'ma. *German and Collaborationist Loss in Belarus during the Second World War (1941–1944): An Analysis of the Results*. Minsk: Logvinov, 2012.
Lastouski, Vaclau. *Кароткая гісторыя Беларусі* [An Overview of the History of Belarus]. Minsk: Kukhty, 1992.
Lindner, Rainer. *Historiker und Herrschaft. Nationsbuildung und Geschichtspolitik in Weißrußland im 19. und 20. Jahrhundert*. Munich: R. Oldenbourg Verlag, 1999.
Loïka, Pavel. *History of Belarus: Textbook for the 7th Grade*. Minsk: Public Education, 1993.
Lukashenko, Alexander. *The Historical Choice of Belarus*. Minsk: State University Press, 2003.
Lukashanko, Alexander. "Preface." In Alexander Kovalenya, *Великая Отечественная война советского народа (в контексте Второй мировой войны). 11* [The Great Patriotic War of the Soviet People (In the Context of the Second World War). 11th Grade]. Minsk: Belarusian State University, 2004.
Lukashenko, Alexander. "The problems of textbooks." *Teachers' Journal* 55 (April 2000).
Namer, Gérard. *Halbwachs and Social Memory*. Paris: L'Harmattan, 2002.
Novik, Evguenii. *История Беларуси 1917–1945. 10* [History of Belarus 1917–1945. 10th Grade]. Minsk: Public Education, 2012.
Petrykau, Petar. *Гісторыя Беларусі. 11* [History of Belarus. 11th Grade]. Minsk: Public Education, 2002.
Recher, Stephen. *Self and Nation*. London: Sage Publications, 2001.
Rothberg, Michael. *Multidirectional Memory. Remembering the Holocaust in an Age of Decolonization*. Stanford: Stanford University Press, 2009.
Sahanovitch, Henadz. "Ten years of Belarusian historiography (1991–2000)." *Critical Review of Belarusian History* 8 (2001).

Schissler, Hanna. *The Nation, Europe and the World: Textbooks and Curricula in Transition*. New York: Berghahn Books, 2005.
Sidartsou, Uladzimir. *Падручнік Гісторыя Беларусі. 9* [History Textbook Belarus. 9th Grade]. Minsk: Public Education, 1993.
Sierp, Aline. *History, Memory, and Trans-European Identity*. London: Routledge, 2014.
Trechtchenok, Yakov. *The History of Belarus*. Mogilev: University of Mogilev Press, 2005.
Zaiko, Leonid. *National Interests of Belarus*. Minsk: Skakoun, 1999.

List of Contributors

Sven Brajer works at Technische Universität Dresden and received his Master of Arts from this institution. His main research fields are revolution and nationalism studies as well as critical examinations of current discourses of globalism. In his dissertation he analysed the völkisch spectrum in Dresden, which stood in stark contrast to the revolutionary Social Democracy of the German Empire and the Weimar Republic. In addition, he has published numerous articles on the political history of East Germany.

Irakli Chkhaidze is Assistant Professor at the Institute of Cultural Studies, Faculty of Humanities, Ivane Javakhishvili Tbilisi State University (TSU). He received his PhD in Cultural Studies from TSU in 2016. Chkhaidze's research interests revolve around nationalism, populism, identity forming and nation building processes in the post-Soviet space. His publications include: "A National Figure as a Memory Site: Reinterpretations of Ilia Chavchavadze in the 1910s-1940s," *Caucasus Survey* (2021), co-authored with Ketevan Kakitelashvili, and "The Image of the West in Georgia after Independence (Key Tendencies)," Civilization Researches 16 (2018): 18-39.

Alicja Curanović is Associate Professor at the Faculty of Political Science and International Studies, University of Warsaw. She holds a PhD in Political Science from the University of Warsaw. Her main research interests include Russian foreign policy, the religious factor in international relationsm as well as identity, status, and messianism in politics. She has conducted research *inter alia* at Harvard University, Columbia University, Stanford University, the Russian State University for Humanistic Studies and MGIMO. Her articles appeared in *Problems of Post-Communism, Politics and Religion, Nationalities Papers or Religion, State and Society*. Her latest monograph is *The Sense of Mission in Russian Foreign Policy: Destined for Greatness!* (Routledge 2021).

Frank Jacob is Professor of Global History at Nord Universitet, Norway. He received his PhD in Japanese Studies from Erlangen University, Germany in 2012 and just recently finished a DBA at Jean Moulin University Lyon, France. His research foci include transnational anarchism, revolution theory and the comparative study of revolutionary processes, as well as modern German and Japanese history. Jacob is the author or editor of more than 80 books and his recent works include the monographs *Ernst Papanek and Jewish Refugee Children: Genocide and Displacement* (De Gruyter, 2021) and *East Asia and the First World War* (De Gruyter, 2022) as well as the edited volume *Wallerstein 2.0* (Transcript, 2022).

Inessa Kouteinikova, PhD, is an independent scholar, art and architecture historian, as well as a photographic researcher, living in Amsterdam. She studies Russian Central Asia, Russian and International Orientalism and Colonialism, and is currently completing a monograph on the development of photographic industries in Islamic Central Asia, the emergence of *albumania*, reception, representation and display of Russia's major colony, the rise of the museums with Orientalist and photographic collections in the Empire (Routledge: 2022). She curated the first large-scale exhibition *Russia's Unknown Orient* in the Netherlands (Groningen Museum, 2010-11) and was a convenor of *Russian and Soviet Orientalism through Production and Education* (Cambridge, UK, November 2014) Her research addresses the 19th century history of collecting in Russia and Europe, with specific reference to Islamic culture and photography. She works for private collections in Europe, the Middle East, and Oceania.

Muhammad A. Z. Mughal is Assistant Professor of Cultural Anthropology in the Department of Global Studies at King Fahd University of Petroleum & Minerals, Dhahran, Saudi Arabia. He received his PhD from Durham University, UK. His main research fields are time, space, globalization, mass media, rural social organization, Pakistan, identity and environment. Mughal's recent publications include "Children's Perception of Social Boundaries: The Intersectionality of Age and Social Group Affiliation in Rural Pakistan," *Children & Society* (2021), "Ethnicity, Marginalization, and Politics: Saraiki Identity and the Quest for a New Southern Punjab Province in Pakistan," *Asian Journal of Political Science* (2020), and "Rural Urbanization, Land, and Agriculture in Pakistan," *Asian Geographer* (2019).

James Okolie-Osemene, is a Lecturer in the Department of International Relations and the Coordinator of the General Studies Unit at Wellspring University, Nigeria. He received his PhD and MA degrees in Peace and Conflict Studies from University of Ibadan, Nigeria. He is alumnus of the Pan African Doctoral Academy, University of Ghana and Research Fellow at the French Institute for Research in Africa (IFRA-Nigeria). His main research fields are among others Global Security, Pan-Africanism, and Cross-Border Security. His work counts more than 50 publications (local and international peer reviewed scholarly journals and book chapters). Recent publications include "Nigeria's Security Governance Dilemmas During the Covid-19 Crisis," *Politikon Journal* (2021) https://doi.org/10.1080/02589346.2021.1913802 and "Trans-Saharan Human Trafficking as a Crime Against Humanity: Patterns, Evolution, and Implications for People-Centred Development in Africa," in *The Routledge Handbook of Africana Criminologies* (2021).

Tetiana Perga is senior researcher at the Institute of the World History at the National Academy of Science of Ukraine and received her PhD from Kiev State University in 1998. She was a DAAD fellow at IOS Regensburg (2018). Her main research fields are: eco-nationalism, state building as well as national, regional and global environmental policy. Recent publications include "Confronting Nuclear Tyranny: Role of Eco-nationalism in Development of Environmental Movement in Ukraine," *Cultural and Religious Studies* 6, no. 9 (2018): 539-547; "The Fallout of Chernobyl," in *Nature and Iron Curtain. Environmental Policy and Social Movements in Communist and Capitalist Countries (1945-1990)*, eds. Astrid Mignon Kirchhof and J.R.MaNeill (Pittsburgh: Pittsburgh University Press, 2019), 55-73; "Eco-nationalism, 'Green World' Association and Path to the Independence of Ukraine in late 1980s – early 1990s," *Bulletin of Cherkasy University: Historical Sciences* 1 (2021): 97-105.

Carsten Schapkow is J.R. Brammer Presidential Professor in History at the University of Oklahoma where he also serves as the Director of the Center for Study of Nationalism. Schapkow received his PhD in 2000 from the Free University Berlin. His main research interests are German-Jewish history, Sephardic History and Culture, and the history of nationalism. He is, among other publications, the author of *Role Model and Counter Model: The Golden Age of Iberian Jewry and German Jewish Culture during the Era of Emancipation* (Lanham: Lexington Books, 2016) and co-edited *Jewish Studies and Israel Studies in the 21st Century: Intersections and Prospects*, eds. Carsten Schapkow and Klaus Hoedl (Lanham: Lexington Books 2019).

Johannes Schütz teaches and Researches at the Technical University of Dresden. He received his PhD from the Georg-August-Universität Göttingen. His main research fields are the history of knowledge and practices of national identities. Johannes Schütz's recent publication is *Die neue Mitte? Ideologie und Kritik der populistischen und extremen Rechten*, co-ed. with Raj Kollmorgen and Steven Schäller (Böhlau, 2021).

Anna Zadora is researcher at University of Srasbourg and received her Habilitation degree from University of Corsica and PhD from University of Strasbourg. Her main research fields are history teaching Name's recent publications include Roger Giner-Sorolla, Denis Hilton, Hans-Peter Erb, Anna Zadora, « Assigning moral roles within the Second World War in Europe: National similarities, differences, and implications for group-level moral representations," in the *Asian Journal of Social Psychology,* and "Les historiens sous la pression politique: entre soumission et résistance. Quelques réflexions autour du contexte biélorusse," in *Clio in Real Socialisms, ed.* Stefano Santoro (Milan: Unicopli, 2020).

Index

AAPC (The All-African Peoples' Conference) 92, 93, 100, 102–4, 111, 112
accident 180, 182, 184 *see also* Chernobyl
Accra 93, 103
activism 34, 185, 191
– social 177, 184, 192
– anti-nuclear 181, 183, 185
activists 46, 160, 161, 168, 185–91
AfD (Alternative for Germany) 44, 46, 63
Africa 91–103, 105–113, 125
– development of 109, 110
– for Africans 100, 110
– liberation of 105
– natives of 99
– people of 94, 99
– post–colonial 112
– independent states of 104
African 91–113
– affairs 96, 106, 107
– countries 101, 105, 108, 110
– culture 95, 196, 112
– dream 91, 92, 101
– leaders 105, 106, 108, 110, 112, 113
– peoples 94, 104, 110, 112
– solidarity 92, 93, 111
– states 102n47, 103, 105–7, 108, 110, 111
agenda 16, 27, 28, 29, 33, 35, 105, 106, 124n8, 132, 160
AHRU (Americans for Human Rights of Ukraine) 189, 190
ANZAC 15
Arabic 104, 127n13, 128, 164
Armenia 24, 177
army 17, 18, 21, 23, 24, 127, 133, 202
– Red 201, 203, 210, 212
– Ottoman 17, 18, 20, 30
art 46, 47, 121, 126, 129, 132, 134, 150, 157
Asia 108, 121, 163, 168
– Central 9, 120–7, 129, 132, 134, 135
Atatürk, K. 15–17, 19–21, 26–33, 35, 36

authorities 22, 25, 81, 122, 129, 133, 146, 150, 151, 181, 182, 186, 187
– political 195, 196, 202, 205, 206, 209, 211, 220
– Soviet 146, 181, 182

Baghaturia, J. 153
Balkan Wars 16, 17, 22
Baltic 46, 124n8, 212
Barth, T. F. W. 97, 98
Belarus 9, 195–200, 202–20
– history of 195–200, 203, 206, 213, 214, 219
– independent 197, 198, 211
– President of 205, 213
– Soviet 195, 197, 213
Belarusian *see* Belarus
Berlin 46, 50, 51, 54
Bhabha, H. 158, 162
Bismarck, O. von 45, 46
black 91, 92, 94, 98, 100, 103, 105, 112
– consciousness 91, 92, 101, 112
– people 91, 95, 96, 104, 105, 108, 109
Black Sea 23
Borggräfe, H. 42, 43
Brandenburg 44, 45, 62
Breuer, S. 43
British 17, 22–5, 27, 32, 120, 131, 163
– India 163, 169, 170
Bush, G. 148, 149

Canovan, M. 141, 144
capitalist 29, 59, 94, 103, 105, 198
Caspian Sea 123
catastrophe *see* Chernobyl
Cebesoy *see* Fuat, A.
Chernobyl 177, 180–191
children 129, 139, 152, 189
Children of Chornobyl Relief Fund (CCRF) 190
citizenship 76, 77, 92, 150, 151, 168
colonialism 100, 102, 106, 107, 113, 162, 179
colonies 101, 121, 134, 135
communism 53, 64, 101, 148

Index

Communist Party
- of Soviet 147, 191, 197, 198, 201–3, 211–13
- of Ukraine 183n24, 187n33, 188

Dardanelles 15, 19, 22, 26, 32
Dawson, J. 177, 185
death 25, 191, 133, 220
decolonization 92, 100, 101, 112
democracy 1, 7, 31, 64, 101, 111, 151, 179, 186, 187, 198, 199, 220
diaspora 36, 91, 103, 110, 112, 157, 168, 188–90, 192
disaster *see* Chernobyl
DNVP 51, 53, 55, 64
Dostoyevsky, F. 132
DuBois, W. E. B. 95, 101, 102

Empire
- British 75
- Ottoman 15, 21–4, 27, 29, 32, 33, 35
Ecology and Peace (Simferopol) 183
elite 21, 28, 77–9, 81, 83, 85–7, 106, 109–10, 142, 144, 146, 152, 160, 179, 209
Erdogan, R. T. 6, 17, 29, 33, 35
ethnicity 79, 97, 140, 145, 151, 162, 168
EU 33, 35–6, 41, 64, 151
Euro-Atlantic 145, 150, 153, 155
European Union *see* EU

Facebook 158, 160, 165, 167
Federal Republic of Germany *see* FRG
fight 8, 9, 101, 146, 147, 191, 201, 202, 212
foreign affairs
French Revolution 21
FRG 57–9, 61n72
Fuat, A. 23

GDR 56–62, 64
Gellner, E. 144, 159
Georgian Parliament 150, 153, 154
German Democratic Republic *see* GDR
German National People's Party *see* DNVP
Germany 22, 31, 43, 44n17, 45, 51, 53, 57–60, 62, 63, 181, 195, 212
- East 41, 43–6, 50, 62

Ghana 92, 93, 102, 103, 105, 107, 109, 111, 113
ghetto 208, 216, 219
globalization 1, 5, 7, 9, 41, 112, 195
Guhr, R. 46–9, 52, 53, 63
gypsies 215, 216, 218, 219

Hanioglu, S. M. 22, 26
Heimat 60–2
Hitler, A. 31, 55, 49, 216, 219
Hitler Youth 210
Holocaust 56, 195, 203, 204, 208, 214–19
human 2, 3, 98, 101, 126, 133, 182, 216
- dignity 95, 106, 130, 204
- rights 95, 151, 152, 204, 217

ideals 28, 73, 83, 85, 87, 105, 108, 147, 185, 202
ideology 26, 42–4, 49, 92–4, 100, 104, 112, 134, 141, 147, 163, 177, 206
imperialism 17n9, 21, 58, 69, 72, 95, 102, 103, 107, 135, 149, 179
India 120, 124, 132, 161, 163, 167–70
Islam 19, 21, 26, 28, 29, 33, 35, 64, 130, 157, 163, 164, 167, 168

Jansen, C. 42, 43
Jewish 56, 63, 207, 218, 219
- community 201, 204, 208, 210
- people 215–217
- population 50, 215, 217
Johnson, B. 6
justice 95, 103, 109, 128, 134n25, 216

Kalasha 167, 168
Kemal, M. 8, 15, 16, 18–28
Kemalism 26, 34, 35
Kemalist 17, 26, 28, 29, 32–35
KGB 182, 186, 187, 189
Khmelnytskyi 183, 187, 190
Khiva 121, 122n4, 132
Kurdish 16, 34

Lavrov, S. 83, 84
Law on Citizenship 150, 151
leadership 16, 18, 22, 25, 31, 92, 95, 102, 105–13, 147, 179, 186, 202

legacy 31, 70, 78, 86, 87 *see also* Soviet legacy
Lepore, J. 4, 8
liberalism 6, 51, 53, 64, 136, 141
Liman von Sanders, O. 17, 31
Lithuania 177, 185, 196, 198, 201, 204, 210
London 17, 92, 95, 132
Lukashenko, A. 205

mausoleum 28, 30
May, T. 6
Mecklenburg 44–6, 53, 55, 63
messianism 69, 71, 73, 74, 83–5, 87
Minsk 204, 205, 208, 210, 216, 218, 219
Molotov-Ribbentrop Pact 203, 210, 213
Moscow 128, 129, 179, 184
Munich 54, 133
Muslim 19, 21–3, 34, 121, 122, 124n8, 128, 157, 163, 164, 166–9, 170n46
– world 19, 120n3, 124n8

Nazi
– Germany 31, 195, 212
– invasion 210
– occupation 195, 208, 215
Nigeria 111
Nkruma, K. 92, 93, 101, 103–5, 107–8, 111, 113
nuclear 179, 181, 183
– death 191
– energy 179, 182, 186
– power 179–81, 183–7, 190, 191

Olijnik, B. 191
ontological security 71, 75, 76, 78, 79, 84, 87
online 158, 160–2
Orientalist 2, 127, 134, 135

Pain, E. 77, 78
Pakistan 9, 158, 163–71
Pan-Africanism
pandemic 4, 5
Paris 92, 95, 99, 100
Parrot, B. 72
perestroika 183, 188, 196–8, 200–201, 203, 204, 207, 209
Petukhov, V. 78, 80, 81

photography 119, 122, 123, 125–30, 134, 135
Poland 45, 196, 209
Pomerania 45, 53, 55
populism 6, 7, 141–5, 148–50, 153–5
postcolonial 4, 140, 158, 159, 162
Putin, V. 6, 83, 86

race 91, 94, 100, 112, 140, 159, 162, 182
regime 18, 78, 123, 141, 182, 203, 216, 217
– occupation 195, 215, 218
– *see also* Soviet regime
religion 28, 42, 79, 148, 153, 155, 159, 162, 163, 168, 209
revolution 8, 15, 21, 22, 24, 53, 63, 112, 151, 154, 209
Romanowski, D. 73
Rowley, D. G. 73, 77
Russia 7–9, 24, 69–71, 77–87, 119, 120, 123, 126, 129–34, 150, 152, 155, 177, 178, 185, 188, 195, 196, 200, 204, 208, 209, 212, 220
– post-Soviet 69, 71, 77
– 19th-century 120n3 121, 130

Saakashvili, M. 151, 154
Samarkand 121, 123, 125, 127, 128, 132, 133, 135
Saxony 44, 45, 51, 53–55, 60, 62, 63
Soviet 24, 63, 70, 146, 147, 148, 155, 177, 179–81, 185, 187, 191, 196–8, 201–5, 207–14, 219, 220
– authorities 146, 181, 182, 187
– empire 179, 192
– legacy 204, 205, 208, 210, 220
– people 180, 197, 202, 215, 216
– period 195–7, 200, 201, 206, 212
– post- 69, 71, 77, 79, 84, 139, 141–3, 145, 154, 195, 198, 200, 202–4, 211
– regime 148, 177, 178, 182, 184, 189, 191, 203
– Union 5, 8, 77, 83, 141, 147, 150, 177–9, 181, 182, 185, 186, 191, 192, 198, 204, 211, 216
– *see also* Communist Party
– *see also* Belarus
SSRB 196, 197, 203, 212
St. Petersburg 122, 123, 128, 132, 133

Tashkent 121, 122n4, 123, 125, 126, 128, 129, 131, 132, 135
Tbilisi 148
Thuringia 44, 45, 55, 62, 63
totalitarian 7, 177, 178, 186, 191, 192, 196, 198, 201, 204 *see also* Soviet regime
tradition 20, 35, 46, 57, 60, 74, 83–5, 120n3, 164, 178, 213, 214
transnational 1, 5, 6, 8, 9, 17, 33, 35, 41, 43, 91, 92, 96, 97, 100, 102, 104, 107, 109–11, 113, 120, 157, 160, 167, 178, 188, 192, 203
Trump, D. 3, 6, 7
Turkestan 120–2, 125–33, 135
Turkey 16, 18, 20, 21, 23–31, 33–6
– modern 19, 21, 32, 33
Twitter 158, 160, 165–7

Ukraine 9, 177–80, 182–91 *see also* Communist Party
USA 8, 149, 152, 160, 168, 178, 180, 190
USSR 77, 78, 83, 87, 147, 178–81, 185, 191, 192, 196–99, 202, 203, 210–12, 214, 219

Vereshchagin, V. 132–4
victory 15–21, 24, 25, 29, 31, 32, 82, 86, 146, 147, 198, 201–4, 212, 213
violence 8, 42, 51, 61, 62, 215

Wagner, R. 48, 49
Weimar 46, 52, 53, 55, 64

Yavuz, H. M. 34
Yeltsin, B. 78
Youtube 158, 165, 167–70

www.ingramcontent.com/pod-product-compliance
Lightning Source LLC
Chambersburg PA
CBHW071739150426
43191CB00010B/1631